SATHER CLASSCIAL LECTURES

Volume Seventy-Seven

# The Small Stuff of Roman Antiquity

The publisher and the University of California Press Foundation
gratefully acknowledge the generous support of the Joan Palevsky
Imprint in Classical Literature.

The Joan Palevsky  Imprint in Classical Literature

In honor of beloved Virgil—

"O degli altri poeti onore e lume . . ."

—Dante, *Inferno*

Luminos is the Open Access monograph publishing program from UC Press. Luminos provides a framework for preserving and reinvigorating monograph publishing for the future and increases the reach and visibility of important scholarly work. Titles published in the UC Press Luminos model are published with the same high standards for selection, peer review, production, and marketing as those in our traditional program. www.luminosoa.org

# The Small Stuff of Roman Antiquity

# The Small Stuff of Roman Antiquity

Emily Gowers

UNIVERSITY OF CALIFORNIA PRESS

University of California Press
Oakland, California

© 2025 by Emily Gowers

This work is licensed under a Creative Commons [CC BY-NC-ND] license. To view a copy of the license, visit http://creativecommons.org/licenses.

Suggested citation: Gowers, E. *The Small Stuff of Roman Antiquity*. Oakland: University of California Press, 2025. DOI: https://doi.org/10.1525/luminos.217

Library of Congress Cataloging-in-Publication Data

Names: Gowers, Emily, author.
Title: The small stuff of Roman antiquity / Emily Gowers.
Other titles: Sather classical lectures ; 77.
Description: Oakland, California : University of California Press, [2024] | Series: Sather classical lectures ; 77 | Includes bibliographical references and index.
Identifiers: LCCN 2024025225 (print) | LCCN 2024025226 (ebook) | ISBN 9780520413146 (paperback) | ISBN 9780520413153 (ebook)
Subjects: LCSH: Miniature objects—Social aspects. | Material culture—Social aspects. | Rome—Social life and customs. | Rome—Antiquities.
Classification: LCC NK8470.G69 2024 (print) | LCC NK8470 (ebook) | DDC 745.59280937—dc23/eng/20240826

LC record available at https://lccn.loc.gov/2024025225
LC ebook record available at https://lccn.loc.gov/2024025226

33  32  31  30  29  28  27  26  25
10  9  8  7  6  5  4  3  2  1

*To John Henderson and in memory of Neil Hopkinson*
   e magnis parva

CONTENTS

*Foreword* ix
*Texts and Abbreviations* xv

1. The Good of Small Things  1
2. Sallust's Salient Snails  29
3. Brief Lives: The Case of Crispus  52
4. Tiny Irritants: Itching Eyes, Stones in Shoes, and Other Annoyances  73
5. Diminishing Returns: Tales of the Diminutive  96

*Notes* 121
*Acknowledgments* 143
*References* 145
*Index* 159

FOREWORD

Luckily for me, it wasn't until well after I finished my term at UC Berkeley that I spotted the following dreadful words in Sterling Dow's history of the first fifty years of Sather lectures:

> The Sathers . . . began with emphasis not only on importance, but on grandeur . . . Subsequent lecturers have hardly deviated. Admittedly not all the subjects treated have been equally important . . . certainly none treats a trivial subject . . . or treats its subject in a trivial manner . . . Thus even the comparatively few volumes that verge on being humdrum are worth reading, and provoke thoughts in us. That is the virtue of treating large and important subjects. (Dow 1965, 11–12)

Dow (Sather Professor himself in 1964) continues mercilessly:

> The invitation to deliver the Sather Lectures has a strong effect . . . In many instances, probably, it is the most compelling challenge the scholar ever received . . . Some scholars resolve to . . . write "the great book" they've always intended to write. (Dow 1965, 12)

I was at least as cowed as any of my Sather predecessors, so what made me "deviate" toward "small and unimportant subjects"? A different kind of panicked response to the same pressure? A sense of not fitting into a seat occupied by some very great men and women before me, always conflated in my mind with the geriatric-looking armchair that greeted me in the Sather Professor's office? The timing of my appointment—when COVID-19 had held sway for two years— gave me, I figured, a certain leeway. I even convinced myself that my small topic was wildly appropriate for an era marked (in the least bad scenario) by experiences of shortchanging, half measures, frustration, tiny joys, short-term views into the future, and limited academic resources. But I underestimated what an affront it was to the grand Sather tradition.

As things have turned out, I am privileged to have been able to turn an extraordinary invitation into a book that comes from the heart. In many ways, this is a return to beginnings. As a typical product of late twentieth-century humanist academia, I always had a soft spot for small and marginal things, in my case those at the lower end of the Latin literary canon. When I was a student, this enthusiasm was nurtured by two legendary Cambridge teachers, Neil Hopkinson and John Henderson—not forgetting Roger Dawe, who taught me all I know about those littlest of words, the Greek particles. Unlike other books I have written, this one has been produced at relative speed. It puts out feelers, forages in (for me) unusual places, and taps into what has felt increasingly like a live vein. This has made it both a pleasure to write and a good excuse for avoiding other tasks. As Callimachus tells us in his *Hymn to Zeus*, even Ptolemy Philadelphus (a pro at time management) preferred to get the small things on his to-do list done right away and leave the big things till the evening.

More generally, the topic of smallness felt timely and predictable—a manageable, even comforting theme with which to hunker down in the face of global disaster and late capitalist fatigue. In 2020, shortly after deciding on my subject, I came across a blog that Nandini Pandey (now of Johns Hopkins) had compiled for the Society for Classical Studies.[1] She based her call for contributions on two recent Radiolab podcasts. One was on Cold War doomsday scenarios, those government-sponsored lists of objects slated for preservation in the case of nuclear war, from the Declaration of Independence to the log of the USS *Monitor* and Lincoln's autopsy report. The other recalled physicist Richard Feynman's challenge to his students in 1961, to say which key piece of wisdom in the shortest number of words they would choose to pass on, in the event of a similar cataclysm where all other scientific knowledge was destroyed. In her turn, Pandey asked a number of current classicists to say what "cataclysm sentence" or thing for each of them best encapsulated what they had learned from classical antiquity, what they hoped to give their students, and what they would choose to leave to posterity.

The choices her interviewees made were quite revealing. Never the obvious monumental remains—the Parthenon, Plato's *Republic*, the *Aeneid*, the Colosseum. Instead, everything lay at the smaller end of the scale. Amy Richlin, for example, chose the "Pietrabbondante rooftile," a piece of miraculously preserved clay in which two enslaved women once squarely plonked their feet, leaving behind a record, in Oscan and Latin, of the job and their names for all time. Samuel Ortencio Flores chose a tenth-century BCE ceramic toy horse on wheels—a token, he says, of our shared humanity, in that we can never know if it belonged to a king's child or a slave's (figure 1). The same spirit emerged from short *sayings* chosen by other contributors. Alice Mandell picked the female tavern-keeper's invitation to Gilgamesh, stopping on his quest, to submit to immediate pleasures like dancing,

FIGURE 1. Toy horse on wheels, tenth century BCE, Kerameikos Archaeological Museum, Athens. Photo: Sharon Mollerus; Wikimedia Commons.

hot baths, a child's hand, and a wife's embrace. Dan-el Padilla Peralta democratized the Lucretian tag, "Even good King Ancus closed his eyes to the light," by adding, "But why did George Floyd have to die? Ahmaud Arbery? Breonna Taylor?"

It wasn't hard to spot a common focus: on the intimate, childish, feminine, everyday, random, subaltern, domestic, bodily, individual, mutable, and perishable. On conventionally slight things that have survived and become disproportionately meaningful: short tags about randomness, transience, or small concrete stuff, and objects made by or for ordinary people. True, the choices reflect pressing concerns in the field—about diversity, equality, rehabilitating the oppressed and the overlooked, and appreciating the messiness and the varied perspectives of antiquity. They also bear witness to a time when life seemed more than usually random and derailed, when the focus had to be on what was in front of us and what really mattered. Small things do matter now, far more than we might have predicted: from the inhabitants of tiny islands speaking out at the forefront of the climate crisis, to the young girl who heads a global environmental movement, to the infinitesimally tiny mutating virus—at the time of the lectures, omicron, "little o"—that has wreaked havoc across the world. In Alice Mandell's words: "It is . . . therapeutic to think through what we assign lasting value and why."

Berkeley was still a ghost town while I was there, but at street level its charms were never masked: an allotment where one could buy a handful of herbs for a few cents; little free libraries; a bijou coffee shop. I sampled sweaty salsa, hot tubs, goat yoga, and, further afield, Palm Springs bungalows and the Mojave Desert. I enjoyed the company of Kristina Chew, Mark Griffith, Erich Gruen, Leslie Kurke, Kathleen McCarthy, Carlos Noreña, Nelly Oliensis, John Shoptaw, and Dylan Sailor, chair of the Department of Ancient Greek and Roman Studies, who wrote a wonderfully tongue-in-cheek letter to persuade the US Embassy in London that my visit was in the national interest. A phenomenal group of graduate students inspired me to think harder about Statius. Among them, my Sather assistants Tommaso Bernardini and Lauren Nguyen always went the extra mile to produce beautiful handouts and slides. Alex Purves and Kathryn Morgan invited me to UCLA; Dorota Dutsch and Helen Morales invited me to UC Santa Barbara. Subsequent audiences in Beer Sheva, Cape Town, Cambridge, Nottingham, Santa Cruz, and Basel kindly listened to and improved some of my chapters. Two people above all changed my thinking entirely, fed me new theoretical frameworks, and boosted my morale at every dress rehearsal: Mario Telò and Anna Uhlig. I could not have written this book without them.

Away from the office, Ann and Aldo Arnold provided a delightful haven and excellent pizza. Anne Marxer rented me the perfect garden cottage, a yellow feathered Baba Yaga hut with lemons for the reaching. All around me, delicious vegetation proved that new starts were possible. For her short saying, incidentally, Hannah Čulík-Baird picked Praxilla's hymn to dead Adonis, revealing that what he misses most from life is not just the sun, moon, and stars but also ripe cucumbers, apples, and pears. As a sun, fruit, and vegetable lover, I have always preferred to read this as being about leaving California.

One day, while jogging along Berkeley's flowery streets, I was stopped in my tracks by a garden fence on McKinley Avenue, apparently sprouting with poems. They had been pinned there, it turned out, by local poet Gary Turchin, and one of them had almost the same title as one of my lectures:

> A THOUSAND LITTLE IRRITANTS
>
> The way mail piles up
> the way we argue
> the way we fail
> and keep failing
> the way we age
> and carry grudges

> the way we hurt ourselves
> and each other
> the way we smell
> or others smell
> the way we have to wait
> the way we have to hurry
> the way no one cares
> the way we don't care
> the way our government doesn't understand
> the way our understanding doesn't matter
> the way we live
> or don't live
> the way we die
> or will die
>
> and tomorrow
> the Sun
> like a giant ball of wonder
> will bounce up happy and yellow
> inventing each day
> like it's the only thing that matters

I was tickled to find my theme already endorsed at the grass roots. But Turchin's words also remind us that, however much we may sweat the small stuff, we do well to keep things in perspective. I only hope that this book, limited and exploratory though it is, will encourage its readers to keep pondering what matters, in antiquity as in the present.

TEXTS AND ABBREVIATIONS

For classical journals, I have used, where available, the abbreviations used in *L'Année Philologique*. For titles of ancient texts, I have followed, where available, the abbreviations used in the *Oxford Classical Dictionary* (3rd ed.). Translations are my own, except where otherwise indicated. I have used standard editions of ancient texts: Oxford Classical Texts or recent volumes of the Loeb Classical Library.

Other abbreviations:

| | |
|---|---|
| Cornell | *The Fragments of the Roman Historians*. Edited by Timothy Cornell. 3 vols. Oxford: Oxford University Press, 2016. |
| Courtney | *The Fragmentary Latin Poets*. Edited by Edward Courtney. 2nd ed. Oxford: Oxford University Press, 2003. |
| Fotheringham | *Eusebii Pamphili Chronici Canones*. Edited by John Fotheringham. London: Humphrey Milford, 1923. |
| K-T | *Menandri quae supersunt*. Edited by Alfred Koethe and Andreas Thierfelder. 2 vols. Leipzig: Teubner, 1957–59. |
| Klotz-Schoell | *M. Tulli Ciceronia scripta quae manserunt*. Edited by Alfred Klotz and Fritz Schoell. 8 vols. Leipzig: Teubner, 1923. |
| Laks-Most | *Early Greek Philosophy*. Edited by André Laks and Glenn Most. 9 vols. Cambridge, MA: Harvard University Press. 2016. |
| OLD | *Oxford Latin Dictionary*. Edited by P. Glare. Oxford: Oxford University Press. 1982. Rev. ed., 2012. |

| | |
|---|---|
| Perry | *Aesopica*. Vol. 1, *Greek and Latin Texts*. Edited by Ben E. Perry. Urbana: University of Illinois Press. 1952. |
| RRC | *Roman Republican Coinage*. Edited by Michael Crawford. 2 vols. Cambridge: Cambridge University Press, 1974. |
| W | *Remains of Old Latin*. Edited by E. H. Warmington. 4 vols. Cambridge, MA: Harvard University Press, 1936. |

# 1

# The Good of Small Things

*Everything is strange. Things are huge and very small. The stalks of flowers are thick as oak trees. Leaves are high as the domes of vast cathedrals. We are giants, lying here, who can make forests quiver.*
—VIRGINIA WOOLF, *THE WAVES*

Small things are all around us. They surprise us, touch us, even scare us. The summer hallucination Virginia Woolf describes here is heightened and surreal, but it conveys something universal, as well: the momentary disorientation all humans experience in their regular adjustments to differently sized surroundings.

Sometimes, small things gesture to us silently from the past. Perhaps no one captures the uncanny communicative power of small things from another time better than John Updike in this early episode of his long short story "Museums and Women." Remembering childhood visits with his mother to a local art collection, the narrator singles out certain "strange, small statues" for their disconcerting effects on him—emotional, even neurological:

> Each, if it could have been released into life, would have stood about twenty inches high and weighed in my arms as much as a cat. I itched to finger them, to interact with them, to insert myself into their mysterious silent world of strenuous contention—their bulged tendons burnished, their hushed violence detailed down to the fingernails. They were in their smallness like secret thoughts of mine projected into dimension and permanence, and they returned to me as a response that carried strangely into parts of my body. I felt myself a furtive animal sitting in the shadow of my mother. (Updike 1972, 10)

To a small boy these bronze figurines, the size of babies or pets, whose native American and mythical Greek subjects evoke two different cultural origins, seem touchable and imaginatively coextensive with his own body. At the same time, they are oddly unreachable—little forerunners, perhaps, of failed connection in his adult relationships. Immobilized, reduced, and silent as they are, they pose no obvious threat. Yet they generate almost electric bodily reactions, stir quasi-parental tenderness, empty out and restore fetal interiority. Their hidden reserves of energy give them a special charge for the child who sees them close up but distanced by age, size, and inability to move or speak. The urge they stimulate to touch ("I itched to finger them") and lunge ("as much as a cat"; "a furtive animal") corresponds in its arrested potential to the menace concentrated in those tiny, miraculously incised fingernails.[1]

Updike brilliantly conveys the complexity of the "object relations" between human beings and small external things—often circular in mechanism ("like secret thoughts"), often conceived in relation to our own feelings and memories of smallness.[2] Antiquity's survivors, much older and often much smaller as they are, preserved in material form or embedded in literary texts, emit a charge that is correspondingly intense. If we associate ancient civilizations superficially with large things—monuments, governments, economics, empire-building—in what remains it is often the small things that stand out. The most endearing and most photographed exhibit at the recent "Islanders" show at Cambridge's Fitzwilliam Museum (2023) was a black copper model of a crawling baby, just a few inches long (figure 2). Its expectant face and chubby bottom made it seem utterly familiar, even though it belonged to another era and miniaturized by many degrees the proportions of a real infant. This tiny sculpture had lain for over three millennia in a cave in Crete, waiting to be cradled again in a human palm.

But this is not a book about "the miniature" or the poetics of the miniature.[3] Nor is it about fragments.[4] Instead I am interested in how and why things dismissed as "minor," "superfluous," "undervalued," "peripheral," or even "useless"—things that by rights should not take up imaginative space and attention—often end up doing so anyway, and in the process pack a surprising punch, or punch above their weight. There is plenty to learn from the unexpected survival of things that should not matter, as well as from the ancients' encounters with what they consider small and trivial, onto which they sometimes project themselves—sometimes sentimentally, sometimes uncomfortably. Put more ambitiously: it is often via engagement with the small stuff that an individual or a society's overarching values, priorities, and sense of proportion and justice are most acutely probed and challenged.

It is easy enough to make the case that most people in antiquity, as now, spent most of their lives "sweating the small stuff," doing and thinking about minor things.[5] When Cicero scoffs at an urban official who busies himself making decrees "about trenches, sewers and the most minor disputes about watercourses," he could have adapted his contempt to many other walks of life.[6] Classical scholars are no exception, as they pore over minutiae (detached or incomplete relics, like particles, fragments, and potsherds) and engage in minor disputes about dates and textual variants—habits that expose us to scorn in the outside world (perhaps in the rest of academia, too). Like it or not, encounters with smallness and lack are meat and drink to us, as they were to the hoarding encyclopedists of the late

FIGURE 2. Figurine of crawling baby (copper alloy), 1600 BCE–700 BCE, Psychro Cave, Lasithi plateau, East Crete, Ashmolean Museum, Oxford, AN1938.1162. Credit: @Ashmolean Museum.

Roman Empire. Still, they need not make us defeatist. Small things reward the attention we give them, out of all proportion to their size. Fragments even force us to confront the essential incompleteness of antiquity, something that can never be received in a perfect state nor be restored to one. Incidentally, this is a plea that in the humanities we might be allowed to go on being curious in ways that are not necessarily about reconstructing the past, but more about sitting comfortably with its brokenness, its odd and often disputed priorities, and its apparently minor preoccupations.

But how much of a plea do I really need to make, when smallness has been a topic of huge intellectual curiosity for some time now, at least since Gaston Bachelard, Susan Stewart, Alfred Gell, John Mack, and others championed the power of tiny things to fascinate us and answer our physical and psychological needs for privacy, control, play, and intimate contact?[7] Their close-up inspection of dolls' houses, shells, nests, pocketbooks, amulets, and matchstick models has inspired many contemporary classicists to rethink "little antiquity," combining a myopic vision with ambitions that go beyond traditional philological scrutiny: Michael Squire with miniature tablets, Verity Platt with seal-rings, Fanny Dolansky dolls, Jessica Hughes votives, Victoria Rimell tiny dwellings and tight spaces.[8] At the

University of California alone, Alex Purves is probing "micro-Sappho" and Mike Chin "tiny alive things" in Christian literature. James Ker has explored the quotidian; Rachel Love has rescued historical epitomes as creative readings, as has Irene Peirano the Appendix Vergiliana. Cat Lambert has discovered in ancient bookworms—those clandestine, indiscriminate word-eaters—a focus for larger anxieties about bad reading practices.[9] Everyone seems to be drilling away into overlooked spaces and extracting rich fodder. Even the building program of middle-Republican temples has recently been described, by Dan-el Padilla Peralta, as a case of "repetitive smallness."[10] In many cases, the rhetoric has changed: small things are being justified less as objects of study in their own right (specimens in a catalogue tradition) and more as indirect symptoms of larger phenomena, behavioral habits, even sociopolitical movements.[11]

## THE CALL OF THE SMALL

I am hardly the first, then, to justify looking at antiquity through a "small" lens; indeed, my instincts show me to be squarely a creature of my time.[12] Anthropologist Nicole Boivin is typical in calling for closer attention to "the things that go unnoticed—the pots and pans, the highways and pens, and teacups and computers, fishing hooks, doorways, building blocks, religious relics, conveyer belts, spears, carpets, parks, antennae, pendants, perfumes, appliances, museum objects . . ."[13] Yet even this recent surge of interest is none too surprising, given that smallness was an enduringly productive concept, theoretical and political, for twentieth-century thinkers such as Freud, Arendt, Adorno, Foucault, Deleuze, and Derrida; when "small, ordinary, vulnerable, and incomplete" has been identified as the core aesthetic of modernist poetry (think William Carlos Williams's plums in the ice box); and when so many alienated citizens of the modern world have sanctified domestic space—insulated from, if usually enabled by, capitalism and industrialization—in a turn that Hannah Arendt in *The Human Condition* dismissed as "the modern enchantment with 'small things.'"[14] Small things can hardly claim to be neglected in academic circles when we have histories of dust, shit, pockets, and fungi. Nearly fifty years ago now, James Deetz's *In Small Things Forgotten* argued for the silent eloquence of humble artefacts from the insular societies of early modern New England: broken crockery; the placing of a single chair; angel images on gravestones, with their minute variations.[15] Around the same time, Georges Perec invented the term "infraordinary" to denote the background details and quotidian nonevents he challenged himself to represent in his experimental writing.[16]

Even so, a debate still simmers in the humanities and social sciences over the pluses and minuses of microanalysis: granular, nuanced, precise, individual, and uncorporate, on the one hand; over-specific, parochial, safe, and underpoliticized, on the other. Digital historian Tim Hitchcock has played devil's advocate against the big-data approaches that characterize his subject. Along the way, he salutes the long-term contribution of the *Annales* school to local, small-scale history, Marxist historians to personal and emotional history, and Michel Foucault to the structures of everyday life (not forgetting New Historicism for giving dignity to unheard voices and uncanonical texts). Hitchcock's conclusion is understandably much quoted: "If today we have a public dialogue that gives voice to the traditionally excluded and silenced—women, and minorities of ethnicity, belief and dis/ability—it is in no small part because we now have beautiful histories of small things."[17]

If "beautiful histories" have had such far-reaching consequences, then the politics of smallness cannot so easily be separated from its aesthetics.[18] Cultural critic Mark Seltzer has identified the academic trend toward "one-downmanship," as a turn "from large events to small (non)events," a collective response to the pressures of globalization:

> with respect to the novel, there is a turn to the study of minor characters; with respect to affect, minor feelings; with respect to political forms, little resistances, infantile subjects, minute, therapeutic adjustments; with respect to perception, the decelerated gaze and a prolonged attentiveness; and so on. (Selzer 2011, 727)

Symptomatic of this "minor" but highly charged approach is *Ordinary Affects* (2006), anthropologist Kathleen Stewart's experimental prose essay on the "jumpiness" inherent in small, mundane events. She presents modern life as a daily barrage of instant shocks and repercussive aftershocks (a blip in air traffic control, heat-induced road rage, a neighbors' spat) that condition in us reflexes of "watching and waiting" which threaten to escalate at any moment. In her words: "The ordinary registers intensities—regularly, intermittently, urgently, or as a slight shudder . . . The ordinary is a circuit that's always tuned in to some little something somewhere."[19]

Tapping into a similar vein is Sonya Huber's memoir, *Supremely Tiny Acts* (2021), which follows James Joyce, Virginia Woolf, and Nicholson Baker (and before them Seneca in his letters) by compressing a lifetime into the action of a single day. Huber's account of her one-off intervention in world events—a court appearance after being arrested at an Extinction Rebellion protest in New York City in November 2019—is interspersed with mundane repetitive actions: using the restroom at Grand Central Station; recording small frustrations in small notebooks; remembering the "thousand little failures" of teaching creative writing. The word *tiny* becomes a leitmotif: tiny plastic bags, tiny nudges, tiny victories, a tiny sadness, a tiny glass egg, a tiny inch-long squiggle of cabbage in a fish taco. Yet the *Supremely* of Huber's title claims a kind of grandeur even for grassroots gestures. If observing microaggressions counts as a valid form of political protest, then her fine-grained logging of daily experience registers as an activist's hyper-vigilance.[20]

Arundhati Roy's *The God of Small Things* (1997), whose title I have tweaked for this chapter, set the trend by probing Indian politics, the caste system, global migration, and other "Big Things" through a small lens, whether that lens is pointed at a moth, a glass bead stuck up a child's nose, peanuts in a narrow paper cone, or "toy histories of India that rich tourists come to play with." Stewart, Huber, and Roy all operate with the kind of telescoping mechanism Stephen Greenblatt has termed "foveation"—that is, putting an intense focus on small things and letting the large ones recede into a vaguer penumbra.[21] This is something we will see in Roman authors, too, when they absorb themselves in what is close at hand, seemingly to the exclusion of all else, but in fact in uneasy or avoidant relation to what Roy calls "the Big Things that lurk unsaid."[22]

In popular culture, too, "smallness" has exploded as a slogan and an attitude—especially since COVID-19—to judge from a slew of titles randomly spotted on planes and bookstands: movies and TV shows like *The Map of Tiny Perfect Things*, *Little Boxes*, and *Tiny Beautiful Things*; nonfiction like *Minor Feelings*, *Small Fires*, *Small Bodies of Water* and *The Joy of Small Things*; novels like *Small Things Like These* and *little scratch* (its title defiantly printed in lower case). Superficially modest, "twee," or hipster in spirit they may be, but together they raise a shrill chorus of minoritarian and countercultural voices. When dozens of such separate minor outbursts are repeated or combined, their collective impact reveals "where things can go," as Kathleen Stewart puts it, "taking off in their own little worlds, when something throws itself together."[23]

My own tic of gathering tiny items into lists incidentally suggests further questions. Does collecting small things together enhance their significance or lessen it? Is tension between individual and plural a feature special to small things (after all, it applies to Cyclopes as well as bees)?[24] When they are not unique, small things tend to come in undifferentiated swarms, rashes, sprinkles, dust storms, and viral loads. In their plurality lies their disposability—and their power.

## A BRIEF HISTORY OF ANCIENT SMALLNESS

Along with closer attention to small things in literary texts and human histories has come a new attitude to the small material objects of the distant past. These are far less likely to be patronized as mere substitutes for complete, original, or life-sized wholes now that we appreciate how their handleable size invites tactile engagement and manual dexterity and radiates a different kind of charisma. The editors of *The Tiny and the Fragmented: Miniature, Broken or Otherwise Incomplete Objects from the Ancient World* (Martin and Langin-Hooper 2018) argue for the autonomy and versatility of things formerly overlooked as cheap or inadequate replicas of larger artefacts: "These objects have a particular command over the viewer, enticing him or her into personal interactions, demanding specific modes of looking and touching, and encouraging the displacement of personal identity."[25] They rightly add the proviso that size is always relative and has a complicated relationship to power in the ancient world. On the other hand, the editors' decision to combine deliberately small things with accidentally broken or fragmented ones has attracted criticism.[26] If I am guilty, for my part, of confusing the small with other categories, the material, trivial, oppressed, brief, minor, fragmentary, pointless, and childish—and I will be—then the blame lies partly with the parallel hierarchies of size and value that have so often bound these concepts together.

How much, then, of our current thinking about smallness is determined by, or resists, ancient orthodoxies? The organizers of a 2015 conference in Toulouse on artistic miniatures, "Think 'Small,'" claimed that the qualities typical of little artefacts—handleability, portability, economy, frugality, preciousness, minute detail, prettiness, and strangeness—have remained essentially stable throughout history.[27] To their list we could add familiarity, intimacy, vulnerability, funniness—and why not scariness, too? But the question remains whether the Greeks and Romans looked at small things differently from how we do. Richard Neer, for example, has emphasized wonder, naïve or rational, as a frame for ancient responses.[28] Equally intriguing—and hard to get past—is how *we* look at *their* small things: half as any human might, with a combination of sentimentality, fetishism, wonder, affection, closeness, and patronizing contempt, but half as observers from a greater distance.

Susan Stewart once memorably claimed that we imagine childhood, that miniature chapter in all our pasts, "as if it were at the other end of a tunnel, distanced, diminutive, and clearly framed."[29] Supposing we viewed antiquity as another miniature chapter, a kind of shared *cultural* childhood, then do the small things of the past exaggerate those diminishing effects? Does a fragile papyrus or doll (or miniature baby) that has survived thousands of years summon in us greater feelings of tenderness and longing than its contemporary equivalents do? And are these feelings focused on the found things themselves or on the absent humans to whom they once belonged? Does close contact with small things help us feel that we can better possess or grasp antiquity, perhaps lighten its pressure? Or does it make us melancholy, reminding us of what we have lost?

If small things have been clawing back their rightful significance after centuries of being dismissed and underrated, then it must be conceded from the outset that classical antiquity is not always to blame. In fact, ancient thinkers deserve much of the credit for questioning the low status of smallness right from the beginning. It is to them that we can trace all three of the central threads in the history of the topic that I pull out briefly here: scale and value; presence and contact with the real; and nostalgia and loss.

Taking scale and value first, it is undeniable that antiquity, along with the automatic impulse to downplay small things, also hands us the tools for thinking about large and small in creative and counterintuitive ways. Platonic philosophy is usually charged with confirming the standard hierarchies, for aligning large with important, abstract, ideal, lofty, complete, adult, divine, and powerful, and small with trivial, material, real, humble, fragmented, childish, subhuman, and powerless. Correspondences between size and value remain embedded in Greek and

FIGURE 3. Fragmentary Roman doll, bone, late third century CE, J. Paul Getty Museum, Villa Collection, Malibu, California, gift of Dr. and Mrs. Marvin J. Teitelbaum, 79.AI.208. Digital image courtesy of Getty's Open Content Program.

Latin vocabulary, as in English. Latin *paruus*, for example, translates primarily as "small," but by extension as "ignorable, worthless, of little account"; *nihil*, "nothing," literally means "not worth a speck" (*ne-hilum*), *hilum* now being the name for the tiny scar that records where a plant's seed broke off from its original sac.[30]

On the other hand, it is the ancients who launch the first, early challenges to these rigid categories, from Homeric similes that reduce warriors to flies on milk (the divine perspective) to the tiny insect of fable that terrifies the larger beast (the subaltern's perspective) to the thorn in a shoe that causes devastating pain (the human or animal perspective). Small-scale or minor genres such as lyric, epigram, elegy, fable, and satire regularly champion alternative priorities, cemented in Callimachean and neoteric manifestos. Antiquity consistently gives a platform to countercultural value systems that make the greatness of armies, statesmen, and empires evaporate next to the *je ne sais quoi* of a beloved's face, a whiff of perfume, a pinch of spice, a lock of hair—even the banality of a chamber pot.[31] Claims to inferiority and weakness, from the elegiac lover, the screwed-over camp follower, or the belated literary successor, may of course only be "passive-aggressive" indicators of superiority (in refinement, virtue, or wisdom) in disguise, ones that indirectly render their targets coarse, bullying, and pompous.[32]

Modernist poets are notorious for focusing on the small and the perishable: "William Carlos Williams's plums, Frank O'Hara's charms, Lorine Niedecker's granite pail, George Oppen's single brick, John Ashbery's cocoa tins, Bernadette Mayer's puffed-wheat cereal, Thomas Sayers Ellis's balloon dog, and Rae Armantrout's cat, bubble wrap, and 'rubber band, chapstick, tin- / foil, this pen, things / made for our use'" (in Sianne Ngai's evocative list).[33] But Latin poetry, centuries before, had made space for long catalogues of equally insubstantial things. The dust, chalk, cobwebs, feathers, seeds, and barely felt insects' feet traced by Lucretius (not to mention his unruly, giggling atoms), Juvenal's mantlepiece ornaments, Martial's party favors and Statius's shopping list of rubbishy Saturnalian gift ideas— lampwicks, figs, snails, onionskins, wine dregs, and so on, and so on—add up to something and nothing at the same time.[34] Indeed, it is when Lucretius grasps at analogies with seeds and fluff to conjure the lightness and mobility of the soul's constitution that he first splits his all-important nothing (*nihil*) into its component parts (*ne . . . hilum*)—a linguistically opportune "proof" that marks the perverse centrality of insignificant things to the operations of the cosmos: *nec defit ponderis hilum* ("[the soul's] weight fails not a whit"; *DRN* 3.182).

For all Homer's generous vision, the polarity between large and small was a central tenet of the first Greek philosophers, the Pre-Socratics.[35] Yet even they were refreshingly open to the idea that size is both relative and expandable. There is always something larger than the largest thing, and something smaller than the smallest thing, claimed Anaxagoras, while conceding (centuries before Virginia Woolf) that the same thing could be conceived as both large and small.[36] Plato would distinguish more subtly between small-large oppositions and strive to unravel their apparent contradictions. In the *Phaedo*, for example, Socrates draws a practical real-life conclusion—if Simmias is tall relative to Socrates but short relative to Phaedo, then he must be tall and short at the same time—only to pronounce dogmatically that abstract opposites, as opposed to empirical ones, are truly incompatible: "Greatness itself will never admit the small."[37] Even so, small men like Socrates (and Aesop) who concealed moral greatness in their squat and unremarkable bodies were walking incarnations of this very impossibility.[38]

Small and large were differently aligned via analogy—another kind of relationship crucial to philosophical and scientific teaching.[39] Anaxagoras is credited with the theory of *homoeomeria*, which posited (via the fallacy of division) that the infinitesimal atoms that constitute a puddle are themselves wet, or those that compose a rock are themselves hard.[40] The *Phaedo* also happens to be the work where Socrates imaginatively cuts the world down to size, comparing the earth to a twelve-faced leather ball and the peoples of the Mediterranean to ants or frogs living around a pond.[41]

Nor were small and large ever simply polar opposites as they pivoted around that accepted template for scale, the human body. When Aristotle carves out his aesthetic midpoint between the two in the *Poetics*, he belittles the two extremes equally: large is impossible for the eye to take in; small too fused together to be properly picked out.[42] Homer was praised by Quintilian for embracing both perspectives at once: "No one surpasses Homer in sublimity where big things are concerned, and in attention to detail where small things are concerned."[43] The first poet's dream of a totalizing purview is realized by Iris when she warns King Priam about the advancing Greeks by casting immeasurable size in terms of innumerable small things: "Never have I seen such a great army as this; for they cross the plain exactly like leaves or grains of sand."[44] Yet a goddess's comprehensive vision, panoptic and microscopic at the same time, lies beyond mortal reach, such that a poet's encounter with unthinkable size or unnarratable detail becomes a "selection crisis" that only confirms human limitations.[45] Kant's "mathematical sublime" is expressed as much in Homer's hand-wringing appeals about the uncountability of waves or sand as in descriptions of mountains. Depending on perspective, the Shield of Achilles is a colossus and a miniature at the same time.

Conversely, when the third-century BCE poet Posidippus captures the unexpected sublimity of an epigrammatized pebble, beaming from its miniature frame, he complicates the "small is beautiful" and "less is more" mantras usually associated with Hellenistic aesthetics and pushes epigram's innate claim to embrace *multum in parvo* to its limits.[46] As Jim Porter argues, "Small objects are calculated attention-grabbers: they demand to be viewed from up close . . . What was once tiny is now gigantic, even grand. It is a sublime object."[47] He echoes Gaston Bachelard in *The Poetics of Space*: "Values become condensed and enriched in miniature. Platonic dialectics of large and small do not suffice for us to become cognizant of the dynamic virtues of miniature thinking. One must go beyond logic in order to experience what is large in what is small."[48] Such "illogical" relationships between large

FIGURE 4. Unknown (Greek), engraved scarab with lion's head and two mice, cornelian, second quarter of fifth century BCE, J. Paul Getty Museum, Villa Collection, Malibu, California, 81.AN.76.29. Digital image courtesy of Getty's Open Content Program.

and small, we will see, are found throughout Greco-Roman culture. They come in many forms: analogous, fractal, metonymic, concentric, inter-entangled . . .

Small and large could, for instance, operate as a continuum. The childhood of the gods presented an attractive subject to Hellenistic poets not simply because of its innate sweetness but also because its miniature proportions contained all the promise of a divinity's future growth.[49] Just so, the *nescioquid magnum* (something big) that is the *Iliad* is already furled up inside the *Achilleid*, Statius's prequel to the Iliadic Achilles.[50] Poets extrapolate backward to imagine epic poets' youthful productions, tracing Virgil's final scene of anger back to the ferocious buzz and sting of a tiny mosquito (*Culex*) in his made-up juvenilia or finding the germ of Homeric wars in the miniature battles of frogs and mice.[51] The small could also be embraced concentrically (and peaceably) *inside* the large: pastoral subsumed by epic; the smallholding or secluded valley protected by empire; a herb-specked cheese (pseudo-Virgil's *Moretum*) replicating the stirred-up cosmos of which it is the tiniest part.[52] So, too, in the contemporary world—as Sianne Ngai has shown in her work on cuteness—fluffy animal toys are the soft, sentimental center of the hard global industry that mass-produces them.[53]

Another type of paradoxical relationship—large compressed *into* small—characterizes the textual phenomenon known as "epitome," the abridgment of a predecessor's longer narrative. The best surviving example, Trajanic author Florus's miniature of Livy's monumental history, relinquishes none of the original's ambition, instead forcing all its characters and events to fall in line with its abbreviating mission, so Jared Hudson has argued.[54] Florus's topographical short cuts (*compendia*) are matched by textual ones: swift execution on the ground complements skilful précis in his script; anecdotes and pointed statements sum up larger actions; individual performances stand for multitudes. Capturing a complete panorama in one imperialist sweep, his minimizing survey takes on a grandeur of its own:

> Therefore, if anything else is, this too is worth the effort to know [*hoc quoque operae pretium sit cognoscere*]; and yet, since its very magnitude stands in its way, and the variety of its subject matter breaks the sharpness of concentration [*magnitudo rerumque diuersitas aciem intentionis abrumpit*], I shall imitate those who depict the lie of the land: I shall encompass its entire representation in, as it were, a small portrait [*in breui quasi tabella totam eius imaginem amplectar*], thus, I hope, contributing something to the admiration of this leading people, if I succeed in displaying altogether and all at once their entire magnitude [*insemel uniuersam magnitudinem*].
> (Florus *Epit.* 1 *praef.* 3)

As Hudson puts it, "Celebrating and comprehending *magnitudo* becomes, paradoxically, a matter of cutting massiveness down to size."[55] And, we might add, of preserving a sharp focus (*aciem intentionis*).

Do small things always need to work harder to defend their prestige and impact? Flaubert's aphorism, "The story of a louse can be as beautiful as the story of Alexander the Great," comes with the caution, "Everything in art depends on the execution."[56] Writers like Lucian who wrote elegant paradoxical encomia to such challenging subjects as flies and gnats would have agreed: workmanship was paramount.[57] But it did not always have to involve intricacy. The ancients prized minimalism and ordinary realism, too, to judge from two kinds of artwork mentioned by Pliny the Elder: the ever-thinner lines drawn by Apelles and Protogenes on an otherwise blank canvas, passing for nothing at all (*inani similem*) among the masterpieces in Augustus's palace but apparently far more "seductive" (*allicientem*) than more prestigious paintings; and the lowly barbers' shops, cobblers' stalls, donkeys, and food scenes of Peiraicos the "painter of trash" (*rhyparographos*), which gave "greater pleasure" and commanded higher prices than "larger pictures."[58]

It is when conventional correspondences between size and importance or value do not line up that things become interesting, and Roman authors express dissent or outrage on this theme surprisingly often. To start late with a more conventional or even fundamentalist response, here is Tertullian directing his spluttering indignation and rhetorical glee at the paradoxical alignment of small scale and market value, in this case the eye-watering cost of women's jewelry:

> From the smallest boxes [*de breuissimis loculis*] is produced an ample inheritance [*patrimonium grande*]. On a single thread is suspended a million sesterces. One delicate neck carries around it forests and islands. Slender earlobes exhaust a fortune; and the left hand sports several purses on every finger. Such is the strength of ambition—equal to bearing on one small body, and a woman's at that [*uno et muliebri corpusculo*], the product of such copious wealth. (Tert. *De Cultu Feminarum* 1.9.2)

Pliny the Elder appears far more liberal when it comes to including insects in his simulacrum of the world, the *Natural History*, a work of superhuman ambition that demands a focus simultaneously macroscopic and microscopic.[59] His apologies for "sterile" subject matter that nevertheless contains all life (*sterilis materia, rerum natura, hoc est uita, narratur*) are disingenuous enough.[60] But Pliny also plays with different perspectives in his lengthy preface to the first book. At his most finicky, he approaches the emperor with a deliberate misquotation from Catullus's opening poem, itself a high-stakes challenge to conventional hierarchies of value:

> namque tu solebas
> nugas esse aliquid meas putare
>
> For you used to think my trifles were worth something . . . (Cat. 1.3–4)

As Pliny reminds his readers, what Catullus actually wrote was *meas esse aliquid putare nugas*: "for he, as you know, by interchanging the first syllables made himself a trifle harsher [*duriusculum*] than he wished to be considered by his 'darling Veraniuses and Fabulluses.'" By improving so infinitesimally on Catullus's original, he drives it home that minute attention to detail, in a project this capacious, must always be on a par with comprehensiveness.

Pliny introduces his insects cautiously, as a conscious supplement to a catalogue of larger animals. Book 10 ends with these words: "For these remain to be covered" (*haec namque restant*).[61] Book 11 heralds a topic of "enormous intricacy" (*inmensae subtilitatis*), one that matches the complexities of insect bodies themselves:

> In these minute creatures, so close to nothing, how exceptional the intelligence, how vast the resources, and how ineffable the perfection [*in his tam paruis atque tam nullis quae ratio, quanta uis, quam inextricabilis perfectio*]. Where has she compressed so many senses as in the gnat—not to mention even smaller creatures [*et sunt alia dictu minora*]? (Plin. *HN* 11.1.1)

Then, drawing in his audience, Pliny bows to the same old prejudices:

> I must beg my readers, for all the contempt they feel for many of these objects, not to feel a similar disdain [*fastidio*] for the relevant information I am about to give, seeing that, in the study of nature, none of her works can seem superfluous [*superuacuum*]. (Plin. *HN* 11.1.2)

14     THE GOOD OF SMALL THINGS

Insects hover between being minimal but welcome components of his cosmic inventory and supplementary *parerga* on the margins of consideration. And the ones "too small even to mention" (*dictu minora*) remain on the margins.

The idea of superfluity also inflects Seneca's *De brevitate vitae* (*On the Shortness of Life*), a treatise that is predictably self-conscious about its economy in relation to its subject—all the way from its little mottoes (*uita breuis ars longa*, "Life is short, art is long," and *exigua pars est uitae qua uiuimus*, "It is a tiny part of life that we actually live") to its broader existential claim that a backward glance from the moment of death shrinks even millennia into the narrowest of spans. All the while, Seneca is redefining the concept of a life well lived, spent not in joining the rat race with the other frenzied *occupati*, embroiled in "focused concentration on useless work" (*in superuacuis laboribus operosa sedulitas*), but in mindfully contemplating the eventual day of reckoning.[62]

This is a shortish work—how could it not be?—but oddly permeable to superfluities of its own. One sentence starts misleadingly, "It would be superfluous to mention" (6.3 *superuacuum est*), before proceeding to mention, at least as a nameless group, all the other people who repent too feebly and too late of having spent all their time working and underestimate their life's span as *superuacuum* in another sense ("baggy" or "capacious"), in that they assume it will keep on giving: "but you allow it to disappear like something that is negligible and replenishable" (6.4 *superuacuam ac reparabilem*). Seneca makes himself an exception to the preoccupied masses, permitting himself to concertina his text and his thoughts at will. Similarly, intellectual distance gives Pliny the Younger a broader perspective on the triviality of his daily urban routine: "The things you do every day seem necessary, but when you reflect that you do them every day, they seem pointless [*inania*], the more so when you are away from them" (*Ep.* 1.9.3).

By default marginal or supplementary, small things usually help to absorb and defuse the threats posed by larger bodies or images.[63] But this does not mean that they cannot sometimes be the focus of intense centripetal force—as if miniaturization entailed concentration, the decoction of bland large-scale ingredients into a denser brew.[64] Seizing a loftier metaphysical vantage-point in the *Natural Questions*, Seneca goes further in minimizing human ambition by reducing the physical terrain we occupy to a mere speck compared with the infinite realm of the mind:

> It is a pinhead [*punctum*] on which you sail, on which you wage war, on which you arrange tiny kingdoms: they are the smallest things even when the ocean meets them on either side. (*QNat.* 1 *praef.* 11)

He is recalling the *Dream of Scipio*, as imagined by Cicero in his *Republic*: "Now the earth itself seemed to me so small that I felt ashamed of our empire, with which we touch as it were only a pinprick [*quasi punctum*] on the earth's surface."[65]

No sooner is the *punctum* mentioned than it galvanizes a change of perspective. Far from maintaining a cosmic viewpoint that shrinks armies to swarms of ants and stares out at tsunamis and earthquakes, Seneca starts to pull back and undermine himself. How wrong-headed, he says, to dread huge threats like these when danger and disaster lurk closer to home, in the tiny things found within our immediate surroundings:

> The man who fears lightning bolts, earthquakes, and gaping cracks in the ground esteems himself highly. But is he willing to be aware of his own frailty and to fear a cold in the head? That, to be sure, is how we were born, having been allotted such excellent limbs, having grown to this stature! And for this reason we are not able to die unless sections of the world are moved, unless the sky thunders, unless the earth settles! The pain of a fingernail, and not even of the whole nail but just a split on one side of it, finishes us off! [*unguiculi nos et ne totius quidem dolor sed aliqua ab latere eius scissura conficit!*] Also, should I fear an earth tremor because a thick catarrh chokes me? Am I to fear the sea moved from its place and the tide with a greater rush than usual, pulling more water and drowning me when a drink has strangled some people as it slipped down the throat the wrong way? How foolish to fear the sea when you know you can die from a drop of water! (Sen. *QNat.* 6.2.4–5; Loeb, trans. Gummere, adapted)

He has a point, when many of us have recently been more terrified of droplets than tsunamis. Note how the fingernail pokes its way in again, a tiny homunculus with the potential to produce excruciating pain. Or rather, not even the whole fingernail, this time (*unguiculi . . . et ne totius quidem*), but the fingernail's miniature: the side-tear, the smallest site of human sensitivity.[66]

Contradictions of scale come to a head in *Epistle* 89, where Seneca twists Aristotelian polarities into a paradoxical loop: "I shall do what you demand and divide philosophy into parts but not into scraps [*non in frusta*] . . . Just as it is hard to take in what is indefinitely large, so it is hard to take in what is indefinitely small . . . Whatever has grown larger is more easily identified if it is broken up into parts; but the parts . . . must not be innumerable and diminutive in size" (*innumerabiles . . . et paruulas*).[67] For overanalysis (says Seneca, overanalyzing) is faulty in just the same way as no analysis at all; "whatever you cut so fine that it becomes dust is as good as blended into a mass again" (*simile confuso est, quidquid usque in puluerem sectum est*).[68] Infinitesimal change and asymptotic progress had long been the stuff of Greek philosophical paradoxes—Sorites's heap and Achilles and the tortoise.

In another letter, Seneca restages the notion that human life is compressed into a minute span: "Our life is a moment, or even less than a moment" (*punctum est quod uiuimus et adhuc puncto minus*).[69] All the more vital for it to have a purpose (or point); life is far too short to spend reading trash (*superuacua*).[70] Here, the *punctum* stands for the tiniest unit of time, rather than space—though in both cases it could be defined as the minimum surface area or interval consistent with the maximum impact and concentration of energy. When Seneca advocates vein opening as the most efficient method of suicide, he notes that the prick of a small scalpel offers the most reliable way out (*puncto securitas constat*), suggesting, as

James Ker puts it, "an aesthetics of the *punctum* that matches the already minuscule temporal and spatial dimensions of human life."[71] Livy repeats a well-known saying about warfare: "A single instant [*punctum temporis*] is often the turning-point of a great event [*maximarum rerum momenta uerti*]."[72] If there is a single word that binds together all my forays into smallness in this book, it is this. Whether it is an insect's sting, a sharp point, or a shaft of wit, the *punctum* marks the spot where the apparently pointless becomes pointful.

## REALITY EFFECTS

Small details also stand out in larger literary texts thanks to their remarkable ability to create convincing reality effects.[73] Like small material objects from the past, they evoke an unsettling sense of familiarity that bridges the gap between the ancient world and our own. But does this always come at the cost of their larger symbolic significance? Not according to Erich Auerbach, who isolated minor details as the open sesame to many canonical works in *Mimesis* (1946), a book that, like Homer's epics and Pliny's encyclopedia, sweeps enviably between micro- and macro-perspectives.[74] Auerbach subtly identifies different relationships between details and wholes, especially in connection with narrative time. His readings span the Western canon from Homer to Virginia Woolf, all the way from the "luminous" primeval clarity and surface coherence of the nurse Eurycleia's discovery of Odysseus's scar to the woolly mismatch between Mrs Ramsay's brief exchange with her son about a too-short brown sock, and the long intervening sadness that the sorry item generates, expressed in the overspill of her deepest thoughts.[75]

Not by chance, details in visual art—traditionally subordinate, or the rarefied preserve of connoisseurs—were being reevaluated around the same time, driven by developments in photography, film and psychoanalysis.[76] In his *Essai sur la connaissance approchée* (1927), Bachelard isolated the cognitive dilemma involved as the eye moves between details and whole: while details stimulate close sensory engagement, wholes inspire more abstract overarching generalizations. Art historians have since made their own sense of such aporetic or schizophrenic viewpoints. Georges Didi-Huberman explains an anomalous splash of paint on a Vermeer canvas as a disruptive, unexplainable "symptom" of painting itself, while Daniel Arasse sees details not as translatable from some agreed language of symbols so much as arresting entities in their own right, "sending a shiver down the spine in a moment of transhistorical contact," as one of his readers puts it (the phrase itself suggesting a minute stabbing or shivering sensation).[77] Such phenomena call for radically new kinds of interpretation.[78]

Literary critics have long faced similar dilemmas. Is the textual detail a quirk, an unassimilable *parergon* or supplement, or a microcosmic building block that serves the construction of the whole? Is its meaning available on the surface or a symptom of something buried? Does it signify materiality for its own sake or is it tied to some broader symbolic purpose? Via intertextuality or intratextuality?[79] I remember a panicked experience as an undergraduate once, having to construct an entire exam answer about Terence and his Greek models from a single piece of memorized information: that in his *Andria* Terence had omitted Menander's original prescription for a tonic containing four egg yolks. Menander's fragmented script runs as follows: "Give her a bath at once . . . and after that, my dear, the yolks of four eggs." Terence bleaches this into "Afterwards give her what I said to drink, in the quantity I specified."[80] Hard though it would be to argue, Auerbach-style, that eggs are metonymically central to Menander's plot, their absence from Terence speaks volumes about his taste for purging detail and his neoclassical boundaries for what is admissible.[81] Later, gastronome-cum-encyclopedist Athenaeus would catch many such small comic delicacies in his capacious net. An unexpectedly modern perspective on reality effects is taken by Seneca the Elder, when he singles out an eccentric orator for including "sordid" things like vinegar, flea-mint, lanterns, and sponges in his speeches. Not only was Albucius reluctant to look pretentious, he says, but his "sordid" things actually created a kind of extraneous background noise (*superuacuus strepitus*), which worked as backing (*patrocinium*) for his other arguments.[82]

Do textual details commit us, then, to making an exclusive choice between salience and background noise? Serendipitously, an egg appears in one of my favourite passages in Latin literature, which happens to illustrate how compatibly the low-level hum of Greco-Roman reality (what Georges Perec would one day call the "infraordinary") can coexist with the throbbing salience of individual small things.[83] Book 7 of Pliny the Elder's *Natural History* (the book about "the human animal") includes a wonderfully inconsequential list that celebrates the randomness of life—or, rather, the randomness of sudden death, something Pliny calls "life's greatest happiness."[84] Starting with Sophocles and Dionysius of Sicily, who both died of joy on receiving prizes for their tragedies, Pliny moves from a mother who expired happily on seeing her son back alive after he had been reported dead at the Battle of Cannae to a grammarian who died of shame on being unable to answer a senior philosopher's question (every academic's nightmare). Then to two Caesars (father and uncle of Julius) who died early in the morning when putting on their sandals. Next comes a group of men who died coming out of their houses: Q. Fabius Maximus on the very last day of his consulship (equivalent to our December 31, a neat and a random death, at once); C. Volcatius Gurges while setting off for a walk; Q. Aemilius Lepidus after leaving his bedroom and stubbing his big toe on the doorstep; C. Aufidius tripping on the floor of the Comitium; Cn. Baebius Tamphilus while asking his slave the time; Mn. Juventius Thalna while offering a sacrifice; C. Servelius Pansa while standing by a shop in the forum, leaning on his brother's shoulder; a judge while granting an extension of bail; M. Terentius Corax when writing on tablets in the forum; a knight while whispering in the ear of an ex-consul in front of the ivory statue of Apollo in the Forum of Augustus. The surgeon C. Julius died dragging a probe through his eye while applying ointment; several men died at dinner, either reaching for a cake, or drinking mead, or coming out of the bathhouse drinking mead and sucking an egg at the same time; two men died in flagrante, two knights died inside the same male pantomime actor. And finally comes the crowning glory in the shape of a beautiful pileup of happy ingredients, "the painstakingly contrived serenity" (*operosissima securitas*) of the appropriately named comic actor and playwright M. Ofilius Hilarus, who staged a feast on his birthday, asked for a hot drink, and, after putting on his mask again and his garland on top of it, lolled there in sheer contentment. And no one noticed that he had grown stiff until his neighbour leaned over to tell him that his drink was getting cold.

This magical assemblage of casual but decisive events was so loved by Montaigne that he updated it in his *Essais*, adding that his own brother had died of apoplexy five hours after being hit by a tennis ball.[85] In a short space, Pliny's account covers a broad range of ancient experience, along with some central polarities in Greco-Roman thought: tragedy/comedy, sorrow/joy, real merit and staged victory (Sophocles and Dionysius), surgery/self-harm, the heat of life/the chill of death, sex/death, banquet/death, survival/death, victory/death, birthday/deathday, randomness/appropriate closure, momentary time/calendrical time, comic mask/death mask, reality/mimesis, knights/consuls, senators/people . . .

At the same time, the special vitality and appeal of this passage surely derive from the insignificant material details that interlard it. The simplest explanation for their presence is that they provide circumstantial evidence and a basis in empirical reality. Things that seem far too innocuous to be fatal instruments flick a critical switch between life and death, measured timewise as the "twinkling of an eye."[86] There are a few specific local resonances (deaths on leaving the house, for example, are ominous because that is where a Roman funeral procession would start; men who die tripping up or stubbing their toes perform the symbolic links Roman divination made between falling and dying). But most of the details feel arbitrary and mundane at a more universal level. They stand in close physical relationship to the deceased individuals: food and drink, incompletely absorbed (egg, cake, wine); body parts or synecdochic stand-ins for the body (sandals, shoulder, ear, toe, mask); or points of near contact with the outside (eye probe, threshold). Props from the immediate environment, they anchor or dislodge the human agents; they are not obviously metaphors for anything else.

For modern readers, though, these props have an extra vibrancy independent of any authenticating or symbolic function. They pop up like punctuation marks or little shocks, producing bumps and frissons of disconcerting familiarity—not unlike a toe-stubbing, a cracked eggshell, a nudged shoulder or a probe grazing the eye. Not only do they evoke Daniel Arasse's shivers of transhistorical contact: they also recall the effect of arresting details in photos, to which Roland Barthes long ago gave the Latinate name *punctum*, the very word Seneca used for the pinhead limit of worldly experience. Barthes translates it variously as a "sting, speck, cut, little hole—and also a cast of the dice," adding, "A photograph's *punctum* is that accident which pricks me (but also bruises me, is poignant to me)."[87] As he notes, it is not always the most obvious aspect of a picture that produces such frissons. In Duane Michals's celebrated photograph of Andy Warhol covering his face, "the *punctum*," Barthes says, "is not the gesture but the slightly repellent substance of those spatulate nails, at once soft and hard-edged."[88] Once again, the fingernail steals the attention: piercing the membrane between image and viewer; not just feeling but generating feelings, too.

Pliny's history is all about physical matter, which means that details like these get easily lost in the middle of a kaleidoscopic encyclopedia. But what happens when small details stand out in a more abstract narrative? Take the notorious example of Aristophanes's attack of hiccups, recorded in Plato's postmortem account of a banquet, the *Symposium*. This bodily eruption, all too appropriate for the off-schedule events of a philosophical drinking party, is the more conspicuous in a dialogue that, as Plutarch observed, is festive but still relatively purged of material detail.[89] The hiccups turn out to be a plot derailer with huge consequences for the set order of speeches about love, whose schedule plays out differently depending on whether Aristophanes speaks as planned or whether he is displaced (as he is, thanks to the hiccups) by the doctor Eryximachus, whose practical attempts to cure his companion act as backing for a speech that conceives love as a physiological process. But what is truly remarkable is that Plato mentions the path not taken at all, actually bothers to superimpose real and shadow versions of what happened.[90]

The hiccups have provoked a wide range of responses, from Guthrie, who writes that the change in sequence caused by something so trivial serves "to warn the reader that the order of the speeches is not significant but accidental," to Plochmann, who concludes: "I like to think that these hiccups are one of the surest indications in the *Symposium* that nothing is really casual . . . Plato . . . is composing a work of incredible, if often unappreciated, tidiness."[91] These polarized statements of course come at the same truth from different slants. No literary selection of material is ever entirely casual, but the *Symposium* gives special (and contrived) prominence to the casual element in the way things turn out right from the start: characters run into each other, the guest-list is tweaked, Socrates is late, and so on. The immediate build-up to the hiccups contains the maximum concentration of accidental events:[92]

> Aristodemus said that Aristophanes should [*dein*] have spoken next, but by chance [*tuchein*], either because he was full or for some other reason [*ē hupo plēsmonēs ē hupo tinos allou*], he was afflicted [lit. they fell upon him, *epipeptōkuian*] by hiccups, which prevented him from speaking. (Pl. *Symp.* 185c)

For all that, most interpretations focus far more on the consequences, narrative or symbolic, ricocheting from Aristophanes's pulsing diaphragm, than on the incident itself. The hiccups have been made to stand for the exuberance of Aristophanic humor and for Plato's revenge on Aristophanes for mocking Socrates in the *Clouds*. They have been blamed for the exclusion from the speakers of Aristodemus, Socrates's current admirer, a little man (*smikros*), who might just be the unnoticed absent presence of Eros in the drinkers' midst.[93] Aristophanes's speech is thought to prick the pompous certainty of the first run of speeches retrospectively; relocated with Agathon's and Socrates's, it helps to confirm Eros as a fullness or an emptiness (of which hiccups are the bodily instantiation).[94]

Yet there is a simpler interpretation, one far more in keeping with the overall spontaneity of the text: this ruffle or stutter is no more and no less than an uninterpretable tease, a blip with repercussions, the butterfly's wingbeat that unsettles (and *stands for*) the dynamic nonlinear process that is a drinking party, or any of its possible narratives. One of the doctor's remedies is to tickle Aristophanes's nose, which brings to mind psychoanalyst Adam Phillips's thoughts on tickling: "To tickle," he writes, "is to seduce, often by amusement. Does it not highlight, this delightful game, the impossibility of satisfaction and of reunion, with its continual reenactment of the irresistible attraction and the inevitable repulsion of the object, in which the final satisfaction is frustration?"[95]

These words get to the heart of the hiccups, too. All foreplay and no climax, their eruption captures the quintessence of Eros that cannot be pinned down, while readers who were never there are tantalized all the more with the question of how much meaning a small accidental interruption, deliberately included, can be made to contain. Reviewing two books by Gilles Deleuze, Michel Foucault once wrote: "To pervert Platonism is to search out the smallest details, to descend (with the natural gravitation of humor) as far as its crop of hair or the dirt under its fingernails [nails, again!]—those things that were never hallowed by an idea."[96] Deleuze, he says, successfully "points out its interruptions, its gaps, those small things of little value that were neglected by philosophical discourse." Foucault notes that Plato himself was the first to undermine Platonism in the *Sophist*, but he does not recognize that he had already done so in the *Symposium*.

The teasing hiccups are of a piece with the larger readerly frustrations with Greek literature that Richard Hunter has discussed in his essay, "The Morning After":[97]

> The characters of the *Symposium* are recreated for us through a veil of hearsay and second-hand reports, which seems to dramatize both our own frantic efforts to discover "what actually happened" in the Athenian past and the impossibility of ever being sure . . . The *Symposium* feeds both our sense of insecurity about the past and our indomitable hopefulness that, despite everything, we are in touch with it. (Hunter 2004, 114)

In touch, almost more than metaphorically? Do small things give us that extra handle, an even stronger illusion of "being in touch" with the past?[98] Brooke Holmes has called for an approach to antiquity "that . . . confront[s] more vividly the paradox of things that are at once buried in layers of time and right here in our hands, animals whose blood can be warmed."[99] She is echoed in a political key by Sonya Huber, who offers her life-in-a-day project *Supremely Tiny Acts* as a serious attempt to cling to what remains reliably present and authentic: "I think we have to get to the real, to catch the facts we have, to hold on to what we see . . . in this time where lies are currency."

## NOSTALGIA AND LOSS

At the same time, Hunter reminds us that small things prompt feelings of nostalgia and loss as often as they foster closeness. According to Bachelard and Stewart, this has everything to do with their connections with toys, childhood, and childish scale.[100] We might at this point reflect that the whole idea of taking something small from the burning house of antiquity (Nandini Pandey's brief for her sample of classicists) had been seared into Roman mythical tradition ever since Aeneas snatched up the Penates, the household gods, on fleeing Troy. Once established in Rome, these portable gods continued to embody presence and loss at the same time. They conjured up the Romans' collective past and identity as a migrant people even when permanently installed in the *penetral* (inmost quarters) or *penus* (storeroom, of a house or temple), according to various etymologies of their name. Seemingly without batting an eyelid, Virgil in the *Aeneid* can describe the Penates at one moment as "little Penates" (*paruos . . . penatis*), when Aeneas is worshipping on the move at Evander's house, then at another as "great Penates" (*magnos . . . penatis*), when Ascanius swears in their name.[101] The easy swing in adjectives from small to large says everything about how compatible small things are with outsize, magnetic power.

There is another legend about Aeneas: that, along with the Penates, he brought another statue, the Palladium ("little Minerva") to Rome.[102] Cicero clearly has this image in mind when he recalls heroically snatching up his personal mascot of the goddess in 58 BCE and dedicating it to Capitoline Jupiter before Clodius could burn down his house: "I, who did not allow the guardian of our city to be polluted by impious hands during the universal ruin of my house and property, and carried her safely from my home to the home of Jupiter the father himself."[103] The act of protecting a miniature goddess allows this self-appointed guardian of the city to devolve his own need for divine safekeeping and make his helpless passivity into something active and heroic.

Normally, Cicero has a firmer sense of the hierarchies of scale. In *De natura deorum* (*On the Nature of the Gods*), he extrapolates from animal warrens to human domestic buildings to the cosmos, claiming stubbornly, "Just as we would never think a human house could be built by mice or weasels, so we must believe in a divine creator of something as complex as the universe."[104] In their own godlike capacity, the Romans built plenty of miniature houses on mouse or

FIGURE 5. Fragment of the panel of the Ara Pacis Augustae in Rome with the scene depicting Aeneas's sacrifice to the Penates. Photo: Anderson; Alinari Archives, Florence.

weasel scale, from the pet-sized structures that housed their favourite deities to parrots' cages (Statius describes a deluxe example) to transparent beehives, like the one Pliny tells us was constructed by a retired consul who wanted to inspect its interior workings.[105] Roman domestic shrines were populated by statuettes

THE GOOD OF SMALL THINGS    23

FIGURE 6. Dale Copeland, "Lares et Penates," 2016, assemblage of found objects. By kind permission of the artist.

of mini-deities—"divine menageries," as John Bodel has called them.[106] Roman emperors' collections of statuettes of holy men and heroes in their *cubicula* (private rooms) or personal *sacraria* have given biographers from antiquity onward penetrating glimpses into their intimate affections and allegiances.[107]

Miniature houses continue to guard their ancient secrets. A Roman moneybox depicts a helmeted Mercury standing in the doorway of a *mise en abyme* house, inside an imitation tholos tomb whose terracotta walls would have to be smashed to get the coins out (figure 7).[108] Tiny silver-lead temples like those found on a ship sunk near Comacchio were mass-produced across the empire as ex-votos or devotional objects, complete with little cult-figures and rings for hanging.[109] Nostalgic relics of childhood, family and home, souvenirs of personal and spiritual formation, these keepsakes even have something in common with a modern secular photo corner, or the "little free libraries" visible on the streets of Berkeley and

FIGURE 7. Roman moneybox, terracotta, Johns Hopkins Archaeological Museum, Baltimore, AN 395. Image courtesy of the Johns Hopkins Archaeological Museum, photography by James T. VanRensselaer.

other civilized neighborhoods—tiny model homes whose cultural treasures can be swapped and shared.

Domestic deities, moneyboxes, and miniature temples are just a few examples of small objects that surrounded the Romans in their everyday lives, conjuring up the past, evoking the wider world, holding secrets, and fostering personal connections with the divine as larger-scale ones could not. For dolls, a different fate lay in store. Dedicated to Venus or the Lares on a girl's marriage, they miniaturized, then ossified a cast-off stage of life.[110] The best-known surviving Roman doll, made of ivory, with its own tiny jewel-box, combs, mirrors, and key, was found in the premature burial of a Roman teenager, Crepereia Tryphaena (figure 8). Maurizio Bettini sees it as a forlorn, scaled-down simulacrum of Crepereia's girlish self—"of a time (or of a person) that had vanished over the farthest horizon—the one remaining piece of evidence from a world made up of tiny tables and household goods reproduced

FIGURE 8. Ivory doll from Crepereia Tryphaena's grave goods, second century CE, Museo Centrale Montemartini, Rome. Photo: Stefano Ravera; Alamy Stock Images.

and reduced as if by a pantograph, tiny clothes that can be put on and taken off, hair that is styled with elaborate care or tousled impatience." He adds: "The doll abandoned in the temple stood for the rigid equivalent of a lost age (physical and cultural) that could never return. It is an object full of the past (because we know, of course, that the past is still with us, hidden away somewhere)."[111]

No matter that Fanny Dolansky has recently reinterpreted dolls not as simulacra or relics of past lives but as aspirational, future-oriented objects: princesses and Barbies for Roman girls.[112] Bettini's response shows just how instinctive it is to look at small past things with a sentimental tug, almost as if they were vulnerable orphans (as the doll *was*, in a sense, thanks to her owner's early death). If the Romans saw little inner shrines as cherished composites of family and individual histories, and little things as receding into the distance, *exuviae* of their former selves, do we also tend to grasp at the small relics of antiquity and superimpose on them small lost pasts, both theirs and our own?

A clue can be found in the Romans' own reactions to stumbling on the experience of their ancestors, their *maiores*: literally "bigger people," but often in habits and stature smaller than their descendants. Suetonius, for example, is struck by the doll's house size of the future Emperor Augustus's rural nursery: "A very small room like a pantry" (*locus . . . permodicus et cellae penuariae instar*).[113] At the same time, this humble room contained the seeds of its occupant's future augustness (the name *Augustus* may come from *augere*, to grow bigger), and even gave off a magnetic aura; the story goes that after spending the night there, the new owner of the birthplace was found inexplicably prostrate on the floor the next day. Seneca is equally in awe of the tiny bathhouse in Scipio's ruined villa: "It was a great pleasure [*magna uoluptas*] for me to contrast Scipio's ways with our own. Think, in this little nook [*in hoc angulo*], the 'terror of Carthage' . . . used to bathe a body wearied with work in the fields!"[114] Cicero, likewise, stresses the small size of the villa where he was born and where his grandfather lived "in the old manner, like Curius on his Sabine farm."[115] Cato the Elder, too, was inspired to live more thriftily by contrasting the tininess and meanness of Curius's villa (*parua . . . uilla*) with his future greatness.[116]

Nowhere is the conceptual analogy between childhood, smallness, and the distant past more clearly outlined than in the preface to Florus's epitome of Livy's history, which tells the city's life story in human metaphors: the regal period was its infancy, the early Republic its youth, the late Republic up to the reign of Augustus its manhood or "robust maturity," and the imperial period its feeble old age (except, predictably, for a brief rejuvenation under Florus's own emperor, Trajan).[117] This classification is "yet another way to grasp in intimate, 'human' scale something immense and extensive," in a work that, as we have seen, repeatedly emphasizes its brevity along with its panoptic vision.[118] In a study of votives, Jessica Hughes has suggested that the switch in antiquity from tiny anatomical images to larger ones (at least according to the surviving evidence) enabled Greeks and Romans to make similar links between miniaturization, nostalgia, and archaism.[119] Usually, however, such neat progress from small to large belongs in the realm of the imagination. Historically, expansions and shrinkages followed a wider variety of sequences. I have already mentioned, for example, the claim that the temples of the Middle Republic in Rome represented a turn towards smaller-scale, repetitive building; this, it turns out, was relative both to the grandeur of the earlier Capitoline temple and to later imperial monuments.[120]

Morally speaking, though, the small-scale past often trumped the expanded present. One of the friends with whom Cicero reminisces in *De finibus* about places that evoke history offers a curiously paradoxical take on this theme. In the mind's eye, Piso claims, the recently extended Curia Hostilia, haunted as it is by dead culture heroes Scipio, Cato, Laelius, and his own grandfather L. Piso Frugi, actually looks smaller in its current enlarged state than it ever did in its humbler but more glorious past incarnation.[121] In Piso's palimpsestic vision of the past, small and large coexist, and even switch roles. The paradox "small but impressive" was entrenched enough for Plutarch to single out a crushing joke that Antony made at the expense of the Megarians. He called their senate-house "Small but—shabby."[122]

## PREAMBLE

Cute apologies for modest or trivial subject matter are not hard to find in Latin literature. I could follow Columella ("little column"), who heralds his supplementary hexameter poem on gardening (*superest ergo cultus hortorum*), following nine prose books on agriculture, as "material that is very meager and almost devoid of substance" (*tenuem admodum et paene uiduatam corpore materiam*) and "so inconsiderable" (*tam exilis*) as to be only "a tiny fraction" (*particula*) of the whole work.[123] His imagined version of the horticultural section that Virgil had lacked time and space to add to *Georgics* 4 is presented as a "tiny remaining instalment" (*reliquam pensiunculam*) of the tithe Columella owes his patron. Broken into its component parts, gardening is conceived as a fractal miniature of the larger topic of agriculture:

> For, although there are many branches [*quasi membra*] of the subject, so to speak, about which we can find something to say, they are, nevertheless, as unimportant as the imperceptible grains of sand out of which, according to the Greek saying, it is impossible to make a rope [*tamen eadem exigua sunt, quod aiunt Graeci, ut ex incomprehensibili paruitate harenae funis effici non possit*]. (*Rust.* 10 *praef.* 4)

We are back with Homer's Iris, scanning innumerable sand armies from above.

More upbeat is the note struck by Aulus Gellius, that obsessive collector of trivia, in the preface to his *Attic Nights*:

> My readers . . . should ask themselves whether these observations, slight and trifling though they are [*minutae istae admonitiones et pauxillulae*], do not after all have the power to inspire study, or are too dull to amuse and stimulate the mind; whether on the contrary they do not contain the germs and the quality to make men's minds grow more vigorous, their memory more trustworthy, their eloquence more effective, their diction purer, and the pleasures of their hours of leisure and recreation more refined. (*NA* 1 *praef.* 16; Loeb, trans. Rolfe, adapted)

I cannot claim such improving effects as Gellius does for the baggy holdall that is this book, but I am less defeatist than Columella. Like him, I have chosen variety over depth in my short and incomplete forays into smallness. In chapter 2,

I return to textual details via an inconspicuous element of Sallust's *Jugurtha* and, by contrast with Aristophanes's hiccups, build on it a huge edifice of overinterpretation that takes in microhistory and creeping temporality. In chapter 3, I consider a very brief Suetonian life in relation to the humor and politics of not-yet-ness and the durability of punchlines. Chapter 4 is about minor emotions, microaggressions, tiny irritants, and their special uses, mostly in Cicero. My final chapter is on the uses of useless-seeming diminutive words in Latin prose and poetry. Grains of sand, all of them, but together they might begin to make something of a rope.

## 2

# Sallust's Salient Snails

*Because often in war tiny variables can have huge consequences . . .*
—JULIUS CAESAR, *BELLUM CIVILE*

Ten years ago, I bought a postcard of a painted snail: side-on against a bright yellow ground, crawling from left to right (figure 9).

FIGURE 9. Postcard (detail of image in figure 10). Author's photo.

It was clearly a detail (when would a snail take up a whole picture?).[1] But I did not know at the time that it was part of a fifteenth-century Annunciation, usually attributed to Francesco del Cossa, now hanging in the Gemäldegalerie Alte Meister in Dresden (figure 10).

Nor did I know that an interpretation of this very painting, focused specifically on the snail, French art historian Daniel Arasse's essay "Le regard de l'escargot," had just been translated as "The Snail's Gaze" in *Take a Closer Look*, a posthumous collection published by Princeton University Press (Princeton is where I bought the card).[2] Arasse (mentioned in the previous chapter for his iconoclastic approach to visual detail) is a chatty and disarming guide who crawls excitedly all over del Cossa's painting, knowing full well that his readers will accuse him of overinterpreting. That may be true, but what he says is eye-opening for students of artistic and literary details alike.

For a start, Arasse has no truck with traditional Warburgian iconology, according to which del Cossa's snail is merely a tactful emblem of the dewy hands-off insemination of the Virgin Mary.[3] For him, by contrast, it is nothing less than an existential gauge of time, scale, and even truth. Why, otherwise, he reasons, would such a striking visual link be made between the silhouette of the snail (lower right) and the tiny flying figure of God (upper left)? It is clear that something humble and real has been put in diametric equivalence with something infinite and unreachable. Surely it must mean more than that God was simply slow to send his son to Earth?

More curious still is that, while God is small, the snail is outrageously large—even outsize, compared with the angel's foot. When Arasse went to Dresden to see the painting, he had a revelation: it is actually the snail that is life-size and the rest of the painting that is on the small side. His conclusion: the snail's gripping, out-of-place realism, as it crawls along the bottom line of the inner frame, half-inside, half-outside the scene of the miracle, makes us question the truth value of the deceptively painted (and relatively miniaturized) annunciation, and thus ultimately the mystery of God made flesh. The blindly gliding snail tells us what we have all failed to apprehend—namely, "the emergence of the invisible into the field of vision."[4] To echo Arasse himself: "All that with a mere snail?"[5] Patricia Simons, who has since nuanced his reading in her essay "The Salience of the Snail" (a title I have borrowed here), agrees that the creature "encapsulates a short-sighted, spiritually barren focus on the here and now"; it is "marginal yet blatant."[6]

Salience is a quality I want to claim in this chapter for some "marginal yet blatant" literary snails, which in this case might seem even more outrageous when they come into view for just a narrative second, crawling between some rocks in the African desert. But, like Arasse, I will take a closer look and push for the larger significance of what seems like just a passing detail. My reading here will be more constructive than with Aristophanes's hiccups (interpreted in the previous chapter as a textual glitch or stammer that signifies nothing more nor less than

FIGURE 10. Annunciation, Francesco del Cossa, Gemäldegalerie Alte Meister, Staatliche Kunstsammlungen, Dresden. Photo: Hans Peter Klut/Elke Estel; Wikimedia Commons.

the randomness of things). Why? Partly intuition, again, but it has something to do with the different relationship I see in this case between detail and whole. Both hiccups and snails are random phenomena with striking domino effects for their overall narratives. But while the hiccups are a tease, a necessary quirky supplement that shadows a path not taken, the snails, as we will see, quite literally reveal a path, which makes them integral microcomponents of the world-shaking events they unwittingly set in motion. The path is not a straight one, but the story cannot do without it. Along the way, I will make a larger claim: that in challenging the whole idea that details have only a small part to play in such narratives the snails also have consequences for Sallust's principles of historiography. At the same time, this *is* something of a plea for overinterpretation.

One factor to keep in mind from the outset is that the snails belong to a text that is panoramic and limited at the same time. Sallust's second monograph after *Catiline*, *Jugurtha* tells the story of a Roman campaign to maintain a delicate power balance in the kingdoms of North Africa in the late second century BCE, some eighty years before he wrote. Sallust says he chose the war not only because it was important and exciting but also because it led to a seismic political shift in Rome, the first substantial challenge to the aristocratic status quo in the shape of its star player Marius, "new man" and radical reformer, whose speech of self-promotion imagined here voices the author's own challenge to elite values. Sallust had himself experienced Africa Nova as its undistinguished governor in the forties BCE: it provided the wealth that enabled the forced retirement (he was tried on the usual charges, for extortion), which he spent writing this history.

In his hands, the Jugurthine War is a capsule episode, a symptom in an overarching diagnosis of Roman imperial growth and moral decline. David Levene has even argued that Sallust presents it as a fragment, in that it lacks obvious closure and appeals to larger continuities, past and future.[7] This gives it metonymic and metaphorical resonance, both for events at home with which it is so closely intermeshed and for the long history of the Roman Republic. As William Batstone puts it, Africa, with its "shifting sands, ambiguous boundaries, treacherous landscape," suggests the other world of Roman politics, "with its shifting sands, ambiguous boundaries, treacherous landscapes."[8] In other words, small-large, periphery-center and real-symbolic relations of the kind that will interest me on the microlevel are already essential to the overall makeup of *Jugurtha*.

The moral message of Sallust's histories is far more difficult to pin down. His Africa is a theater for Roman enterprise and resilience, a testing ground for his heroes' ability to live the lessons laid out in the prefaces to both monographs: keep to the true path of virtue, avoid deviant tendencies—above all crookedness (*prauitas*), greed and desire (*cupido* and *lubido*), and trust in chance (*opportunitas*). All his protagonists will fail the test in turn: Jugurtha sells himself to Rome; the Roman general Metellus goes native, outwitting Jugurtha with his treachery. And nothing hides the fact that it is luck, drive, and treachery that propel

Marius and his successor Sulla Felix, "Lucky Sulla," to the top, then over the top, far more quickly and more successfully than conventional virtue could do. So it is that postmodern historiographers have found in Sallust both a sympathetic mistrust in straightforward teleology and a failure to separate virtue from vice that is symptomatic of Roman imperialism.[9] In the preface to *Catiline*, Sallust is confessional about his complicity with a broken system: this proto-Augustine went off the rails in adolescence but was redeemed by the intellectual life from which politics had diverted him.[10] Writing history becomes his "talking therapy," an attempt to reclaim language and master material in a system that binds him in its toils.[11] What hope can there be for his integrity or that of his heroes, when, as Sallust says, even ordinary men (*etiam mediocris uiros*) are so easily sidetracked (*transuersos*) by the hope of rich pickings (*spe praedae*) that opportunity (*opportunitas*) throws in their way?[12]

## SNAIL TRAILS

As the end of the work approaches, one such ordinary opportunist *is* sidetracked by rich pickings, so galvanizing a crucial twist in Roman fortunes. The African campaign has reached a stalemate. Metellus has been overtaken by the new energy of Marius, who has just captured the snake-infested city of Capsa, while Sulla, an even greater force of nature, is coming up the ranks. Meanwhile Jugurtha, whose name means "overtaker" in Berber, has outstripped his brothers and peers to become a new Hannibal, a tricky, evasive master of elephants and winding paths.[13] The challenge Marius now faces is a steep one: an unnamed fortress where the king's remaining treasure is stored, on top of a hill, in the middle of a deserted plateau, with just one narrow, well-guarded path to the top . . .

Until, that is, a nameless Ligurian auxiliary goes off-piste in search of water—and this is where the snails come in:

> But after many days and much labor had been expended, Marius began to ponder anxiously whether to abandon the attempt since it was fruitless, or to await the favor of fortune, which he had often employed to his success. While he was vacillating as he turned these matters over for many days and nights, by chance a Ligurian, a common soldier of the auxiliary cohorts, when he had left camp to fetch water, noticed snails crawling among the rocks not far from the side of the fortress which was facing away from the battling. As he went after first one and then another of these creatures and then still more, in his eagerness to gather them he gradually emerged at almost the top of the hill. When he realized the deserted nature of the place, his mind was overcome, after the fashion of human nature, by a desire to perform a difficult feat. By chance, a great oak tree had taken root there among the rocks; having grown horizontally for a short distance, it then turned and soared to a great height, in the direction nature encourages all plants to grow. Supporting himself now with the tree branches, now with projecting rocks, the Ligurian reached the level ground of

the fortress because the Numidians as a whole were intent upon and physically engaged in the fighting that was taking place. After examining everything that he thought would be useful later, he returned by the same way, not heedlessly, as he had gone up, but testing and observing everything. Then he quickly approached Marius, told him what he had done, and urged him to make an attempt on the fortress at the point where he himself had mounted; he promised to be a guide for the dangerous ascent. (*Iug.* 93.1–6; Loeb, trans. Rolfe, rev. Ramsey)

This is an extraordinary piece of writing: detailed, intense—hyperreal, even. I am not alone in admiring it: Graziana Brescia has devoted a full-scale commentary to just this and the two surrounding chapters.[14] Frontinus abbreviates the story in his *Strategemata*, complete with snails (in a section called "Attacks from Unexpected Quarters").[15] However, they do not make the cut in Florus' epitome of the Jugurthine War (he prefers the Capsian snakes).[16] In this account, everything really has been observed (*exploratis omnibus*), whether by this eyewitness or some other source. Yet Sallust is typically what Ronald Syme characterizes as a broad-brush historian: " Full particulars about the size of armies, precise intervals of time, or exact itineraries . . . was the function of *commentarii*. Historians are selective, dramatic, impressionistic."[17] From his postmodernist viewpoint, William Batstone sees Sallust's tendency to select and dramatize rather differently: "The narrative . . . is in part about how history sinks into the aesthetics of storytelling. Rather than weighing the evidence and arriving at disinterested and objective conclusions about what happened, Sallust toys with the traces, following from uncertainty to duplicity a story of intersecting forces, uncertain motives, and dangerous consequences. This is history as literature."[18]

The obvious question, then, is why, if Sallust is not known for details, does he give so much space to a minor figure's encounter with some snails and a bendy tree? Is this just a case of unusually myopic precision, or is it "toying with the traces," singling out something small to give it greater aesthetic or historical significance? In such a tightly woven narrative, where the Gracchan reforms and the siege of Capsa get just a paragraph each, and huge events like the war with Carthage and Sulla's later atrocities are simply passed over in pregnant silence (better, says Sallust, than saying too little), the account really has to justify the space given to it.[19]

Snails, though? They should be beneath the notice of any historian. That is what Horace seems to imply in his *Epistle to Augustus*, where he makes excuses for not writing an epic on the emperor's *res gestae* (deeds) by claiming that his humble satires, "crawling along the ground" (*repentis per humum*), would be dwarfed by barbarian kingdoms, rivers, and mountain fortresses (which all sounds suspiciously as if he has been reading Sallust).[20] As isolated spots in the middle of a sweeping historical narrative, Sallust's snails do achieve a special salience—far more so than the fellow snails coiled in their slimy houses (*curuarum domus uda coclearum*) in Statius's catalogue of mediocre Saturnalian gifts (*Silvae* 4.9) or the snails placed at the end of a whole lot of nothing (*nihil*)

FIGURE 11. Mosaic of snails in a basket, fourth century CE, Basilica di Santa Maria Assunta, Aquileia. Photo: Carole Raddato; Wikimedia Commons.

in Martial's epigram 8.33. In a historiographical context, to quote Arasse again, "the anomaly of the snail reaches out to you."[21]

The most basic reason for their presence here must be to create a robust reality effect, one that confirms a bizarre eyewitness account. If anything, it is an effect that works even better on a modern reader than an ancient one. One reason the Dresden snail seems so real to us is because it is the only thing in the painting that has not changed over the centuries. Snails look more or less the same today, so much so that Arasse can securely identify del Cossa's as *Helix pomatia*, the Burgundian (or Roman) snail. Ancient Roman snails looked much the same, too, judging from a mosaic from Aquileia of some gathered in a basket, one randomly falling out and another very determined one setting off in the opposite direction to escape its fate (figure 11).

For all that, there is every reason to suspect the story's credentials. Erich Koestermann calls the snails "too cute to be true" (*zu hübsch um wahr zu sein*), typical of some lost repertoire of ancient military humor (*Soldatenwitz*).[22] Sure enough, there is a suspiciously close parallel in book 1 of Herodotus: Cyrus only succeeded in conquering Lydian Sardis because a man called Hyroeades happened to notice a soldier emerging from a vulnerable spot in the walls in pursuit of a fallen helmet.[23] This gives our adventure a touch of fiction, urban myth, or ben trovato. Further traces of folktale have been detected in its various ingredients: the anonymity and impregnability of the fortress, the anonymity and humility of the Ligurian, the decisiveness of Marius, and success against all odds for men large and small.[24] As an exemplary tale divorced from the surrounding narrative, it has something in common with two legends of local martyrs recalled in the same work: the Philaeni brothers, who allow themselves to be buried alive to increase their people's territory; and the citizens of Thala, who set themselves on fire after feasting—to avoid the same fate at the hands of the Romans.[25]

For literary critics, however, reality effects will always compete with an episode or element's metonymic potential. Is this merely background detail or quirk, or is it a microscopic building block in a larger whole? All I am sure of is that this bit player's small victory with its enormous repercussions is strangely magnified. But I also suspect that the snails are there to unsettle not just our sense of scale but equally our sense of time. Marius, who bookends the chapter, provides the most obvious reason to read it as an allegory or premonition of the success story of a far greater opportunist. The repeated word, *forte*, "by chance"—so often in Latin literature the disingenuous marker of a significant coincidence—makes what follows fall into line with a leitmotif of the work as a whole: the element of fortune in history, particularly in the careers of Marius and Sulla.[26] *Forte* will recur twice more in the episode, culminating in the propping up of Marius's audacious decision-making.[27] The Ligurian's zeal for collecting (*studium legundi*)—his perverse innate desire to do hard-to-do things (*dif-ficilia faciundi*)—thus reads easily as a miniversion of the ambitions of more important characters and their desire to overcome and possess (*potiundi . . . maxuma cupido*) in an imperialist system that Sallust casts as "smash and grab": *ducere trahere rapere* (to take, to snatch, to seize—his spin on Caesar's *ueni uidi uici*).[28]

Quite plausibly, then, Andrew Feldherr calls the episode "an emphatically Marian story," where the smaller *dux* (scout or sherpa) stands in for the greater leader.[29] Again, the snails help join the conceptual dots. As they are to the Ligurian and the Ligurian is to Marius, so the anecdote is to the monograph and the monograph is to universal or annalistic history. As the tiniest things in *Jugurtha*, they are the small acorns from which Marius's big oak will grow (quite literally: the *ilex* here launches a general forever associated with another venerable oak, the *quercus* celebrated in Cicero's *Marius* and revisited in his *Laws*).[30] Over the entire narrative hangs the oracular deathbed pronouncement of King Micipsa, echoing Herodotus on the rise and fall of cities, as he fears the exponential growth of Jugurtha, once his little (*paruum*) adopted son:[31]

> For in concord, small things grow; in discord, great things collapse. (*Iug.* 10.6)

Even so, I wonder if to privilege Marius over the smaller players in this story isn't to misassign metonym and whole, to belittle the combined forces of human, animal, and plant ingenuity that prompt Sallust's reflections on the predictability of all nature in the service of growth and survival. To say the Ligurian acts "according to the natural human desire" (*more ingeni humani*) for a challenge, and that the tree struggles to find the light "in the direction nature encourages all plants to grow" (*quo cuncta gignentium natura fert*), lifts the narrative to a higher plane, an impulse that has been readily dismissed as "folk philosophizing."[32] I think Sallust would have been offended to be called a "folk philosopher." Instead, he is taking time out to reflect on the relationship of man to landscape and on different creatures' instincts for movement and growth, to register what is universal in the energy that drives human history, as well as human nature. After all, the tale's coordinates are plotted along axes of broader historical concern to him: chance versus predetermination: crooked versus straight; detail versus whole; circumstantial anecdote versus world event; the morality of human ambition; and the roots of causality. Backing up to discover the primary origins of events is *his* instinct as a historian. In *Catiline* he traces the origins of the conspiracy back to the dictatorship of Sulla, whereas *Jugurtha* has that dictatorship as a future disaster in its sights. Read together, the two monographs tessellate around a taboo episode in Roman history.

The prefaces to both works make it clear enough. Sallust isn't just a historian: he's a *natural historian*. He thinks of individuals and cities alike as organic forms. He traces predictable cycles from birth to maturity to decay, and roots physical and ethical habits in biological patterns of growth and the forces of physics—dynamic energy (*uis*) and momentum versus inertia (*inertia*). The start of *Catiline* famously echoes Plato's *Republic* in making man a vertical animal who aspires to godlike heights but always risks falling back to join horizontal beasts who march on their stomachs.[33] Topographical and ethnographical classifiers further subdivide the human race.[34] Numidian nomads, for example, are stereotyped as fast runners and quick-thinking deceivers who shelter from the sun in crude huts, hide camouflaged in the scrub, and never settle anywhere for long before vanishing in a swoosh of desert sand.[35]

For all that, there is something unprecedented about this campaign—Sallust calls it its *asperitas*, its prickliness or jagged edges—that threatens to snag all such smooth generalizations.[36] If Marius can conquer nature (*naturam uincere*) through military conquest, the historian, trying to make sense of an unmappable region and period, is often as disoriented as soldiers caught out by a sudden sandstorm.[37] If Sallust's universalizing asides take him off the main track, at least they guide him for a while. Conserving the sediment of accrued wisdom, they are gestures of control against the uncontrollable.

None of this, though, explains the specificity of snails and ilex when Sallust could so easily have done without them. Surely it is the task of any scout to go scouting, tastebuds or not, always to want to see what lies on the other side of the hill? How much, then, does it matter that it is snails he stumbles on, and not locusts and wild honey, or mushrooms, or even silphium? That it is an ilex, and not just any tree?

To start on the ground with practicalities, snails and tree together could be said to trace an alimentary history of Africa, a place where desire, Sallust's primary driver of action and movement, so often takes its most elemental form, hunger.

FIGURE 12. Escargotière, Sidi Mansour, Gafsa (Capsa), Tunisia. Photo: M. Rais; Wikimedia Commons.

Snails are a wholly plausible feature of the African landscape (having evolved from marine to inland habitats). Pliny the Elder calls African ones the most prolific of all.[38] It so happens that the Capsian area of the Mahgreb (that is, eastern Algeria and southern Tunisia) houses the densest prehistoric deposits of snail shells (now called *escargotières*). Indeed, archaeologists believe that snails were once so plentiful as foraged food that they may even have helped delay the onset of agriculture in the region (figure 12).[39] Snail stalls are still routine on the streets of North Africa as a local fast food (or should that be slow food?). Hunger also helps to explain why this is an ilex tree, in country we are told is short on trees, indeed bare of any plants.[40] Again, the specificity gives a ring of truth.[41] The holm oak *is* native to North Africa as to other Mediterranean countries, but it also bears edible acorns, another source of wild food for hungry peoples.

One effect, however, of the Jugurthan campaign was to turn everyone into nomads and scavengers. Not only are the pre-Herculean inhabitants of Africa described as restless and roaming about (*uagi palantes*) but the Roman invaders, too, "roamed about restlessly, wasting the fields" (*uagabantur, et palantes agros uastare*).[42] While Numidian cattlemen take their meat and milk with them (like Tacitus's Germans, not needing the fussy condiments essential to civilized Roman life), Marius commends himself for not giving fancy dinners like his aristocratic rivals.[43] In 46 BCE, Sallust himself had invaded the island of Cercina, off Tunis, to capture Pompey's grain supply.[44] His thoughts about foraging versus luxury (chance versus design, in eating terms) make the snails a serendipitous find from both viewpoints: caviar discovered in the wild, as it were, an image for colonial depredation. This is after all a story of eaters and eaten, hunters and prey. If modern aesthetic theory associates the "cute" with affective responses to powerlessness and commodification, that makes the snails sweet but helpless victims in the history of imperialism.[45] As for the solitary ilex, it suggests an earlier pedigree for the "lone tree and sunset motif," which, as Liv Yarrow has shown in a fascinating article, came to symbolize a safe version of colonized Africa on nineteenth- and twentieth-century coins and medals.[46]

Hunger even explains why the scout is specifically Ligurian. By Sallust's time, this mountainous, forested region between Italy and Gaul had come under Roman control. But in Jugurtha's time, it was still an ambiguous buffer state, scene of frequent skirmishes and once the site of a glorious victory for Mago the Carthaginian. Liguria had poor soil; its inhabitants were the rugged foragers of Europe:

> They are continually hunting, whereby they get abundant game and compensate in this way for the lack of the fruits of the field. Consequently, spending their lives as they do on snow-covered mountains, where they are used to traversing unbelievably rugged places, they become vigorous and muscular of body. Some of the Ligurians, because they lack the fruits of the earth, drink nothing but water, and eat the flesh of both domestic and wild animals and fill themselves with the green things which grow in the land, the land they possess being untrodden by the most kindly of the gods, namely, Demeter and Dionysus. (Diod. Sic. 5.39.3; Loeb, trans. Oldfather)

Ligurians were equally associated with deceit: it was a trickster's ruse that would overthrow the Numidian camp.[47] Hardy, lean, and enterprising, this fish out of geographical water adapts his hunter-gatherer skills to a new, arid environment. But his first impulse, hunger, is in his genes.

In other ways, though, the Ligurian transcends his ethnicity to become a kind of Everyman, driven on by luck, curiosity, and greed, those ethically ambivalent opposites of traditional virtue that seduce all humans ("after the fashion of human nature") and impel them to keep on grabbing and pushing. Plato had warned how easily man's progress from empirical discovery to abstract wisdom, from low desires to uprightness, can be derailed by *pleonexia*, wanting more.[48] Hunger is here just the baseline of an upward story of compulsion and desire. The Ligurian's inch-by-inch decision-making, as he spots first one snail (*unam*), just one more (*atque alteram*), then more still (*dein plures*), recalls the quickfire transitions in Seneca's *Thyestes* from satisfied to renewed appetite, when Atreus, high on his meaty sacrifice, tells the history of the Tantalid house in 1.5 lines: "It's good, it's plenty, it's enough at last even for me. But wait. *Why* is it enough?"[49]

In his 1957 novel *Il barone rampante* (*The Baron in the Trees*), Italo Calvino tells the tale of Cosimo, a boy who rebels against aristocratic mores at the time of Napoleon's drastic deforestation of Liguria by climbing a tree on the family estate, the start of a lifetime's treebound existence and, with it, a uniquely enlightened perspective on human folly. It is my guess that Calvino, born in Cuba to botanist parents but later acclimatized, along with other tropical specimens, in their plant laboratory in Sanremo, was introduced at some point in his classical education to Sallust's description of another Ligurian's escapade.[50] Cosimo's rebellion is precipitated, after all, by his refusal to eat some snails that his sadistic sister, the nun Battista, has served up for dinner, at which point he climbs the nearest tree, which just happens to be an ilex (*leccio*). As with Sallust's greedy Ligurian, Cosimo's motives transcend simple depredation and reach toward the heights of human possibility. As his brother relates, "we spent hours and hours in the trees, and not for utilitarian reasons, like many boys, who climb up just to look for fruit or birds' nests, but for the pleasure of overcoming difficult protuberances and forks, and getting as high as possible, and finding beautiful places to stop and look at the world below, to make jokes and shout at those who passed under us."[51]

Calvino's novel ends by comparing Cosimo's arboreal gymnasium, a rope net of flimsy branches, to his own precarious storytelling, a "thread of ink" that "now twists on itself, now forks, now links knots of sentences with edges of leaves or clouds, and then stumbles, and then resumes twisting."[52] Andrew Feldherr has observed how firmly Sallust's narrative of progress is scaffolded by its horizontal and vertical axes: the fortress, the climb, and the steplike shape of the tree.[53] Yet aslant this grid, to my mind, run some equally well-defined lines, ones that vindicate lateral thinking, maverick behavior, and queer patterns of growth. Spatially and morally, these slanted axes plot alternative routes to success. Democritus had once claimed that twisted plants are more resilient, thanks to the slower distribution of their nutrients.[54] And just as the Ligurian's ascent is described as "random," "unplanned," or "blind" (*temere*), so the thought processes that lead him there are decisive but transverse. We almost feel the neurons fire his flickering glances (*animum aduortit . . . animum alio uortit*), glances as angular as the twisting tree—whose name, on second thought, is perhaps chosen because it *sounds* bendy (*inflexa . . . ilex*).[55] This is man as *polutropos*, looking not straight ahead but behind the fighting (*auersum proeliantibus*). Later, Sallust will take an equally wry squint at the warped oppositions of human morality: "Human affairs are so fluid and unstable [*fluxae et mobiles*], they are always turning into their opposite" [*semper in aduorsa mutantur*].[56]

While both snail and tree have adapted by moving athwart inhospitable terrain, it remains odd that Sallust gives us far more detail about the tree, as it evolves horizontally (*prona*), then bends (*inflexa*) and pushes upward (*in altitudinem*), obeying universal biological laws but with an idiosyncratic shape that consolidates (*coaluerat*) the singular will and history of its growth (traumatopic, whether from lack of light or flattening desert wind). Gerard Manley Hopkins would name this singularity "inscape":

> There is one notable dead tree . . . the inscape markedly holding its most simple and beautiful oneness up from the ground through a graceful swerve below (I think) the spring of the branches up to the tops of the timber. (Hopkins, *Notebooks* = House 1937, 154)

When Hopkins uses the word again in a letter to Robert Bridges, it comes with hints about his own idiosyncrasies: "Now it is the virtue of design, pattern, or inscape to be distinctive, and it is the vice of distinctiveness to become queer. This vice I cannot have escaped."[57]

Other queer trees in Latin literature come freighted with partly hidden messages. The plane, for example, that overhangs Atedius Melior's lake in Statius's *Silvae* 2.3, then dives down only to grow straight up again as if coming from the water's depths, not only conjures the legend of a nymph and a lovesick Pan but also configures decline and revival in the family fortunes of Melior's friend Blaesus.[58] In *Carm.* 1.12, Horace uses an image of a tree's roots for the subterranean endurance of another noble Roman family: "The reputation of Marcellus grows unseen, like a tree, in hidden time."[59] Sallust's tree suggests a similarly precarious version of human history, its branches tracing man's evolution from earthbound beast to mountain climber, always threatened by gravity and an uncertain foothold. As it winds along and up among the rocks (*inter saxa*), first horizontally, then vertically, it tracks not just homo sapiens but also the snails (which also crawl *inter saxa*): a *grandis ilex* mirrors a small helix.

Were it human, Sallust's tree might be called *praua*, bent; instead, it is merely *prona*, then *inflexa*. At least it has agency and personality. The snails just creep, mere specimens of a genus, too low a lifeform to be anything but prey. In 2015, scientists from Lund University revealed how grossly we have underestimated the individuality of snails' bodies and behavior. When they tapped a sample group of 168 snails lightly with tweezers to see how they reacted—with alarm, predictably— then timed how long it took for each one to poke its head back out of its shell, they found strong correlations between speed of response, feeding habits, and thickness of shells.[60] But Sallust's snails tell us almost more about the Ligurian—what happens when gastronome meets gastropod—than about their own lives. For all the parallels between the motor impulses of snails and tree, he seems to have the biological hierarchy the wrong way around—at least according to Plutarch's categories:

> Why do we not say that one tree is less intelligent than another, as a sheep is, compared with a dog; or one vegetable more cowardly than another, as a stag is, compared with a lion? Is the reason not that, just as it is impossible to call one immovable object slower than another, so among all creatures to whom Nature has not given the faculty of understanding, we cannot say that one is more cowardly or more slothful or more intemperate? Whereas it is the presence of understanding, of one kind in one animal, of another kind in another, and in varying degree, that has produced the observable differences. (Plut. *De Soll. An.* 4 = *Mor.* 963; Loeb, trans. Cherniss and Helmbold)

All the contempt Plutarch directs at unmoving plants Sallust diverts to snails, those virtual vegetables.

## SLOW HISTORIES

In the end, we only know one thing about the snails (apart from their plurality and their haphazard patterning): they crawl. Slow locomotion has always been the snail's salient characteristic (English "snail," from Old English "snaegl," has, like "snake," etymological roots in the idea of crawling). When a giant mechanical snail headed the processions of Demetrius of Phaleron, tyrant of Athens in the fourth century BCE, emitting a trail of slime and followed by a string of donkeys, Demochares explained that both snail and donkeys were there to mock the Athenians for being submissive to their overlord, Cassander of Macedon.[61] Plautus calls legal advocates *spissigradissimos*, "sluggish walkers," whose gouty steps make them slower even than snails.[62] But Sallust's snails do not simply evoke slowness. The single descriptor "crawling" (*repentis*) makes us think about space and time at once. In an environment where distances are vast and speed is key, the tiny snails slow down not just the Ligurian's pace but the entire narrative, forcing a microscopic focus before the sweeping overview returns.[63] As Susan Stewart has suggested, it takes longer, slows down time, to look at miniature things.[64]

In short, the snails, with their slow pace and obtrusive tininess, may have something to tell us about Sallust's approach to historiography. After all, when snails have been used or cited in scientific experiments, it tends to be in connection with Sallustian concepts like space and time, chaos and predictability, the momentary and the longer term. Cellular automata, for example, model the spiraling patterns found in nature—in seashells or a romanesco cauliflower; Feldherr even refers to Sallust's "fractal" representations of landscape.[65] One such experiment dates from the 1930s, when Gerhard Brecher tried to give some scientific heft to the claim of nineteenth-century biologist Karl Ernst Von Baer that "the moment" (*der Moment* or *der Augenblick*) can be defined as the smallest unit of subjectively experienced time ("The time we need for our sense organs to be conscious of its impression"), something that varies among different life forms.[66] So it was that Brecher made a snail crawl continuously on top of a floating rubber ball, tapping its belly at the same time and testing the interval between its forward thrusts, to show how intrinsic memory is to the perception of a unit of time—one quarter of a second, in the snail's case (figure 13).[67] Joining the separate stimuli together conceptually, the snail took them as a signal to start crawling forwards in a continuous line.

More surprisingly still, Yale art historian George Kubler adapted Brecher's claims in a paper titled "Style and the Representation of Historical Time" (Kubler 1967). He used the idea that isolated moments create the illusion of a continuum to define artistic style as "a way of imposing space upon time and of denying duration under the illusion that successive events are similar events." "The historian," says

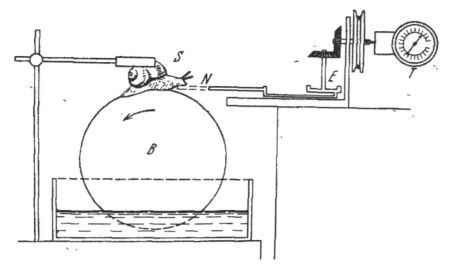

Abb. 3. Versuchsanordnung zur Messung des Schneckenmomentes.
B Ball, E Exzenter, N Nadel, S Schnecke, T Tachometer.

FIGURE 13. Gerhard Brecher's snail experiment (Brecher 1937: 215). Author's photo.

Kubler, "is at liberty to stress either the regularity of artificial periods (centuries, decades) or the irregularity of actual durations"; in both cases, repetitions "induce a *spatialization*, or illusion of coherent surface, which some of us call style" (emphasis original).[68] In the Dresden Annunciation, the snail's slow progress across the canvas has another effect beyond reminding us that God was slow to send his son to earth: it creates the illusion that past miracle and present humdrum reality, del Cossa's and our own, are fused into one glutinous continuity. This kind of realism has quite the opposite effect from that produced by the trompe l'oeil fly that Daniel Arasse remembers, humiliatingly, reaching out to flick off another painting in Dresden. A painted fly, so often an erratic fixture in the still life tradition, is the very essence of momentariness caught in perpetuity.[69] If we tried to flick off the snail, we would expect resistance; time, we would find, would be congealed.

At first sight, no place could be slipperier than *Jugurtha*'s monotonous desert for getting a handle on either time or space (if we borrow Andrew Riggsby's neat definition of space as the thing that "allows for the objects it contains to be related to each other").[70] Sallust even suggests a causal link between the infiniteness of the desert and the infinite warfare it prolongs:[71]

> The land between them was sandy, undifferentiated [*una specie*, "with only one face"], without river or mountain to mark their boundaries. This circumstance kept the people engaged in a great and protracted war [*in magno diuturnoque bello*]. (*Iug.* 79.3)

FIGURE 14. Snail and other small creatures, acanthus frieze, Portico of Eumachia, Pompeii, late first century BCE. Photo: Album; Alamy Stock Photo.

Yet a feature of any landscape with "only one face" is that its small details are far more likely to become salient.[72] After all, the Romans are frequently forced to comb the horizon for outcrops (camouflaged Numidians or protruding elephants) and repeatedly caught out by optical illusions. Pliny writes of phantom men who loom up in the African desert and vanish in a moment.[73] Centuries later, in *The Sheltering Sky* (first published in 1949), Paul Bowles would observe a similar effect in the mirages or visuo-spatial errors generated by the unique sameness of the Sahara:

> The desert landscape is always at its best in the half-light of dawn or dusk. The sense of distance lacks: a ridge nearby can be a far-off mountain range, each small detail can take on the importance of a major variant on the countryside's repetitious theme. (Bowles 2009, 286)

So, too, the eponymous hero of Michael Ondaatje's *The English Patient* reflects on the natural tracking devices of the desert:

> When I was lost among them, unsure of where I was, all I needed was the name of a small ridge, a local custom, a cell of this historical animal, and the map of the world would slide into place. (Ondaatje 1992, 20)

As Andrew Feldherr sees it, the desert's expanse of barely relieved blankness makes a near-perfect (if ungraspable) canvas for thinking about relations between space and time.[74] I would add that the snails function as token gripping points on this treacherous surface. Momentary spots that enter the visual field one by one, then proliferate, they provide an analogy on the ground for sporadic cognitive circuits. We are never actually told whether they left a slimy trail behind; it is the Ligurian who must deduce the path (supposing he dropped the shells, like Hansel and Gretel, he could more easily retrace his steps).[75] But joining the scattered dots conceptually not only provides an accurate route to the desired water-source: it also breaks the narrative's temporal span into smaller units (*paulum . . . paulatim*).

I am reminded of the similar effect that a variant word for a small unit of time, *paulisper* ("for a little while"), produces in a passage of Cicero's *Pro Milone*. As part of his uphill (and ultimately doomed) rhetorical attempt to exonerate his old ally, the thug Milo, Cicero conjures up an interlude of such innocuous domesticity that it would be hard to imagine his client setting off to commit a murder on the Appian Way. In this version of events, Milo returned home from a day at the Senate, removed his shoes and day clothes (we are carefully not yet told how he redressed for the journey) and waited for his wife to get ready:

> But Milo, because he had been in the Senate that day until the Senate was dismissed, came home; he changed his shoes and clothes; for a little while, he waited, while his wife got ready, as men always have to [*paulisper, dum se uxor, ut fit, comparat, commoratus est*]; then he set out at the time when Clodius might have returned, if he had been going to come to Rome that day. (Cic. *Mil.* 10.28)

The preparations are presented in a sentence of little pauses and parentheses for which *paulisper* functions almost as shorthand, a sentence so choppy with stops and starts that both syntax and characters—Milo, who indulgently "waited for a little while" (*paulisper . . . commoratus est*), and his wife, who predictably, like all women (*ut fit*), lingered over her toilette—come to figure the leisurely delaying tactics of the orator himself, as Cicero plays for time to stave off an inevitable conviction.[76]

As I hinted earlier, it is in their capacity as spatio-temporal markers that the snails may have something significant to tell us about historiographical method. Jonas Grethlein has claimed that Sallust's tendency to incorporate alternative teleologies when looking at the same event makes him an early devotee, if he but knew it, of Reinhard Koselleck's "slices of history," *Zeitschichten*, a term coined to denote "the simultaneity of the non-simultaneous."[77] Grethlein explains: "The image of different geological strata that are layered on top of each other, partly separate, partly entangled with each other, is well-suited to express the multitude of times that come together in history: natural history, *longue durée*, microhistories, and so on."[78] Koselleck's "slices" strike me as particularly helpful for thinking about the juxtaposed speeds and natural histories of the cohabitants of this African outcrop: man, snails and tree. Snails (we know now) are among the oldest animals in the world; trees (the Romans knew this, too) are even older. Again, modern readers are even better placed to appreciate the different layers, to read the episode not just as a record of a historical event but also as a time-lapse allegory of man's intervention in the environment, a speeded-up account of the opportunistic raids of the Anthropocene.

## SNAIL OFFENSIVE

We could leave it there: a brief existential pause before the narrative action resumes, a sublime overview of the sluggish locomotion typical of all human endeavour if seen from a distance, by scouts or historians.[79] But there is another aspect to the snails—their practical contribution to the Roman cause, we could call it—that is yet to be revealed. If the Ligurian "checked out all that he thought would be of use in the future," his data-gathering exercise evidently included what he saw on the way up, too. This emerges when Marius orders a reconnaissance party to verify the report:[80]

> Marius sent a party of those present with the Ligurian to test his report. Each one pronounced the task difficult or easy according to his nature. Still, the consul's spirit was somewhat buoyed. And so he sent five of the swiftest from his band of trumpeters and horn-players and with them, for protection, four centurions, and told them all to follow the Ligurian's orders and decided on the next day for the operation. (*Iug.* 93.7–8; Loeb, trans. Rolfe, rev. Ramsey)

Each soldier reacts according to his nature (*ingenium*), in pronouncing the task difficult or easy. Note that Sallust is still dividing human nature into subtypes (though the information also has the virtue of expanding the pool of witnesses).

In what follows, the level of detail continues to be intense:

> Now when it appeared to be time according to Marius's instructions, the Ligurian proceeded to the spot after all preparations and arrangements had been made. Those who were going to make the ascent, in keeping with the previous instructions of their guide, had changed their arms and equipment, baring their heads and feet so as to be able to see better and climb among the rocks more easily. On their backs were swords and shields, but the latter of Numidian design, made of hide, both because of their lighter weight and so that they would make less noise if bumped. And so the Ligurian, going on ahead, fastened ropes to the rocks and roots, if they stuck out as a result of age, so that pulled up by means of them the soldiers might more easily make the ascent. Sometimes he hoisted up with his hand those whom the unusual nature of the route alarmed; where the ascent was a little too rough, he sent men ahead one at a time unarmed and then followed himself, bringing their arms. He was first to test spots that appeared to offer uncertain support, and by repeatedly climbing up and back down the same way, and then at once stepping aside, he bolstered the courage of the rest. Accordingly, after a long time and great exertion, they finally reached the fortress, deserted at that point because all the defenders, as on other days, were face to face with the enemy. (*Iug.* 94.1–3; Loeb, trans. Rolfe, rev. Ramsey)

The little band is well equipped by its Ligurian *dux* to suit the terrain. Heads and feet are left bare, to allow a better view and an easier foothold among the rocks. Shields and swords are carried on backs, the shields made of Numidian hide, apparently lighter and less noisy when struck. But these hides are not just practical and adaptive: they also function as a kind of camouflage. Going native to deceive the enemy, the Romans dress as Numidians, or rather, Numidian beasts of burden. Or even . . .

The snails, it turns out, have given the Ligurian more than just a delicious snack. They have also given him a strategic plan. It is never explicitly stated, but this stumbling, encumbered procession back up the mountain looks like nothing so much as a caravan of snails: bareheaded and barefoot, peering timidly out from under hard but lightweight protective shells. On second thoughts, in this harsh landscape an analogy with its smallest inhabitants is not too surprising. The word used here of the soldiers' exposed extremities, *nudus*, is also Horace's word for snails served without their shells, in a cooking context; Sallust uses it to describe both unarmed soldiers and the African desert, devoid of plants.[81] After all, protection against the elements and lightness of maneuver are among the top essentials for desert survival. What the Ligurian must have noticed on the way up is that snails—humble and profoundly earthbound as they are—have always had the advantage in managing vertical climbs. The soldiers need to make up for lack of suction and slimy grip by attaching ropes and pitons (*claui*) to the rocks and roots that snails just glide past.

In this sun-baked, bare terrain, snails set an example to everyone who takes their house with them for shelter from the elements.[82] They are miniatures of the Numidian nomads, equally amphibious creatures, descended, Sallust tells us, from Persian sailors who settled on the coast and used the hulls of their ships to roof their huts, then gradually moved inland and learned to pitch camp in the desert.[83] From the earliest Greek literature, snails and human travellers have been aligned. The same epithet, *phereoikos*, "house-carrier," is used by Hesiod of snails and by Herodotus of Scythian nomads.[84] As the poet Philemon puts it, "How clever a creature is the snail, by Zeus! If ever he finds himself with a bad neighbour, he just takes up his house and moves away, and lives free from care, leaving those who annoy him behind."[85] At one point on the expedition, when the gradient is particularly steep and the Ligurian offers to carry his comrades' armour for them, they even briefly turn into slugs. This is work that cannot be rushed. Indeed, the little party goes at a snail's pace: arriving finally (*tandem*) and much fatigued (*multumque fatigati*).

For anyone who remains sceptical, another clue that Sallust, like the Ligurian, is thinking all along about the lessons that nature teaches is about to appear. A battle with the Numidians ensues in front of the fortress walls (94.3–6), and the Roman army for the first time on this campaign uses its traditional defensive "tortoise" formation (*testudo*), shields interlocked in a thick, impermeable outer layer.[86] Plutarch describes it as follows, etymologizing *testudo* rightly from *testa*, roof tile: "The resulting appearance is very like that of a roof, affords a striking spectacle, and is the most effective of protections against arrows, which glide off

FIGURE 15. Testudo formation, Trajan's column (from plaster cast in National Museum of Romanian History, Bucharest). Photo: ChristianChirita; Wikimedia Commons.

from it."[87] When it comes to real-life *testudines*, Pliny writes about African land turtles, which inhabit the driest parts of the desert and live on dew, and the turtles of the Indian Ocean, so huge that islanders roof their houses with a single shell or use it as a boat.[88] This takes us straight back to Sallust's description of the Numidian huts with their curved sides, roofed with the hulls of ships. Along with snails and Numidians, turtles adapted early from aquatic origins to arid inland habitats. In the Middle Ages, *testudo* was even interchangeable with *limax* as the Latin word for snail.[89]

To return to the parallel in Herodotus from Cyrus's Sardis campaign, it even turns out that Hyroeades, the man who saw a soldier emerge from a gap in the ramparts to retrieve a fallen helmet, was a Mardian—that is, he came from a tribe of Persian nomads who lived in the mountains bordering the Caspian Sea. What is more, the McGuffin in that story, the cap or helmet (*kunea*) separated from its wearer, functions metonymically, like the snails, for larger themes in the story: vulnerable places exposed and weak points in military defences.

Finally, why do trumpeters and horn players take up such a large section of the party? Five of them to four centurions? Their strategic function is clear enough: to sound a misleadingly loud alarm from the back of the camp to terrify and scatter the enemy. But it may also be because of how their instruments look. The *cornu*, played by a *cornicen*, a horn player, was a twisted G-shaped contraption, whereas

FIGURE 16. Roman limestone relief with funeral procession from Amiternum, showing trumpeters and horn players, Augustan period, Museo Nazionale d'Abruzzo, L'Aquila, Abruzzo, Italy. Photo: Dan Diffendale; Flickr.

the *tuba* was a long straight horn. Does the presence of the instruments complete the picture of these slow-moving travellers by suggesting the snail's projecting eyes, which Pliny calls horns, *cornua*, and which he says the snail uses to test its route in advance (*praetemptans iter*)?[90]

All that with mere snails? At least I hope to have shown how solidly the snails belong in *Jugurtha*, with what determination they own their place, and how unstickable they are from Sallust's multilayered reading of the challenges of desert life. So far, several relationships have emerged between the different narrative levels. It is clear enough that the Ligurian sherpa reads as a miniature of Marius and other human opportunists. Less obviously, he can also be seen as a smaller version of the historian as naturalist or explorer—enthusiastic student of all life-forms and twisted genius, quick-witted and resourceful. Like the Ligurian, Sallust is a collector, for whom the Jugurthine War is a prize specimen, chosen for its exceptional size (*magna*) and shifting colours (*uaria*). In the preface to *Catiline*, Sallust even identifies his tight selection process as "cherry-picking":

> I decided to write the history of the Roman people piecemeal [*carptim*], according to what seemed worth recording. (*Cat.* 4.2)

This suggests both the hunter gatherer, plucking choice gastropods like stationary fruit, and the detached observer from a high place, from which all historical characters, even Marius and Sulla, look small and slow (as Plutarch said, "It is impossible to call one immovable object slower than another").[91] If, like Calvino's tree-climbing baron, the historian is "positioned above the fray," thanks to his "sovereign intellect," here he stoops for just a moment to scoop up the weakest, most microcosmic and beleaguered units of empire-building.[92]

FIGURE 17. "An Incident in the Jugurthine War," *Cassells Illustrated Universal History*, Edmund Ollier (1893–96). Photo: De Luan; Alamy Stock Image.

But George Kubler makes another comparison altogether in the opening paragraph of his essay on the moment and artistic style, which includes this startling sentence: "To spatialize time is a faculty shared both by snails and by historians."[93] Sallust, for one, seems to know what he means. He fills the moralizing preface to *Jugurtha* with indictments of laziness; words like *socordia, inertia* and *torpescere* characterize the human animal at its sluggish worst. But before he knows it, he is fighting for his own reputation. "I believe that some people," he says, "will give my useful labour [*utilis labor*] the name of laziness [*inertia*], people who think it is the hardest kind of work [*industria*] to greet the people and enjoy the pleasures of feasting."[94] The historian is on the warpath against elite values and leisure practices. In Yelena Baraz's words: "*otium* is construed as occupied with a true *negotium*, while his imagined critics' activities, which are more normally seen as the *negotia* of a Roman senator, appear frivolous."[95] Sallust's claim to industry of a different kind—discreet, apolitical, timeless—should make him all too sympathetic to the snails as they wind between the rocks (*inter saxa*) just as he and his human characters navigate tricky historical and political obstacles.[96] The historian may be lofty and detached, but he shares something critical with these lowly creatures: the risk that his life's work will be grievously underrated. I think the special salience of his slow-moving snails shows us the way to understanding that.[97]

FIGURE 18. Roman column base with palm tree and snails (?), Volubilis, Morocco. Author's photo.

3

# Brief Lives

## *The Case of Crispus*

*Life is too short to write long things*

This self-reflexive aphorism may sound like a motto from Seneca. In fact, it comes from a parodic anthology of pocket wisdom by Polish satirist Stanisław Lec, first translated into English as *Unkempt Thoughts* in 1962.[1] Lec's words have worn well in the age of the meme, the tweet, and the soundbite. Do they bear inverting? Are *things* too short now to write long *lives?* Clearly not, if we think of the endless pileup of biographical doorstoppers. Yet short biography seems to be having its moment, too. A recent conference at the University of Bristol, "Flash Histories" (2019), included such papers as "The Long and Short of Writing History" and "Can a Short Life Be a Good Life? Brevity in Historical Biography" (the latter from a former employee of the *Oxford Dictionary of National Biography*, that monument of short life-writing described by its founder Sir Leslie Stephen as a "literary condensing machine").[2] These days, little biographies, even of inanimate objects, are far from modest in their sights. While eighteenth-century England boasted a subgenre of picaresque "little lives" or "it-lives" (the adventures of slippers, rupees, pincushions, and lapdogs), their modern equivalents have distinctly global aspirations.[3] Titles like *Cod: A Biography of the Fish that Changed the World* and *Salt: A World History* have become publishing clichés.

Seen through a wider lens, though, the current trend for contracted lives, lives of subalterns, and lives of mute or inanimate things is not so much a flash in the pan as the latest manifestation of a centuries-old drive to expand the methods and subjects of life-writing and to embrace more individuals, more democratically, in less conventional ways.[4] Its thrust is increasingly political: to reverse past inequalities and injustices for subjects who seem less than significant or whose traces are slight. The effects of its most recent surge have been both radical and widespread.

To repeat Tim Hitchcock's claim from my first chapter: "If today we have a public dialogue that gives voice to the traditionally excluded and silenced . . . it is in no small part because we now have beautiful histories of small things."[5]

Consider the spotlight recently cast on one anonymous Chinese farmer, who met his death in 1661, gunned down in the war with the Dutch over Taiwan.[6] As miraculous biographical resuscitations go, this example is far less celebrated, far more sparsely documented, to be sure, than Menocchio, the sixteenth-century miller in Carlo Ginzburg's *The Cheese and the Worms* (1980), or the nineteenth-century clog-maker in Alain Corbin's *Life of an Unknown* (2001). Indeed, it was a case of mistaken identity that caused the farmer's fatal run-in with history. His death "left a passing impression in the archives," according to historian Tonio Andrade, who recalls discovering him in a contemporary diary, "like a fly pressed between the pages of an old book."[7] In 2010, Andrade gave him a new lease on life (at least in scholarship), using him to argue in the process for the potential interconnectedness of microhistory and global history.[8] Yet in the shadows of this obscure personal tragedy lurks an even fainter trace: a scullery maid who lost her life thanks to the Chinese cannonball that ripped away her left leg while she was doing laundry on the beach below the fortress walls. Again, her death happens to be recorded in a diary from the time, leaving the tiniest hint of a life about which nothing more is known.[9]

Where antiquity is concerned, dredging up submerged individuals tends to be a tougher business. Epigraphic records can be fruitful—above all, the personal statements of Roman freedmen who emerged from obscurity to record their entry into mainstream public service.[10] John Henderson has rebuilt the life of imperial senator Rutilius Gallicus from literary and epigraphic sources combined.[11] Where the lamentably underdocumented life of slaves is concerned, we have the painful speech of the pimp's slave boy (*puer*) introduced to fill a brief interlude in Plautus's *Pseudolus*. This blurted protest against "miseries large and small" hints at the sexual abuse of a defenseless minor (*paruuolus*) before it is abruptly suppressed (*sed comprimenda est mihi uox et oratio*, "but time for me to restrain my speech and end my words").[12]

Even more tantalizing is this two-line life, preserved in the *Prodigies* of Julius Obsequens:[13]

> Seruus Q. Seruilij Caepionis Matri Ideae se praecidit, et trans mare exportatus ne umquam Romae reuerteretur.
>
> A slave of Quintus Servilius Caepio castrated himself for the Mother of Ida and was shipped across the sea never to return to Rome.

In his exquisite meditation on these lines, Shane Butler has attempted to contextualize the mysterious third-person account against a backdrop of slave revolts and the cult of the Magna Mater. But it remains just a heart-stopping moment, or in his words a *membrum disiectum*. "I knew," he writes, "that it was useless to comb the beach from which the slave had departed for other fragments to flesh out the picture."[14] And later: "'History' may be more complete, but it can never offer such immediacy."[15]

In the case of those who have been successfully singled out for posterity, the belief that it is the little things that resonate, not grand CVs, has deep classical roots. Plutarch, most famously, in his *Life of Alexander*, prioritized the slight or short event (*pragma brachu*) over important *res gestae* for nailing the true character of one's subject:

> For it is not Histories that I am writing, but Lives; and in the most illustrious deeds there is not always a manifestation of virtue or vice, no, a slight thing like a phrase or a jest often makes a greater revelation of character than battles when thousands fall, or the greatest armaments, or sieges of cities. (Plut. *Alex.* 1.2; Loeb, trans. Perrin)

So it is that he preserves for us the anecdote about Diogenes telling Alexander to get out of his light, Philip telling his son that Macedonia is too small for him, how Alexander sliced through the Gordian knot, his dreams, dress, taste in food, and so on.

Plutarch's priorities in turn inflect John Aubrey's *Brief Lives* (first published in 1680), that radically experimental work of small-scale life-writing which combines brevity with "trivial" detail. Aubrey responded pugnaciously to the charge that he was "magotie-minded" and "too minute" by claiming that one day he would be properly appreciated:[16]

> Pox take your Orators and poets, they spoile lives and histories. The Dr sayes that I am too Minute; but a hundred yeare hence that minuteness will be gratefull.

Aubrey's *Brief Lives* is indeed revered now, and not just for the memorable details of the people its author chooses to record but also for the outlines of those he leaves behind. In the recesses of his life of Shakespeare, for example, is the intriguing outline of another butcher's son from Stratford-upon-Avon, the same age as William Shakespeare and even known to him, and "held not at all inferior to him for a natural wit . . . but died young."[17] By "brief" Aubrey generally means short in the telling, not short in duration.[18] But one of his subjects compresses both kinds of brevity almost into the vanishing-point of his minimizing experiment: William Saunderson, who had it said of him by Christopher Wren that "as he wrote not well so he wrote not ill," and who, when he died, "went out like a spent candle" even before he could receive the sacrament.[19]

Looking back at antiquity in his "Life of Plutarch," Aubrey's contemporary John Dryden probed the classical origins of this mindset, how "there is withal, a descent into minute circumstances, and trivial passages of life, which are natural to this way of writing . . . you are led into the private Lodgings of the Heroe: you see him in his undress, and are made Familiar with his most private actions and conversations."[20] Aubrey justifies his own emphasis in the prefaces both to his longer *Life of Hobbes* and the first two editions of *Brief Lives* (1680, 1681), always repeating the same Latin quotation lifted from Francis Bacon:[21]

> I humbly offer to the present Age and Posterity, tanquam Tabula naufragii [like planks from a shipwreck] & as plankes & lighter things swimme, and are preserved, where the more weighty sinke & are lost.

Small lives and small details, he implies, are the flotsam and jetsam of history: they make better swimmers, and are more likely to stay afloat until we arrive to comb the beach and piece together their stories. As for Aubrey's own life, he signs it off with modest initials, JA, a mere add-on to his lives of great scientists and thinkers, a nothing that should be "interponed" like a "sheet of wast-paper only in the binding of a Booke."[22] Another fly pressed in the pages, perhaps, but one composed and preserved, even so.

The subject of this chapter is an equally brief *Roman* life, another virtual sheet of wastepaper. Disappointingly, it is not the life of a slave or subaltern—or at least it is that only in a metaphorical sense. Instead, it belongs to someone at the top, who always more or less kept afloat. Indeed, his survival strategies evoke Kathleen Stewart's notion of modern life as akin to the precarious existence of a water bug: "living on the surface tension of some kind of liquid. Seduced by the sense of an incipient vitality lodged in things, but keeping oneself afloat too. And nimble, if you're lucky."[23] Yet in his own way the subject of this brief life is equally a nonperson, known less now for his conventional achievements, his oratory, and the events of his two consulships than for his imperial marriages and a few short but immortal quips (a word that comes from Latin *quippe*, an ironic "to be sure"). Nandini Pandey's brief for the question of what to take from the burning house of antiquity juxtaposed small things—traces of forgotten people and what they made (Amy Richlin's Pietrabbondante rooftile, for example)—with short sayings (like Dan-el Padilla Peralta's Black Lives Matter slant on "Even good King Ancus closed his eyes to the light"). But the possibility of a deeper connection between the two—brief lives and brief sayings—is something Plutarch long ago embraced when he spoke of the phrase or joke that sticks firmer in the memory as a biographical device than any battle or siege does.

## THE BRIEF LIFE OF CRISPUS

Thanks to the tricks of transmission, the life of C. Sallustius Passienus Crispus (from now on Crispus, for short) is preserved as an odd remnant of a much larger lost Suetonian corpus of lives of around a hundred illustrious men, *Viri illustres*.[24] Most of his fellow survivors are poets or grammarians. Crispus's claim to be included, along with C. Calpurnius Piso, is his standing as an orator, though none of his speeches are extant.[25] He is far better known for his bons mots, uttered on the sidelines of history by a spectator of events, not a maker of them. Crispus owes his survival to chance. The one-paragraph biography we have now exists only thanks to a scholion on Juvenal's fourth satire found in two manuscripts (P and S).[26] A shorter variant is preserved in Renaissance scholar Giorgio Valla's collection of Juvenalian scholia attributed to one "Probus."[27] The life comes attached to a sketch of one of Domitian's most impassive courtiers, who was summoned to deal with the unwanted gift of a huge turbot:

> Amiable old Crispus also arrived, a gentle soul, with a character resembling his eloquence. Who would have been a more useful companion to the ruler of seas, lands, and peoples, had he only been allowed, under that plague and disaster, to condemn his cruelty and offer honourable advice? But what's more savage than a tyrant's ear? On his whim the fate of a friend simply intending to talk about the rain, or the heat, or the showery spring, hangs in the balance. So Crispus never swam against the flood [*ille igitur numquam derexit bracchia contra | torrentem*]; he was not the kind of patriot who could speak his mind's thoughts freely and risk his life for the truth. That's how he managed to see many winters and his eightieth summer. He was protected by this armour even in that court [*sic multas hiemes atque octogensima uidit | solstitia, his armis illa quoque tutus in aula*] (Juv. 4.81–93; Loeb, trans. Braund)

As it happens, the scholiast had the wrong Crispus in mind. Juvenal was writing about Vibius Crispus of Vercellae, who lived under Nero and the Flavians (more on him later).

It is possible, then, that Suetonius's biography of our Crispus was somewhat longer in its original form. But short and sweet is how it has come down to us—and short and sweet is how it asks to be read:

> Passienus Crispus, a townsman of Visellium, began his first speech in the senate with these words: "Conscript fathers and you, Caesar" [*"patres conscripti et tu Caesar!"*], and was as a result fulsomely commended by Tiberius, though not sincerely [*propter quod simulata oratione plenissime a Tiberio conlaudatus est*]. He voluntarily pleaded a number of cases in the court of the Hundred, and for that reason his statue was set up in the Basilica Julia. He was twice consul. He married twice: first Domitia and then Agrippina, respectively the aunt and mother of the emperor Nero. He possessed an estate of two hundred million sesterces. He tried to gain favour with all the emperors, but especially with Gaius Caesar, whom he attended on foot whenever the emperor made a journey. When asked by Nero [or: the same person] in a private conversation whether he had had intimate relations with his own sister, as the emperor had with his, he replied "Not yet" [*hic nullo audiente a Nerone (ab eodem) interrogatus, haberetne sicut ipse cum sorore germana consuetudinem, "nondum" inquit*], a very fitting and cautious answer which neither accused the emperor by denying the allegation, nor disgraced himself with a lie by admitting it [*quantumuis decenter et caute, ne aut negando eum argueret aut adsentiendo semet mendacio dehonestaret*]. He died by the treachery of Agrippina, whom he had made his heir, and was buried with a public funeral. (Suet. *Vita Crispi*; Loeb, trans. Rolfe)

Like Crispus following his master Caligula on foot, this courtier's life tags along behind the far more complex and illustrious lives of the emperors. In its current state, it looks complete enough, racing through a lifespan from debut to death, via a bitty selection of details: a place of origin (Visellium, now unknown); a memorable first speech in the Senate; a statue to commemorate good service to oratory; two consulships; two wives; a hefty fortune; a hint that he was bumped off by wife number two; a will in which his property reverted to her, followed by a hollow-sounding public funeral.[28] Crispus's identity is shaped above all by his imperial marriages (in 33 CE and 41 CE) and his performance as a courtier, right from his first speech, where he invents a new form of address, one that Tiberius mirrors fulsomely (*plenissime*), with his own "simulated speech" (*simulata oratione*).

As for Crispus's background, we know that his grandfather was Lucius Passienus Rufus, consul in 4 BCE; his father, another C. Sallustius Passienus Crispus, was adopted by his great-uncle, the historian Sallust—hence his name, along with associations with the pursuit of luxury and observation from the fringes. Crispus *père* receives his own short sketch in Tacitus (such small-scale sketches of unusual people, "paradoxical portraits," constitute an entire subgenre of brief lives in Roman historiography).[29] In achieving influence while avoiding the *cursus honorum*, the father shadowed Maecenas, the imperial archetype of unelected friend to a ruler:

> Thus for him the path to great offices lay clear; but, choosing to emulate Maecenas [*Maecenatem aemulatus*], without holding senatorial rank he outstripped in influence many men who had won a triumph or the consulate, while in his elegance and refinements he diverged from the old Roman school, and in the ample and generous scale of his establishment he tended towards extravagance [*diuersus a ueterum instituto per cultum et munditias copiaque et affluentia luxu propior*]. Yet under it all lay a mental energy equal to important tasks, all the keener for the display he made of somnolence and apathy [*suberat tamen uigor animi ingentibus negotiis par, eo acrior quo somnum et inertiam magis ostentabat*]. So it was that next to Maecenas, while Maecenas kept his influence, and later in the top place, he carried the burden of imperial secrets. (Tac. *Ann.* 3.30; Loeb, trans. Moore and Jackson, adapted)

Both Crispus senior and Maecenas mixed business with pleasure; both their biographies are strung between minimizing the conventionally important and maximizing the conventionally trivial. Both also knew how to negotiate court life. As Seneca wrote, had Maecenas been Nero's contemporary, he too "would have been among the dissimulators."[30]

Our Crispus, by contrast, whose career was far more conventionally driven than his father's, seems to have fully inhabited the dissimulator's role. By far the most memorable factoid in his life belongs to the penultimate sentence, which records for posterity his gloriously fence-sitting one-liner (or "one-worder"): the riposte *nondum*, "Not yet," suspended between two killer alternatives, yes and no—the best, briefest, and most tactful answer a courtier could ever give to such an awkward trap question as "Have you slept with your own sister?" The closest modern equivalent is of course the loaded question "Have you stopped beating your wife?" Except that that "informal fallacy" presumes something that has already happened; its possible "yes" and "no" answers are "damned if you do, damned if you don't." Whereas "not yet" seems to offer a double way out.

As it happens, the wife-beating puzzle has ancient roots. When third-century BCE philosopher Menedemus was asked if he had stopped beating his father, he came up with this careful response: "I have not beaten him and I have not stopped."[31] Far too plodding for any smooth imperial courtier. For wily prevarication on Crispus's level, we must turn to the BBC TV adaptation of Robert Graves's *I, Claudius* and the courtier who gives this riposte to Augustus's question, "Have you slept with my daughter Julia?": "Not slept." At which the emperor (memorably played by Brian Blessed) bellows: "*Ah* . . . ! Not *slept* . . . ! You mean it happened standing up, perhaps! Or in the street, or on a bench!"[32] In fact, read along with Suetonius's analysis ("he neither accused the emperor by denying the allegation, nor disgraced himself with a lie by admitting it") and with Tacitus's sketch of the elder Crispus in mind, our Crispus's *nondum* starts to look positively Tacitean, in countering imperial power with an equivocal response nicely pitched between aggression and flattery.[33]

## THE POINT OF THE ANECDOTE

Brief quip and brief life converge here in an anecdote, a form identified by Joel Fineman in a well-known discussion as a "historeme, i.e. . . . the smallest minimal unit of the historiographic fact."[34] Among mainstream historians, anecdotes still tend to have low status, dismissed as "no-account items."[35] For Fineman, they punch above their weight, standing out from the larger accounts in which they are embedded through their ability (illusory, in his view) to create an effect of the real, often helped by the presence of material "stuff."[36] Hence, as Dryden recognized, the charms of "a Scipio and a Lelius gathering Cockle-shells on the shore, Augustus playing at bounding stones with Boyes; and Agesilaus riding on a Hobby-horse among his Children."[37] This suggests that play is another vitally revealing side-activity in otherwise "important" lives. Eccentricity, too. Helen Deutsch has discussed Samuel Johnson's fetish for collecting and storing old pieces of orange peel while refusing to reveal their purpose as a kind of symbolic hoarding that haunts biographers, from Boswell on, with the limits of their condition: that their subjects can be intimately known, yet never fully known.[38]

If some anecdotes, as in Plutarch's *Lives*, are illuminating incidents in a larger narrative, others are self-contained and as often as not transferable. Anecdotes tend to transcend their surroundings, packing a universal or memorable truth into the context of an everyday encounter and often acquiring a life independent of their original subjects as transferable memes or urban legends. Immanuel Kant is said to have said of the tales clustering around one celebrity: "It seems to me I recall similar anecdotes about other great figures. But that is to be expected. Great men are like high church towers: around both there is apt to be a great deal of wind."[39] Writing on the golden age of the anecdote, Enlightenment France, Lionel Gossman recalls Roland Barthes's thoughts on the self-contained type, known in French as a *fait divers*: "It contains all its knowledge within itself: consumption of a *fait divers* requires no knowledge of the world; it refers formally to nothing but itself; of course its content is not unrelated to the world: disasters, murders, abductions, robberies, and eccentricities all refer to human beings, their history, their condition of alienation, their fantasies." For Barthes, the *fait divers* belongs to the moment and is context-free: "sans durée et sans context."[40]

Even so, there is enough fence-sitting here to keep us pondering about how an anecdote relates to its larger context. Fineman is adamant that the function of anecdotes is to perforate conventional historical narrative: "The anecdote is the literary form that uniquely *lets history happen* by virtue of the way it introduces an opening into the teleological, and therefore timeless, narration of beginning, middle, and end."[41] This is what gives the form its postmodern appeal, dislocated as it is from traditional chronicling (and, Fineman would claim, from historical truth). He resists the fetishization of anecdotes by New Historicists Catherine Gallagher and Stephen Greenblatt, who respond that such unruly eruptions offer special access to the past, in that they belong to the suppressed "history of things that did not happen."[42] Writing about Tacitus in *Wit and the Writing of History*, Paul Plass would seem to agree: "Witty, anecdotal history is authentic even if not factually true, because in its incongruity it is history written at one of its most common denominators."[43]

What connection, then, if any, does the *nondum* story have with what comes before and after it? If anecdotes are interruptions—if they owe their very survival to their success in puncturing an otherwise suppressed (because predictable) routine—something different seems to apply in this case.[44] *Nondum* functions, rather, as a signature or seal, an *imago vitae* (image of life), no less, in capturing some more universal trait of "not-yet-ness" in Crispus's life. I will have more to say about this later. For now, let us consider how *nondum* relates to other "not-words" in Roman historiography. Paul Plass identifies "nicely placed negatives" as a Tacitean speciality: reflecting the imperial "gridlock of contradictory forces" or even the "vacuum of forces, an absence of any effective claim, decision, action or policy," they feature in many of his more epigrammatic statements.[45] Emperor Otho, for example, is associated with *nondum* in one such quip: *Othoni nondum auctoritas inerat ad prohibendum scelus* (Otho did *not yet* have the authority to prohibit crime).[46] This is followed by a nicely placed *paraprosdokian* or sting in the tail: *iubere iam poterat* (but he *already* had the power to order it). Rather than the kind of piety we might expect—for example, "but he already had the best intentions of prohibiting it." Plass writes: "Tacitus' language is not a neutral tool but reflects and . . . in a sense reproduces *in nuce* the substance of Roman politics, in this case a peculiarly self-defeating dialectic of terror."[47] This allows us to start to make a larger claim for Crispus's laconic *nondum*: that it speaks for all cautious imperial subjects and for the limited power of any courtier to suppress fear or to stave off corruption.

If any element of the "Life" is obviously connected to *nondum*, it is the matching opening anecdote about Crispus's first senatorial speech—the difference being that there it is the senator who speaks first and the emperor who responds disingenuously. It is hard to judge the tone of this exchange, or guess why it is singled out, which shows just how successfully Tiberius concealed his inner response, or how insensitive we are to the nuances of Crispus's address. Before the late second century CE, *patres conscripti* alone was the usual senatorial address, even if the emperor was present—in Pliny the Younger's *Panegyricus*, for example, predictably with an egalitarian emperor like Trajan.[48] To supplement it with *et tu Caesar* could be construed either as flattering, because it makes the emperor equal to the senators (which is as much as Tiberius may have wanted, on the surface), or as inept, even insulting, because it puts the emperor in second place.[49] But the heavy emphasis Suetonius puts on the faked quality of Tiberius's response suggests that he was overcompensating for a formula that was uncomfortably misjudged—or uncomfortably prescient. This is only a guess when both parties have, as it were, kept their options open. At least Crispus can see double, has his finger perfectly on the pulse of an ambiguously hybrid and still evolving constitution, as does Tiberius.[50]

## FAMILY AFFAIRS

In the case of the *nondum* anecdote itself, the nagging textual or historical problem remains that it is Caligula, not Nero, who is the obvious Julio-Claudian emperor to provoke a question about sleeping with one's sister (Crispus was already dead when Nero succeeded). For that reason, Tristan Power, most recently, has supported emending the text from *Nerone* to *illo* or *imperatore* or something similarly multipurpose.[51] He argues that it is because the life was excerpted and transmitted by the Juvenalian scholiast that it might in the interim have triggered memories of Nero and his more famous incest with his mother, so prompting the scholiast to interfere and pin the story to him.[52] This all makes good sense in the immediate context because of peculiarities in the Julio-Claudian family tree: Agrippina was both Nero's mother and Crispus's second wife, which made parallels between the two men the more plausible to contemplate. Yet she was also Caligula's sister, so there is a ready parallel there, too.

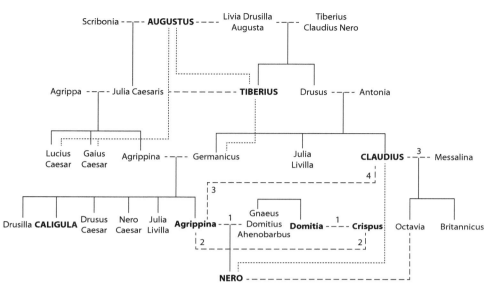

FIGURE 19. Julio-Claudian family tree.

A further complicating factor pointed out by Power is that Agrippina, via her repellent first husband Domitius Ahenobarbus (brother to Crispus's first wife, Domitia, and father to Nero), was already Crispus's sister-*in-law*. And since in-laws (*adfines*, "border people," literally) counted as inside Roman families, rather than outside them, Agrippina *was* a "sister" in the broadest sense, one Crispus *was* about to sleep with, in a marriage that, thanks to his earlier marriage to her aunt Domitia, *was* technically incestuous. As Power says, "this irony in Passienus' reply has been missed by critics."[53] In that case, there is another relevant fact to add: Agrippina is not the only sister in the picture. If she is Crispus's "sister" as well as his wife, then retrospectively that makes his first wife, Domitia, Agrippina's sister-in-law through her brother Domitius, Crispus's "sister," too. In other words: not only had Crispus *not yet* slept with his "sister" Agrippina: he had *already* slept with his "sister" Domitia! Which makes him a trendsetter in the kinds of imperial relationships that would become routine *consuetudines*—literally "habits" ("familiar affairs," we might translate it)—making the bon mot not just an evasion but possibly even a lie, from the man who thought he was avoiding lies. This will be only the first instance of our joker being hoist with his own petard.

As Power admits in passing, though, the emperor's precise question is: "Have you slept with your *own* sister?" (*cum sorore germana*). Agrippina could not have counted as a *soror germana*, since this refers exclusively to a biological relationship, such as Gaius had with the sisters (Drusilla, Livilla, and Agrippina) he was rumored to have taken to bed. On the other hand, there is a problem with chronology if we think this is Gaius referring obliquely to *his* sister Agrippina: it was only in 41 CE, when her first husband, Nero's father Gnaeus Domitius Ahenobarbus, died, that Gaius's successor Claudius had the bright idea of making Crispus marry her. No such neat insinuation about Agrippina could realistically have been in Gaius's mind.

## PUNCHLINES

If the various dynastic relationships have seemed exhausting to disentangle, that is hardly surprising—and must surely be part of the joke. Crispus was truly intertwined with the imperial family, every which way. Just as the full potential of the *nondum* joke lies in the dual or even triple relational identities of the protagonists and their female associates, some of them operating on a subterranean level, so the brilliance of the reply lies in its ambidextrous, dual-purpose nature. The number *two* is already all over the short biography: two consulships; two marriages; two times one hundred *centemviri* equals a fortune of two hundred million sesterces. Does this all imply short measure, in some sense? That Crispus never made it to "three" of anything? Dogged by nonfulfillment and proxyness; brushed out of the way to allow Claudius to marry Agrippina; no children of his own (according to Suetonius, anyway); only a suffect consul the first time (27 CE), and only an ordinary consul the second time (44 CE), expected to relinquish office within just a few days.

The double-headed quality of jokes was observed long ago by Freud, who noted how they give pleasure both in their original conception and in the ricochet of amusement back from the listener who appreciates them. He distinguishes "The Janus-like [in the original: *double face*], two-way-facing character [of jokes], which protects their original yield of pleasure from the attacks of critical reason, and the mechanism of fore-pleasure" from "the further complication of the technique," which "takes place out of regard for the joke's third person."[54] Later, he adds: "Nothing distinguishes jokes more clearly from all other psychical structures than this double-sidedness and this duplicity in speech."[55] Freud's favourite joke, at least according to Iris Murdoch in *The Sea, The Sea*, was an old chestnut that goes back to Roman times and requires similar reflection on the false symmetries of familial relationships:[56]

> The king meets his double and says, "Did your mother work in the palace?", and the double says, "No, but my father did."

In Crispus's case, we are told nothing about the emperor's response, whether he was tickled or silenced by the courtier's clever reply, or how the pleasure flowed, if it did. But the joke keeps on giving—not only to its begetter, who thinks he is hedging his bets against all eventualities, but also to its wider audience, who can see how it ties its speaker in knots with its double bind.

What, then, are we to make of the detail that there were no witnesses to the exchange (*nullo audiente*)? If the audience was a private one, then who leaked the joke: the emperor or the smug courtier? Some fly on the wall?[57] Was the emperor amused, despite being beaten at his own game? Or do we really need to care at all about historical realism, as regards either the anecdote's publication or its timing? Rather, it asks to be read across the longue durée of Crispus's life, *as if* Gaius, or whichever emperor is speaking, already knew the outcome: two imperial marriages, with many attendant complications. So it is that, like so many other anecdotes, this one takes on the flavor of an urban myth or teaching *exemplum*, one adaptable to any immoral overlord and any evasive courtier. For a recent incarnation, we need look no further than Christopher Nolan's 2020 sci-fi thriller *Tenet* and the scene where the "Protagonist" (played by John David Washington) is put on the spot by Russian oligarch Sator (Kenneth Branagh): "Just tell me if you've slept with my wife yet." The reply, after a moment's hesitation: "Er no, not yet."[58] Incidentally, the Protagonist's answer to Sator's follow-up question, "How would you like to die?"—"Old"—is more in the spirit of the self-preserving Vibius Crispus, who saw out his eightieth winter, or the courtier in Seneca's *De ira* who, when asked how he had achieved old age ("that thing most rare in a palace"), replied: "By accepting wrongs and giving thanks."[59]

## CRISPUS AT LARGE

Let us hold onto the word *nondum* now and allow it to guide us through some other traces of Crispus in the surviving literary record: four more anecdotes that add up less to a rounded portrait of an individual than a kind of mini joke-book, something like the sour apophthegms of Georg Christoph Lichtenberg or the anticommunist one-liners of Stanisław Lec. Themes of duplicity, twinning, evasion, inversion, and incest will magically reappear, as if generated by some central algorithm or algorithms. Together, these anecdotes offer a virtual commentary on the imperial condition from a courtier-observer of the emperors' antics: they are history and not-history, biography and not-biography at the same time.

My first passage is a charming story in Pliny the Elder's *Natural History*, from a section on remarkable trees:

> In the territory around the suburbs of Tusculum, on a hill known by the name of Corne, there is a grove consecrated to Diana by the people of Latium from time immemorial; it is formed of beeches, the foliage of which has all the appearance of being trimmed by art [*uelut arte tonsili coma fagei nemoris*]. Passienus Crispus, the orator, who in our time was twice consul, and afterwards became still more famous as having Nero for his step-son, on marrying his mother Agrippina, was passionately

attached to a fine tree that grew in this grove [*in hos arborem eximiam aetate nostra amauit*]: not only would he lie down beneath it and moisten its roots with wine but he would even kiss and embrace it [*osculari conplectique eam solitus, non modo cubare sub ea uinumque illi adfundere*]. Near this grove is a holm-oak, also very renowned [*nobilis*], the trunk of which is no less than thirty-four feet in circumference; giving birth to ten other trees of remarkable size, it forms of itself a whole forest. (Plin. *HN* 16.242)

As in Suetonius, Crispus is introduced as an orator who was twice consul. But Pliny immediately corrects himself: what later made Crispus more famous (*clarior postea*) was his close family relationship to Nero and his mother. Celebrity is then extended to trees as well as humans. A giant ilex that sprouts ten other huge trees is called *nobilis*, "noble, renowned," playing on a long tradition of parallels between human and tree pedigrees.[60] Even so, Crispus's inflated social credentials pale next to the ignoble eccentricity given center stage: his passionate adoration of a prominent beech tree, expressed through kisses, hugs, and offerings of wine. There is evidence enough of tree worship in Rome, but this level of response has been judged overamorous—less dutifully religious than mindlessly perverted.[61] Wine pouring, again, was a known practice (wine was considered good plant fertilizer), but *adfundere* suggests a maudlin outpouring of emotion as well as liquid. The precious orator Hortensius once walked out of a court case because he so badly needed to irrigate his prize plane trees with wine.[62]

In fact, the closest parallel for Crispus—a good example of the kind of portable meme mentioned earlier—is Aelian's critique of Persian potentate Xerxes, who once "honored" a plane tree by draping it with ornaments and even giving it a bodyguard:

> In Lydia, they say, he saw a large specimen of a plane tree, and stopped for that day without any need. He made the wilderness around the tree his camp, and attached to it expensive ornaments, paying homage to the branches with necklaces and bracelets. He left a caretaker for it, like a guard to provide security, as if it were a woman he loved. (Ael. *VH* 2.14; Loeb, trans. Wilson)

Aelian supplies the analysis we need to understand Crispus's behavior. He claims that Xerxes "was enslaved to the plane" and showered it with pointless offerings "as though it were a woman he loved." Apply this to Crispus and it becomes clear that his extravagant expression of erotic love (*amauit*) for a tree diverts him from unproductive involvement with the imperial family (Nero is called his *priuignus*, stepson, not his son). The tree crush is even troped on the futility of an extramarital relationship. Not only does the beech grove grow with the apparent artificiality of topiary (*uelut arte tonsili coma fagei nemoris*)—which is then reflected in the artificiality of Crispus's rhetoric—but the clipped quality of its foliage is already "naturally" expressed in humanoid terms (via *tonsilis* "shaven" and *coma* "hair"), anticipating the ornamental beauty of a tree that somewhat resembles an elegiac mistress. If the verb *cubare* (lie) most obviously channels incubation in a god's temple, it is also the root of *concumbere / concubare*, the origin of our "concubine": thus Crispus "lies with" as well as "under" his exceptional (*eximiam*) tree.

Yet for all the generous sprinkling of liquid fertilizer, the union does not result in offspring. The adjacent ilex with its multiple side-growths seems to taunt Crispus with his ineffectual contribution to the imperial stemma, indeed reproaches the entire Julio-Claudian house for the contortions and ramifications with which they disguised their biological deficiency.[63] This was partly screened by the imposingly propagandistic nemus Caesarum, a grove of laurel trees located on the Via Flaminia and grown from a sprig that a chicken once dropped into Empress Livia's lap, each of which bore the name of an emperor and withered when he died, a grove that has been called "a living genealogy of the *triumphatores* of the *gens Iulia*."[64]

On the other hand, Crispus's hugs and kisses could be read as courtly gestures as much as amatory ones, palace fawning adapted to smothering a safely static, unreactive object. Two of the key players named here, Nero and Agrippina, were known for their ambiguous mutual embraces:

> Already lascivious kisses, and endearments that were the harbingers of guilt, had been observed by their nearest and dearest. (Tac. *Ann*. 14.2; Loeb, trans. Moore and Jackson)

> Nero ... escorted her on her way, clinging more closely than usual to her breast and kissing her eyes; possibly as a final touch of hypocrisy, or possibly the last look upon his doomed mother gave pause even to that brutal spirit. (Tac. *Ann*. 14.4; Loeb, trans. Moore and Jackson)

Similar charades took place between courtiers and emperors—for example, after Seneca fails to be granted retirement by Nero:

> Nero followed his words with an embrace and kisses—nature had fashioned him and use [*consuetudo*] had trained him to veil his hatred under insidious caresses [*fallacibus blanditiis*]. Seneca—such is the end of all dialogues with an autocrat [*qui finis omnium cum dominante sermonum*]—expressed his gratitude [*grates agit*]. (Tac. *Ann*. 14.56; Loeb, trans. Moore and Jackson)

For all this, Crispus's adoration of his tree is not just eccentric: it borders on transgressive. The human incest to which his imperial marriages make him so susceptible is displaced only temporarily here onto whatever one calls the plant equivalent of bestiality.[65] Innocent as it looks, the anecdote indirectly seems to confirm not only Crispus's infertility but also the fact that it is only a matter of time before the firmest prohibition of all is overturned: *nondum*, again.

Another of Crispus's sayings is recorded with approval in the preface to Seneca, *Natural Questions* 4. Here, the theme is flattery:

> I never knew a man more subtle in every matter than Crispus Passienus, especially in distinguishing and curing faults of character. He often used to say that we only put-to the door against flattery, and do not shut it [*saepe dicebat adulationi nos non claudere ostium sed operire*], much in the same way as in the face of a mistress [*amicae*]. If she gives it a shove, we are pleased, still more pleased if she smashes it down [*quae, si impulit, grata est; gratior, si effregit*]. (Sen. QNat. 4 praef. 6)

Crispus is credited with the diagnostic and curative powers of a shrewd observer of character and faults ("especially in distinguishing and curing faults of character"), like some post-Aristotelian Theophrastus or other ethically concerned comedic observer. His advice about resisting flattery gently to let it flow even more may be specifically directed to the emperors, objects of his own courtly approaches, as he cynically advises them to hide their desire to be pursued by their subjects (recall his flattering—or inept or insulting (?)—senatorial debut, to which Tiberius responded in characteristically hypocritical fashion).

The mistress figure (*amica*) has already appeared as a metaphor in the tree story, but the striking door image here puts her to different work. Doors are usually emblems for the barriers presented by patronage, or thwarted love, or both at once; for example, in Ovid's *Tristia* 1.1, where the supreme patron, the emperor, is cast in the image of an imperious unreceptive *domina*. In this scenario, the situation is inverted. Far from the lover being excluded from the mistress's house, usually by a stubborn door or doorkeeper, now the mistress is the one forcing an entry, either by pushing the door open or—more gratifying still—by smashing it down. This image of a passionate, assertive *amica* switches the agency from lover to beloved, or, as in the tree story, credits a normally stationary object of adoration with agency and desire. At the same time, it offers a fantasy of power to those on the inside who do not have to lift a finger.

As Isidore would explain in his survey of Latin door terminology, reversibility is a quality intrinsic to the inner doors of a Roman house:

> Now this [*ianua*] is the first entrance of a house; others, inside the front door, are generally called doorways [*ostia*]. A door-way (*ostium*) is that by which we are prevented from any entrance, so called from impeding (*ostare*, i.e. *obstare*) [or it is doorway (*ostium*) because it discloses (*ostendere*) something within]. Others say doorway is so called because it detains an enemy (*ostis*, i.e. *hostis*), for there we set ourselves against our adversaries—hence also the name of the town Ostia at the mouth of the Tiber, because it is set there to oppose the enemy . . . 'Door panels' [*foris*] or leaves [*valva*] are also elements of a door, but the former are so called because they swing out (*foras*), the latter swing (*revolvere*) inward, and they can be folded double [*duplices conplicabilesque sunt*]—but usage has generally corrupted those terms. Barriers (*claustrum*) are so called because they are closed (*claudere*). (Isid. *Etym.* 15.7.4–5; trans. Barney et al. 2009, 311)

Among these inner doors is the *ostium* referred to by Crispus. Isidore's etymologies variously convey its bidirectional quality: it is called *ostium* either because it stands in the way (*ostando*) of anyone coming in, or because it is a defense against an external enemy (*(h)ostem*), or because it reveals (*ostendit*) something further inside (*intus*). As for other inner doors, *fores* turn outward (*foras*) and *ualuae* turn inward (*intus*), but both are classed as "double and folding" (*duplices conplicabilesque*), or, translated differently, "duplicitous and complicated." The double valence of these adjectives (when Isidore not a door?) recalls the doors and windows that provide such apt material backdrops to the machinations of lover and beloved in the first book of Ovid's *Amores*: the slatted window that frames Corinna's gradually yielding striptease (*pars adaperta fuit, pars altera clausa fenestrae*, "half the window was open, the other half closed"); the folding doors in which the eavesdropper hides to learn female duplicity (*me duplices occuluere fores*, "the double doors hid me"); or the tiny slit in a housedoor (*ianua*) that is all the emaciated lover needs to gain admission (*aditu fac ianua paruo | obliquum capiat semiadaperta latus*, "make the door, half-ajar, contain me sideways-on in its slender opening").[66]

In Crispus's case, the half-open *ostium* suggests affinities with his various double roles.[67] First, as a prominent courtier, he is the doorkeeper who mediates between emperor and world, at once the object and the subject of flattery. Secondly, as an *adfinis*, an in-law on the margins of a family, he is neither in nor out. Isidore writes elsewhere that the wives of two brothers call each other *ianetrix* "as if the term were 'frequenting the doors' [*ianua* + *terere*] or through the same 'door' having 'entry' [*ianua* + *iter*]."[68] Crispus's *ostium* (a passage, or, correctly etymologized, a kind of mouth) gives material form to his *nondum*, that swing-word that offers two convenient exits. When the philosopher Menedemus was told he really needed to answer "yes" or "no" about whether he had stopped beating his father, he replied: "It would be crazy to comply with your rules when I can stop you at the gates."[69]

Every comic needs a fall guy, and in Crispus's case that role goes to his first, older wife Domitia. Usually cast as mean and spiteful, she appears in a more innocent light in one Suetonian anecdote about a fatal encounter with her nephew Nero:

> To matricide he added the murder of his aunt. When he once visited her as she was confined to her bed from constipation, and she, as old ladies will, stroking his downy beard (for he was already well grown) happened to say fondly, "As soon as I receive this, I shall gladly die," he turned to those with him and said as if in jest: "I'll take it off at once." Then he bade the doctors purge the sick woman too aggressively and seized her property before she was cold, suppressing her will, that nothing might escape him. (Suet. *Nero* 34.5; Loeb, trans. Rolfe, adapted)

This is a story about hurried transmission down the generations, not to say opening the sluice gates of inheritance. Nero distorts the natural time of aging and succession by fastforwarding Domitia's death and his own puberty simultaneously, seizing her property while she is *not yet* dead (*necdum defunctae*)—a case of *nondum* unnaturally sped up.

By contrast, the anecdote that links Domitia with Crispus involves a horizontal relationship. It is Quintilian who records it, as an example of the courtier's supreme tactfulness in the law courts, as in the imperial court:

> There are also milder kinds of summing-up [*leniores epilogi*] in which we do justice to our opponent, if he is the sort of person who deserves respect, or when we give him friendly advice and encourage him towards a settlement. This method was admirably adopted by Crispus Passienus when he pleaded in a suit brought by his wife Domitia against her brother Ahenobarbus for the recovery of a sum of money: he said a great deal about the relationship [*necessitudo*] between the two parties and then, referring to their wealth, which was in both cases abundant, added, "There is nothing either of you needs less than the subject of this dispute" ["*nihil uobis minus deest quam de quo contenditis*"]. (Quint. *Inst.* 6.1.50)

The algorithm that generates this story is Crispus's evenhanded mildness (witness *leniores, amice, concordiam*); his "handling" (*tractatum*) of legal conventions is as exceptional (*egregie*) as his handling of the two rivals. Once again, the quip hinges on family relationships, specifically sibling ones. Hard though it is to capture in an English translation, it looks as if Crispus is compressing all his understanding of the situation—a rich brother and sister, neither of whom needs the sum over which they are quarreling—into a neat pun on *necessitudo*, either "need," "necessity," or, as used here, "family relationship."[70] Brother and sister are united twice over, once through blood ties and once through abundant wealth; the combination of an actual *necessitudo*, a family tie, with a spurious one, poverty, makes their legal conflict doubly absurd (the required phrase *non necesse est*, "it is not necessary," is paraphrased in *nihil uobis minus deest*, "there is nothing either of you needs less").

The scenario also reads as a variant on the *nondum* anecdote, with its double bind. Crispus pinpoints the relationship between a wealthy brother and sister that makes their resort to litigation inappropriately antagonistic—a civil war that reveals the hatred that is the usual underside of all sibling love but that in the imperial family tended to erupt without restraint into divorce, murder, prosecution, and expropriation. By contrast, in the *nondum* story Crispus successfully bats away, via semi-denial, an emperor's aggressively familiar enquiry about his own putative sibling relationships. If Crispus concedes that incest runs in the imperial family—is the new normal, *consuetudo*—he does at least disclaim any urgency in his own needs. But if he now says "much," *multa*, about the *necessitudo* of sister Domitia and brother Domitius, it sounds as if he already knows about the twists that his own future marriage to Agrippina, Caligula's sister and Domitius's widow, will give to any simple brother-sister bond. Incidentally, Crispus's gentle reprimand pales next to a much funnier joke involving Domitia: the riposte thought up by Junius Bassus, which Quintilian calls "more biting" (*mordacius*). When Domitia complained that he was attacking her by accusing her of selling old shoes, Bassus retorted: "I never said anything of the sort. I said you *bought* old shoes."[71]

Finally, Crispus makes a short appearance in Tacitus's *Annals*, where he is wheeled on to make a typically Tacitean assessment of two emperors. And here comes a rival contestant for his most famous quip. As the original context makes clear, Crispus is referring to the future emperor Gaius (Caligula) and his grandfather, Tiberius:

> About the same time, Gaius Caesar, who had accompanied his grandfather on the retreat to Capri, received in marriage Claudia, the daughter of Marcus Silanus. His monstrous character was masked by a hypocritical modesty [*immanem animum subdola modestia tegens*]: not a word escaped him at the sentencing of his mother or the deaths of his brothers; whatever mood Tiberius assumed each day, his grandson adopted the same attitude, and his words were not very different [*qualem diem Tiberius induisset, pari habitu, haud multum distantibus uerbis*]. For that reason, in due course, the orator Passienus invented a bon mot that was often repeated: that there had never been a better slave nor a worse master [*neque meliorem umquam seruum neque deteriorem dominum fuisse*]. (Tac. *Ann.* 6.20; Loeb, trans. Moore and Jackson, adapted)

Gaius comes across here as a perfectly trained dissimulator, a man who clothed (*tegens*) natural cruelty with modesty, who in mood and words shadowed Grandpa Tiberius, the man who put on (*induisset*) a different face every day. Unsympathetic Gaius may be; his surface behavior, however, is akin to the stoic endurance of all those subjects, from Herodotus's Harpagus to Seneca's Pastor, who suck up in silence the royal feasts for which their relatives supply the food ("not a word escaped him at the sentencing of his mother or the deaths of his brothers").[72] The vague temporal marker *mox* suggests that Crispus's bon mot was uttered after both reigns—which is hardly surprising.

Once again, the plot thickens unintentionally. Tacitus's formula, "Whatever the mood Tiberius assumed each day, his grandson adopted the same attitude, and his words were not very different," sounds suspiciously like a prescription not just for the ideal imperial heir but more generally for the ideal courtier—as revealed in Horace's *Epistles* 1, for example. Gaius escorting Tiberius on his retreat to Capri (*discedenti Capreas auo comes*) reminds us that Crispus, too, will be remembered for currying favor with the emperors, with Gaius above all (Suet. *Crispus: omnium principum gratiam adpetiuit, sed praecipue C. Caesaris*), and specifically for following his travels on foot (*quem iter facientem secutus est pedibus*). In short, it takes one to know one. "His words were not very different" (*haud multum distantibus uerbis*) again recalls the flexible *nondum*: the best response to changeable Tiberius is a courtier's approximative reply.

In his preface to *The Joke*, Freud quotes two predecessors in the study of humor. One is Theodor Lipps, who wrote, "A joke says what it has to say, not always in a few words, but in too few words—that is, in words that are insufficient by strict logic or by common modes of thought and speech. It may even actually say what it has to say by not saying it."[73] The other is Kuno Fischer, who made the additional suggestion that jokes "must bring forward something that is concealed or hidden."[74] Both formulations are helpful for dissecting the joke here, though both authors assume that a joker is in full control of his double meanings. Like Gaius's modesty, Crispus's bon mot is already *subdolus*, freighted with subterranean treachery, in suggesting an identification of slave and master even as it seems to polarize them. How so? Because in due course Gaius will turn from being the best slave into being the worst master, a worse one even than Tiberius—in another instance of dual identity. This is confirmed by the evolving history of another piece of tyrannical shorthand. Tiberius is said to have subtly modified the stage tyrant's quip, *Oderint dum metuant* ("Let them hate me so long as they fear me") to *Oderint dum probent* ("Let them hate me so long as they approve of me"). Gaius was not shy of using the bleak original.[75]

Yet for all that Crispus intends his targets—Gaius and Tiberius— to be specific and limited, any extrapolation further down the pyramid makes him the victim of his own joke. Not only will his witticism go viral (*percrebuit*), so will the imperial *habitus*: ever-adaptable Crispus will in turn become the best possible slave to Gaius, even to the point of following his carriage on foot. Thinking about both parties to a joke, the begetter and the receiver, Freud concludes: "A joke is thus a double-dealing rascal who serves two masters at once."[76] The full truth of Crispus's witticism will only be revealed sometime in the future. It's not that we've *never* seen a better slave and a worse master—it's just that we *haven't* seen them *yet*!

Looking back to Suetonius's biography, one might conclude that Crispus's *nondum* is actually farsighted, in correctly predicting a future era of full-blown Julio-Claudian incest. And if Domitia counts as his sister, loosely speaking, Crispus could even be regarded as a pioneer in this area. In other ways, his career, as suggested earlier, could be summed up as a case of "not yet" or "not quite": curtailed consulships and backfiring marriages made him a shadow and stooge—a follower, not a leader. Or is it that imperial Rome tout court was a case of "not yet" or "not quite," a slippery slope into repression and decline gradually licensed by earlier precedents? As Seneca, for example, writes in *De beneficiis*: "In Augustus' reign, men's words were not yet [*nondum*] able to ruin them, yet they already caused them problems [*iam molesta*]."[77] Or does "not yet" speak of the uneasy two-way contract between ruler and courtier?[78] "I haven't finished giving you presents yet," says Nero, when he resists Seneca's pleas to retire:

> which is why I am embarrassed that though you are foremost in my affections you do not yet outstrip all others in good fortune [*nondum omnes fortuna antecellis*] (Tac. Ann. 14.55)

Like Suetonius's *nondum* anecdote, the scenario freeze-frames the ruler-courtier relationship for all time.

## FLIES ON THE WALL

"Indeed, the most intense point of a life [*le point le plus intense des vies*], the point where its energy is concentrated, is where it comes up against power, struggles with it, attempts to use its forces and to evade its traps." These are the words of Michel Foucault, not surprisingly, in his "Lives of Infamous Men," an essay originally published in 1977 that resurrects the experience of individuals expunged by disgrace from traditional biography but traceable in prison archives.[79] His words explain why Crispus's short life is bookended by two such encounters with power, each with its own searing *punctum*, before he is virtually submerged by history. Commenting on a famous detail in Pieter Brueghel's *Fall of Icarus*, art historian Georges Didi-Huberman notes that Icarus's legs have *not quite* been swallowed up by the sea: "A *not quite* is necessary here in order to make visible the signified."[80]

Let us end by renewing our acquaintance with the other Crispus, Vibius Crispus, Domitian's sluggish courtier in Juvenal's fourth satire, the one to whom Valla's "Probus" mistakenly ascribes the Suetonian biography. For he, too, is credited with some memorable quips.[81] In his *Life of Domitian*, for example, Suetonius tells us that when he was alone and had nothing better to do, the emperor used to like to stab flies with a very sharp pen:

> At the beginning of his reign he used to spend hours in seclusion every day, doing nothing but catching flies and stabbing them with a keenly sharpened stylus [*stilo praeacuto configere*]. Consequently, when someone once asked whether anyone was in there with Caesar, Vibius Crispus made the witty reply: "Not even a fly" [*ne muscam quidem*]. (Suet. *Dom.* 3; Loeb, trans. Rolfe, adapted)

Barely longer than *nondum*, and also framed as a negative, the riposte clearly comes from the same stable as our Crispus's quip, though this time the joke hinges on the topical significance of a normally insignificant insect. What it suggests is that there was a whole stage family of Crispuses, each one ready to pop up with a specimen of generic courtly wit, some "very sharp pointer" to nail the current climate whenever the relevant emperor provoked it. Their exuberant buzzes and stings punctuate and puncture larger imperial narratives. As for the jokers themselves, these fly-on-the-wall informers, witnesses to imperial depravity (how did they get in?), end up squashed "like flies between the pages of old books." For all their fleeting moments in the limelight, their identity takes a battering from its sheer replicability; ultimately, the price they pay is self-effacement. By contrast, centuries after Crispus's statue, speeches, and all his other achievements have evaporated, the trail of his dazzling wit remains unextinguished:[82]

The brief and strident words that went back and forth between power and the most inessential existences doubtless constitute, for the latter, the only monument they have ever been granted: it is what gives them, for the passage through time, the bit of brilliance, the brief flash that carries them to us. (Foucault [1977] 2020, 162)

FIGURE 20. Roman bronze ring with insect intaglio.
With kind permission of St James's Ancient Art, London.

## 4

# Tiny Irritants

*Itching Eyes, Stones in Shoes, and Other Annoyances*

*If you think you're too small to make a difference, try sleeping in a closed room with a mosquito.*
—WEST AFRICAN PROVERB

Flies stay on the wall (and in the ointment) as I turn now to a different aspect of small things. Not their doll-like cuteness or their microcosmic potential but their power, often surprisingly strong, to act as irritants. John Mack has this to say in *The Art of Small Things* about idols, fetishes and amulets:[1]

> Small things also "get under your skin." They are potent, irritating, sometimes malevolent.

The ancients, too, knew full well that small things could jab in ways disproportionate to their size—never more than when they came into contact with the skin, that hypersensitive membrane between flesh and world. A Theocritean goatherd quakes sympathetically at the outsize pain caused by a thorn stuck in his friend's foot: "What a tiny wound to overcome such a mighty man!"[2] We have seen Seneca write about the intensely concentrated pain of a split nail (*unguiculus*).[3] In one of his letters, a medium that shrinks space and time into the compass of a single "thought for the day," he pours out a memorable slew of "feeling" diminutives to convey the intense discomforts of seasickness: "the slightest little movement [*motiuncula*] disorients you . . . your feet ache, [the ends of] your limbs [*articuli*] feel tiny little prickings [*punctiunculas*]."[4] In another, he exploits diminutives for their tingling specificity: "instruments of torture arrayed for each separate joint of the body [*singulis articulis singula machinamenta quibus extorqueantur aptata*] and all the other innumerable mechanisms for tearing a man apart bit by bit" [*mille alia instrumenta excarnificandi particulatim hominis*].[5]

Sallust's snails have already raised questions about causality, and I leave behind now the notion of tiny things as catalysts for bigger events (along with their descendants, the proverbial butterfly's wing, and the recycled molecules of Julius Caesar's last breath). Not before mentioning the memorably hyperbolic example produced by John Buchan in a 1929 lecture on "The Causal and the Casual in History," where he traces the defeat of Greece in the Greco-Turkish War of 1919–22 and the consolidation of Kemal Atatürk's authority back to the unlucky death two years before of young King Alexander from the bite of a pet monkey in the palace gardens. "I cannot," says Buchan, "better Mr Churchill's comment: a quarter of a million persons died of that monkey's bite."[6]

For now, my focus is on minor provocations closer to home. Not only do these turn out to infest Roman writers' mental and emotional worlds, both as isolated menaces and in droves and swarms; they also help their victims construct certain identities, both literary and social. Such a claim might seem counterintuitive, to say the least. Surely elite Romans were conditioned to conceal their pettier outbursts and only occasionally succumb to grander ones, the kind we connect with epic, tragedy and political ambition: jealousy, fear, anger, pride, hatred, and love?

Seneca, for example, assures his correspondent Lucilius that he won't stamp his feet or fling his arms around when he expresses his feelings—anything to avoid being melodramatic or inauthentic:

> If it were possible, I should prefer to show, rather than speak, my feelings. Even if I were arguing a point, I should not stamp my foot, or toss my arms about, or raise my voice [*nec supploderem pedem nec manum iactarem nec attollerem uocem*]; but I should leave that sort of thing to the orator, and should be content to have conveyed my feelings to you without having either embellished them or lowered their dignity. I should like to convince you entirely of this one fact,—that I feel whatever I say, that I not only feel it, but am wedded to it. (Sen. *Ep.* 75.2; Loeb, trans. Gummere)

In *De ira*, even though his main business is with one devastatingly powerful passion, he makes space for temporary lurches of feeling, too:

> All the sensations which take place without our volition are beyond our control and unavoidable, such as shivering when cold water is poured over us, or shrinking when we are touched in certain places. Men's hair rises up at bad news, their faces blush at indecent words, and they go dizzy when looking down a precipice; and as it is not in our power to prevent any of these things, no reasoning can prevent their taking place. (Sen. *De ira* 2.2.1)

Cicero, conversely, while indicating that his stomach heaves at the very thought of Caesar, makes a show of suppressing the urge:

> What a shameless thug! What a disgrace is this to the Republic, which scarcely any peace can make up for! But let's stop retching [*sed stomachari desinamus*], let's submit to circumstances, and go to Spain with Pompey. That's the best of a bad situation . . . but so much for this. (Cic. *Att.* 7.18.2)

From this brief survey alone, it is clear enough that minor feelings, such as embarrassment, awkwardness, anxiety, and annoyance, make their presence abundantly felt in first-person Latin literature, to varying degrees and across different kinds of shared performance. But what exactly are they doing there? True, many of the irritants I consider in this chapter transcend historical context, among them pinching shoes, stones in shoes, stubbed toes, minor ailments, the buzz of insects, and the added menace of tiny but excruciating stings. Many, indeed, overlap with the catalysts of sudden death in Pliny the Elder's *Natural History* discussed in chapter 1. They belong to the thrilling set of things that bind "us" and "them" together and produce frissons of unexpected familiarity with the distant past.

Shared experience makes it all too easy to sympathize with Horace when he grouses about diarrhea and mosquitoes on his journey to Brundisium, or with Sidonius when he complains of the smoke that gets in his eyes and up his nostrils in the kitchen of a country inn.[7] We can relate to Juvenal's grumbles about Roman traffic (3.254–61) and to Ovid's advice to unhappy lovers in *Remedia amoris* to focus on subtly annoying defects and so speed up the abrupt reversal of attraction now popularly known as the "ick."[8] The impact of such tiny irritations in our own daily lives tends to be cumulative. Or, as Ovid puts it, in an erotic context, they may be small things in themselves but together they add up to a huge heap:

> Someone perhaps will call them small (for small they are), but things that are no use on their own help when they are many. The tiny viper's bite slays the vast bull: a boar is often caught by a small hound. Only fight with safety in numbers, and gather my precepts all together: many will make a large heap. (Ov. *Rem. am.* 419–24)

All this strikes a familiar enough chord. Yet the Romans never had to deal with frustrating technology, cold-calling, poor Wi-Fi, or not being able to find the end of the sticky tape. So what did bug them? What pricked or stung them? What made them itch or chafe? These questions reveal my actual focus: less on the tiny irritants themselves than on the language of physical irritation, which in Latin, as in English, so often provides the imagery in which negative mental feelings are expressed.

In *Ugly Feelings* (2005), Sianne Ngai pioneered, to critical acclaim, the topic of minor emotions, specifically envy (as opposed to jealousy), paranoia and anxiety (as opposed to fear), and irritation (rather than indignation or rage). She considers them both in their own right and for what they reveal about their subjects' interior orientation to the exterior world. In her chosen area, twentieth-century literature and film, the representational space progressively conceded to small, humiliating emotions does not, she argues, simply shift literary priorities, in validating the minutest registers of human sensation; it also has a distinct social and cultural purpose. Minor feelings, even though she refers to them (unappetizingly enough) as unsublime, flat, ongoing, and ultimately uncathartic, are perfectly pitched, in her view, to express the helpless irrelevance of many modernist artists, frustrated by the seemingly unbridgeable gulf between aesthetics and political action.[9]

Of course, Ngai is dealing with a very specific set of external conditions. But in identifying feebler emotions as expressions of social and political powerlessness while at the same time appreciating the relationship between genre and gradations of affect, she helps us to see something similar at work in Latin literature, too. For if minor emotions suit minor or uncanonical literature, they also help to define it. In the case of the Romans, I will be less concerned with the stimulants of disgust (*fastidium*), so expertly dissected by Robert Kaster and others, and more with those smaller irritants that provoke the feeling called *molestia*.[10] Admittedly, there is a sliding scale involved: *fastidium* has come down a peg or two and now indicates *minor* annoyance in some modern European languages—"mi da fastidio" being standard for "it annoys me" in Italian.

## SLIGHT AND FREQUENT FRICTIONS

Let us start with an anecdote from Plutarch's life of Lucius Aemilius Paulus, the second-century BCE conqueror of Macedon, a man who surprised everyone by suddenly divorcing his first wife. At this juncture in his biography, Plutarch calls up a similar tale that offers limited insight into Paulus's mystifying behaviour:

> No documentary grounds for [Paulus's] divorce have come down to us, but there would seem to be some truth in a story told about divorce, which runs as follows. A Roman once divorced his wife, and when his friends admonished him, saying: "Is she not discreet? is she not beautiful? is she not fruitful?" he held out his shoe (the Romans call it "calceus"), saying: "Is this not handsome? is it not new? but not one of you can tell me where it pinches my foot?" For, as a matter of fact, it is great and notorious faults that separate many wives from their husbands; but the slight and frequent frictions arising from some unpleasantness or incongruity of characters, unnoticed as they may be by everybody else, also produce incurable alienations in those whose lives are linked together. (Plut. *Aem.* 5.1–5; Loeb, trans. Perrin)

We are never told who the anonymous Roman was—and it hardly matters, there are so many possible candidates, given the ease of divorce among the elite. But the story went on to have a rich afterlife. It crops up again in Chaucer and Trollope, and even features in the political theory of John Dewey, who used the privately pinching shoe as a homely symbol of misplaced state interference in citizens' personal concerns.[11]

One approach to the anecdote might be to investigate Roman shoes as archaeological objects, to find out how long they took to wear in and whether their wearers often struggled with a bad fit. Roman shoes were not necessarily tailor-made, as we know from Varro's analogy in *On the Latin Language* for masculine nouns that look feminine in form:

Dissimilar things are sometimes given similar forms and similar things different forms, just as we call shoes women's or men's shoes from the similarity of their shape, even though we know that sometimes women wear men's shoes and men wear women's shoes. (Varro, *Ling.* 9.29.40)

Behind Varro's analogy lurks a rich private history of hidden but intense irritation. Did Paulus ("Little") wear the wife's shoes in his marriage?[12] Women's visible behavior was already irritating enough. Plautus can be confident of a laugh when he says all married women talk too much, in and out of the house: let them carry their themes for gossip off home, so as not to be "annoyances" (*molestiae*) to their husbands, in public and in private.[13]

But far more intriguing than the history of Roman footwear, to my mind, anyway, is Plutarch's decision to assimilate mental irritation to "slight and frequent frictions" (*mikra kai pukna prokrousmata*; where *prokrousmata* literally means "obstacles" or "stumbling blocks"). The solid materiality of the concept of friction, the domestic image used to express it, and the contrasts drawn with both "large, glaring faults" and society's wider expectations, are all, I suspect, typical of the written experience of minor emotion: a disclosure of something intimate and personal, often shaming or embarrassing and reluctantly winkled out, but one that no less courts a community of fellow feelers.

Where should we look for witnesses to this kind of experience? Catullus, Cicero, Horace, and Seneca come immediately to mind. All these first-person authors work hard at giving us disclosures of their inner selves, capturing what it feels like to be caught between exterior presentation and interior sensation. They talk to each other, too. When Seneca points in *Natural Questions* to the powerful discomfort relative to tsunamis and earthquakes of a hangnail (*unguiculus*), a chill (*pituita*), or a choking drink that goes the wrong way, he is clearly rereading Horace in *Epistles* 1.1, where finicky Maecenas winces at his gauche, sniveling friend with the flapping shoes and broken nails.

Recent work on the senses in antiquity has helped to approximate some of the lost resonances of sensory experience, both aesthetic and social.[14] In the ancient language of irritation, all five senses—sight, smell, sound, taste, and touch—turn out to intermingle in various synesthetic combinations. Of these, perhaps sound and touch are hardest to separate. The classic recreation of annoyance at background noise is Seneca's letter on living above a bathhouse at Baiae (*Ep.* 56), where the orchestra of sounds evoked (building works mingled with clients' screams, as they are pummeled by masseurs or getting depilated or jumping into cold water) represents a heightened challenge to Stoic peace of mind. More than that, though: Seneca's hypersensitive phrasing is precisely designed to make the skin tingle, in line with the epidermal torments being described.[15] He even provides a painstaking calibration of levels of annoyance—judging, for example (and many would agree), that intermittent noise is more irritating (*molestior*) than continuous noise.[16]

Writing about dissonance as a ubiquitous feature of the Greek soundscape, Sean Gurd confirms this special link between sound and touch, quoting Brian Massumi, who characterizes affect as "embodied in purely autonomic reactions most directly manifested in the skin—at the surface of the body, at its interface with things."[17] After all, says Gurd, loud noise makes me jump, makes my skin crawl. In *Ugly Feelings*, Sianne Ngai attends to what happens when minor emotions, normatively repressed, are brought to the surface, where they are often registered in terms of skin-deep sensation. Synonyms for *irritation* such as *inflammation, rawness, soreness*, and *chafing* "tend," she writes, "to apply equally to psychic life *and* life at the level of the body—and particularly to its surfaces or skin."[18] This is literally and metaphorically the case in the work that is the focus of her study of irritation, Nella Larsen's novel *Quicksand* (1928), whose heroine feels and expresses racial discomfort via the social exposure of her skin. Ngai concludes: "Irritation's marginal status thus seems related to the ease with which it always threatens to slip out of the realm of emotional experience altogether, into the realm of physical or epidermal sensations."[19] It is relevant for her that Frantz Fanon used a cutaneous metaphor, "epidermalization," to replace "internalization" in his analysis of racism's psychological effects.[20] As we will see, skin as the interface between body and world plays a large part in feeding the Roman vocabulary of irritation, too.

One writer, it turns out, provides such rich fodder that I will not stray far from him in this brief foray into the Roman world of minor emotions. Marcus Tullius Cicero is hardly a typical Roman subject—or perhaps he is all too typical of a certain successful masculine type. But the sheer range of his writings, combined with a colossal ego that straddled aesthetics and politics, with plenty of frustration involved—documents with exceptional openness how tiny irritations work both to convey a fine sensibility, where needed, and to demarcate parapolitical writing in a minor key. Stanley Hoffer has written brilliantly about the metaphor of *stomachus* in the letters, how Cicero's performed suppression of his political fury conveys impotent rage, humor, and resignation, all at once.[21] Here, I consider three more clusters of images in Cicero's writing: annoyingness per se; a minor ailment and its miseries; and a single nagging but indefinite sensation.

## THE TROUBLE WITH *DE ORATORE*

The topic of annoyingness (*molestia*) can be broached via a practical Roman exemplum of how to *avoid* irritation.[22] It is staged in the middle of Cicero's *De oratore*, a work that would seem to belong to the aesthetic sphere but that equally teaches smoothness in rhetoric as a universal key to frictionless social and political interaction. In the Tusculan garden of the orator L. Licinius Crassus, a discussion of rhetoric has been taking place between various friends and relatives when two late arrivals, Q. Lutatius Catulus and his half-brother C. Julius Caesar Strabo, gate-crash the party. Catulus apologizes fulsomely on their behalf. Jon Hall summarizes the incident in his study of politeness in Cicero:[23]

> Three times in just a few lines (*De or.* 2.13–14) [Catulus and Strabo] acknowledge the potentially bothersome and intrusive consequences of their visit: "and you may well think we are being tactless or troublesome" (*vel tu nos ineptos licet . . . vel molestos putes*); "But on my word I was afraid, even so, that our sudden interruption might annoy you" (*sed mehercule verentem tamen ne molesti vobis interveniremus*); "For our part, we are delighted to be here, provided that our sudden interruption does not happen to be a nuisance." (*nos quidem, nisi forte molesti intervenimus, venisse delectat*).

In all three cases, the word for "troublesome," "annoying," or "a nuisance" is *molestus*, from *moles*, a heavy mass or weight. In two cases, *interuenire* (interrupt, break in) makes social intrusion almost equivalent to epidermal rupture. True, such a tiny breach of etiquette is a far cry from the Virgilian sentiment *tantae molis erat Romanam condere gentem* ("So weighty a task was it to lay the foundations of the Roman race");[24] indeed, it would seem to sit at the very opposite pole on a scale of relative pressure. Yet the basic idea of a weight that needs lifting is worth keeping in mind.

That is because behind the delicately competitive dance of refinement that marks the dialogue weighs Cicero's opening disclosure of how he ever came to have so much time on his hands for concerted rumination: he had no choice but to retreat from politics.[25] The dialogue is set imaginatively in 91 BCE, nine days before the death of its host and against a background of civil unrest similar to the atmosphere Cicero found himself in thirty-five years later (*De oratore* appeared in 55 BCE). He opens by introducing himself and pointing to the etymological weight that underpins *molestus* even as he minimizes his suffering and euphemizes his exile:

> For the time of life which promised to be fullest of quiet and peace proved to be that during which the greatest volume of vexations and the most turbulent tempests [*maximae moles molestiarum et turbulentissimae tempestates*] arose. (*De or.* 1.2)

Just so, decades of sectarian violence in Northern Ireland are darkly referred to as "The Troubles." Or is that a false analogy? Should *molestus* rather be understood as an exaggeratedly, humorously *heavy* word for describing minor irritations: not a drag but a juggernaut—catastrophizing, making mountains out of molehills? Cicero seems to oscillate. Later in *De oratore*, his character Antonius will claim that orators, for the sake of their cases, tend to exaggerate "troubles":

> But the orator, by his eloquence, represents all those things which, in the common affairs of life, are considered evil and troublesome, and to be avoided, as heavier and more grievous than they really are. (*De or.* 1.221)

In *De oratore* 2, Antonius will put emotional responses to *molestia*, "annoyance," at the end of a long list of more obviously major emotions that the orator is trained to stir up in his audience:

the emotions which eloquence has to excite in the minds of the tribunal, or whatever other audience we may be addressing, are most commonly love, hate, wrath, jealousy, compassion, hope, joy, fear or vexation [*molestia*] . . . (*De or.* 2.206)

Antonius cautions in all cases against disproportionate emotion-raking—"these rhetorical fireworks . . . in petty matters" (*paruis in rebus . . . hae dicendi faces*); "if we indulge in heroics over trifles" (*si . . . tragoedias agamus in nugis*). But he also makes a substantial point: negative emotions like jealousy, anger, and fear are felt more intensely in the context of private, individual injury than when communally experienced. Fear, for example, "is struck from either the perils of individuals or those shared by all: that of private origin goes deeper [*interior est ille proprius*], but universal fear also is to be traced to a similar source."[26] Along with other, stronger emotions, then, annoyance has two faces: one interior and deeply felt; the other externally shared and apparently milder. Away from the courtroom and in the new context of forced *otium*, Cicero will find it easier to restore his identity as a pre-eminent Roman by publicly sharing those little annoyances that affect the proper orator and the elegant man of leisure alike: "otium tibi molestum est" (ease has become tiresome for you), we might say echoing Catullus, another restless Roman with time on his hands.

Returning to Catulus and Strabo, Hall gives their mollifying preamble a sociolinguistic label. He calls it a strategy of "redressive politeness"—that is, a disarming preemption of one's potential to give annoyance. Such strategies, he says, "offer compensation for the face-threat (or intrusion) inherent in their arrival. They show respect to Crassus by making clear that his compliance is not taken for granted"; they also "aim to ease the tension provoked by the pair's unexpected gate-crashing."[27] If not being *molestus* is the mark of having arrived (literally and metaphorically) as a gentleman, this suggests another hypothesis: that the continued ability to feel *molestia*, to keep on wincing and squirming at small irritations, while appealing to a community of likeminded sensibilities, not only helps to dilute private sensations (often shamefully intense) but works as a lasting badge of refinement, the mark of a man of feeling. Sianne Ngai offers an apt parallel: "'Irritation' qua 'soreness,'" she writes, also signifies "'hypersensitivity', 'susceptibility', and 'tenderness,' words with explicitly affective dimensions easily turned . . . into signifiers of social distinction in the late nineteenth-century discourse of 'nerves.'"[28]

Let us test this hypothesis by going further into *De oratore* 2 and looking at a couple of jokes from the rich collection provided there by gate-crasher number two, C. J. Caesar Strabo, in what Mary Beard has called "the most substantial, sustained, and challenging discussion of laughter . . . to have survived from the ancient world."[29] This is no handbook of jokes, however. While some answer the speakers' criteria of restrained and gentlemanly wit, others infringe it, by being *molestus* in themselves—though, as Beard points out, the criteria are always subjective.

The jokes I single out both concern annoyingness. One of them is about flies, and it is immediately stamped on by Strabo as an example of scurrilous humour (that is, as pertaining to a *scurra*, a shameless entertainer)—a cheap excuse for a laugh. It goes as follows. When a friend of his, Vargula, was hugged in public by a pushy political candidate and his brother (Aulus and Marcus Sempronius), Vargula could not resist responding, "Slave, brush away these flies" (*puer, abige muscas*)—in other words, get rid of these provoking pests.[30] "He just wanted to raise a laugh," says Strabo, "in my view a very poor reward for talent [*tenuissimus ingeni fructus*]."

This seems harsh, to say the least. What Strabo does not bother to mention, perhaps because it is well known to Cicero's contemporaries, is the crucial fact that in this case both brothers bore the family cognomen Musca (Fly). This would seem to make the joke fair game, if not completely irresistible. Anthony Corbeill concludes that Strabo (subjectively, *mea sententia*, "in my opinion") must consider it beyond the pale because from an orator's point of view it is *sine causa* ("gratuitous," Strabo's words again) in having no direct applicability, packing no rhetorical punch in a courtroom.[31] Yet Strabo has just distinguished between two kinds of humor, respectively involving things and words, and has defined the verbal kind as being "provoked by a kind of sharp point in a word or expression" (*uerbi aut sententiae quodam acumine mouetur*).[32] The fly joke perfectly combines words and things in its retaliatory strike against a needling intrusion. In short, it is crying out to be made, in a windfall situation where the Muscae *are* invading Vargula's personal space with their vote-seeking hugs, all too close to the *molestia* associated with the minipests contained in their names. It is just a short hop from the Fly brothers to Mosca, the cringing parasite in Ben Jonson's *Volpone*.

At the same time, to miniaturize the brothers in line with their name and multiply them into a plague of disposable creatures, while giving a lordly wave to some imaginary slave to have them swatted, might be thought offensive to two aristocrats, coming from humble Vargula. I say "humble"; we know nothing about him, except that Strabo has just mentioned him in the company of Granio, another practitioner of scurrilous wit, and Granio was a *praeco* (announcer or auctioneer), an occupation, like that of *scurra*, associated with the upwardly mobile.[33] "What is the difference between Crassus, Catulus and co. and your friend Granio and my friend Vargula?" asks Strabo, admitting conscientiously, "No real distinction occurs to me; no one's wittier than Granio."[34] "Still," he says, "we should not imagine ourselves obliged to come out with a joke whenever the occasion arises."[35] Strabo flails about like this because the distinction is all too obvious but hard to state outright: he is bowing to a double standard based on class, between aristocratic orators and rank and file humorists. Gentlemanly humor always already belonged to the gentlemen.

It is no surprise, then, to find Strabo being far more indulgent to his host, established orator Crassus, who is credited with my second joke, one that pivots on the very word *molestus* (annoying). When a man once asked if it would bother him if he called on him before daybreak, Crassus replied politely, "No, you really won't bother me" (*"tu uero . . . molestus non eris"*). "You mean you'll get someone to wake you up?" asked the man. To which Crassus replied: "[I said:] you won't bother me" (*molestus non eris*).[36] That is, he won't bother with the wake-up call. This time, everyone has to be polite about it because it is Crassus's joke, a choice example of acceptable wit with an intellectual basis in the duplicitous language of politeness. But the humor is surely reinforced by the larger community's tacit agreement that the man's proposal for such an early visit *is* "bothersome," that he doesn't matter enough to be named, and that Crassus's riposte is funny because it is extremely polite and extremely rude at the same time. As Beard puts it more generally, "Crassus' showmanship was dangerously marginal."[37] He gets away with it because he belongs to the rhetorical inner circle, the one from which new man Cicero was so easily excluded as a *consularis scurra*, "a consular comedian."[38]

Back to Catulus's opening apologies, and Crassus's response takes a fascinating turn. He proceeds to claim that minor feelings of annoyance are nothing less than a rich source of cultural capital for the Romans, specifically in relation to the Greeks:

> The Greek nation, with all its learning, abounds in this fault, and so, as the Greeks do not perceive the significance of this plague, they have not even bestowed a name upon the fault in question, for, search where you may, you will not find out how the Greeks designate the "tactless" man [*quomodo Graeci ineptum appellant*]. But, of all the countless forms assumed by tactlessness [*omnium autem ineptiarum, quae sunt innumerabiles*], I rather think that the grossest is the Greeks' habit, in any place and any company they like, of plunging into the most subtle dialectic concerning subjects that present extreme difficulty, or at any rate do not call for discussion. (*De or.* 2.17–18; Loeb, trans. Sutton and Rackham)

How significant it is, says Crassus, that the word *ineptus* (inappropriate or misplaced, which Catullus has just used interchangeably with *molestus*) has no equivalent in Greek: "Search all you like but you'll never find a Greek word for 'tactless' [*ineptus*]."[39] A typical maneuver in this "emphatically 'Roman' work," where even Greek theories of humor are dismissed as laughable in themselves.[40] The reason for the difference, Crassus explains, is that the Greeks of today refuse to observe boundaries: they specialize in doing annoying things (*ineptiae*) and, worse, they are only interested, intellectually, in discussing annoying little things.[41]

This all feels like oversimplification. Of course the Greeks knew tiny irritants and had feelings about them. Theophrastus's *Characters*, for example, activates the same synesthetic blend of sound and touch interference discussed by Sean Gurd. It can be no coincidence that many of Theophrastus's wildly annoying antisocial types operate in more than usual proximity to insects and other small pests: the ungenerous man gets up early to deflea his sofas; the chatterer twitters louder than a swallow; the offensive man has armpits infested by lice; the coward rushes to keep flies off a wounded man in his tent, rather than fight.[42] Isn't this because the "Characters" themselves constitute an album of irritating specimens, all buzzing too loudly, touching too closely, getting under reasonable people's skins?

Insects also feature in Chremylus's assault on Poverty in Aristophanes's *Plutus*: "What benefits can *you* provide, except blisters in the bathhouse and masses of hungry children and old ladies? Not to mention the lice, gnats, and fleas, too numerous to enumerate, that annoy us by buzzing around our heads and waking us up with the warning, 'get up or you'll go hungry!'"[43] The list here is typical of Greek comedy's predilection for weevils, beetles, gnats, fleas, lice, locusts, and other small creatures—swarms of humanoid pests and parasites.[44] Another insect even finds its way, more ominously, into tragedy: the mosquito that wails around insomniac Clytemnestra's head in *Agamemnon*, anticipating Freud's use in *The Interpretation of Dreams* of the fly as metaphor for the nocturnal insistence of thoughts, which must be endlessly thrashed over in our sleep or in our wakeful nights.[45]

For all that, the outrageous claim *De oratore* makes is that sensitivity to minor annoyance is something particularly Roman, is even part of what makes one Roman. The proof: in this case, unusually, it is *Latin* that has the words for it.[46] What do I care, says Horace in *Satires* 1.10, when Maecenas and his cronies have my back, about the peevish attacks of those obscure (mostly Greek-named) literati Pantilius, Demetrius, and Fannius, the first of whom he calls a louse (*cimex*), the second of whom is accused of torturing Horace (*cruciet*) because he plagues (*uellicet*) other people, and the third of whom is just called *ineptus*?[47] Such a swarm of minor irritants must be ritually fumigated to avoid polluting the pure house (*pura domus*) of Maecenas.

The same interaction of individual and community in the performance of irritation attends the thinly disguised self-portrait in Horace's catalogue of antisocial types earlier in *Satires* 1. The poet's sharpened antennae twitch at the thought of his gauche former self (*simplicior quis*) who used to barge in on Maecenas uninvited:

> Take someone a bit naïve [*simplicior*], as I have often freely shown myself to you, Maecenas, interrupting you perhaps while reading or thinking with some annoying chatter? [*ut forte legentem aut tacitum impellat quouis sermone molestus*] "He is quite devoid of social tact" [*communi sensu plane caret*], we say. (*Sat.* 1.3.63–66)

Horace swaps subject position from past self to present self, then to the wider community, who are enlisted to mutter that such behavior is unacceptable, lacks all tact, and is characteristic of a *molestus*—before making the case for greater tolerance himself.

*Molestus* is also the punchline of Catullus 10, an anecdote poem that tells of a three-way meeting between Catullus, Varus, his friend, and Varus's girlfriend:[48]

Varvs me meus ad suos amores
uisum duxerat e foro otiosum,
scortillum, ut mihi tum repente uisumst,
non sane illepidum neque inuenustum.
huc ut uenimus, incidere nobis
sermones uarii; in quibus, quid esset
iam Bithynia, quo modo se haberet,
ecquonam mihi profuisset aere,
respondi, id quod erat, nihil neque ipsis
nunc praetoribus esse nec cohorti
cur quisquam caput unctius referret,
praesertim quibus esset irrumator
praetor, nec faceret pili cohortem.
"at certe tamen," inquiunt, "quod illic
natum dicitur esse, comparasti
ad lecticam homines." ego, ut puellae
unum me facerem beatiorem,
"non" inquam "mihi tam fuit maligne,
ut, prouincia quod mala incidisset,
non possem octo homines parare rectos."
at mi nullus erat nec hic neque illic,
fractum qui ueteris pedem grabati
in collo sibi collocare posset.
hic illa, ut decuit cinaediorem,
"quaeso," inquit mihi "mi Catulle, paulum
istos commoda! nam uolo ad Serapim
deferri." "mane," inquii puellae,
"istud quod modo dixeram me habere,
fugit me ratio: meus sodalis
—Cinnast Gaius—is sibi parauit.
uerum, utrum illius an mei, quid ad me?
utor tam bene quam mihi paratis.
sed tu insulsa male ac molesta uiuis,
per quam non licet esse neglegentem."

My pal Varus had taken me from the
Forum, where I was idling, to pay a visit to
his mistress, a bit of a slut, as I realized at a
glance, and not short on charm or sex
appeal. When we got there, we fell to
talking of this and that, and among other
things, what sort of place Bithynia was now,
how things were there, whether I had made
any money out of it. I answered (which was
true) that these days neither praetors nor

their staff can find any means of coming back more loaded than when they went, especially when they were screwed over by the praetor, a fellow who didn't give a damn about his staff. "At least," they say, "You must have got yourself some litter-bearers. They say that's the place to get them." To make myself look better off than all the rest in the girl's eyes, I say, "Things didn't go so badly with me—even though I got a bad province—that I didn't come away with eight straight-backed men." Truth was, I didn't have a single one, here or there, strong enough to shoulder the broken leg of an old sofa. At this—quite the shameless hussy—she says, "Please, dear Catullus, do lend those slaves of yours for a moment: I want a ride to the temple of Serapis." "Hang on," I said to the girl, "what I said just now about having those slaves, I slipped up; I have a friend—Gaius Cinna—he's the one who bought them. Whoever they belong to, I use them just as if I had bought them myself. But you are really awkward and a piece of work; you never let anyone relax for a minute." (Loeb, trans. Goold, adapted)

The raconteur's first impressions of Varus's new squeeze are favorable, even if coolly registered with familiar Catullan diminutives and double negatives: "a bit of a slut" (*scortillum*) and "not short on charm or sex appeal" (*non illepidum et non inuenustum*). But there is a nasty surprise in store when she calls him out on the brag he invents to impress her (that his unrewarding spell in Bithynia at least scored him a litter with eight bearers) by asking if she can borrow it forthwith. Having in reality not even an old chair leg to stand on, Catullus fumbles for an excuse and ends up taunting her defensively.

Modern readers have recoiled from what appears to be a string of misogynistic insults (*scortillum*, lit. "little whore"; *cinaediorem*, "characteristic of a passive male homosexual"; *insulsa* "tacky"; *molesta* "gauche").[49] The vocabulary is indeed belittling and crudely sexualizing, a form of microaggression that William Fitzgerald rightly aligns with the macroaggressions of Roman imperialism: "The role of Varus' woman in this context is to act as a kind of secondary province."[50] Whatever one thinks, one does not call someone *molestus* to their face (unless this is imagined as a thought bubble coming out of Catullus's head). If one does, it is outrageous enough that the social interaction (and the poem) must end right there.

Or is that right? In the casual world of *neglegentia* Catullus inhabits, a gray area is reserved for plausible deniability. One can be a committophobe in words as in actions (see Catullus 16), because those *au fait* with the rules, people on one's wavelength, will never take them quite at face value. This means that there is a tacit game or test focused on the words *molesta* and *insulsa*: "gauche," "tacky," "a pain," "party pooper" or "piece of work"—and, since *molestus* literally means "heavy" and *insulsus* "unsalty," attendant hints of pedantry and literal-mindedness. The bind is this: only if the girl really is *molesta et insulsa* will she take the insults literally; if she is *neglegens*, she won't. Between the lines, Catullus credits her with being a fellow-*cinaedus*, a shameless opportunist and a wriggler out of tight spots, like himself. In fact, *molesta uiuis* begins to feel like grudging praise, an ironic concession that he has met his match in this person who has called him out—as a glutton for punishment, a sexual and economic loser, and a thorn in other people's sides (whether they are provincial governors or challenging women). Likewise, *insulsa* is not so much a rethink of *non illepidum et non inuenustum* as a reinforcement of the girl's annoyingly good ability to sniff out what is fraudulent.

All of this anticipates a similar episode in Horace's *Satires* 1.9 where the poet is hounded by his nemesis, a pushy stranger, through the streets of Rome. Horace is incapable of being rude except behind people's backs, though he shares with the reader (or rather, whispers to a textual proxy, his slave) irritation so overwhelming that it causes floods of sweat to drip invisibly into his shoes.[51] He cannot vent his feelings without breaking the politeness contract. The fact that the anonymous nuisance is usually known in English as the "Pest" suggests that Horace has succeeded in getting his readers on side. But later he himself will be given the polite slip by a close friend, Aristius Fuscus:[52]

> male salsus
> ridens dissimulare (*Sat.* 1.9.65–66)
>
> The sick joker laughed, pretending not to understand

Horace's parting insult to Fuscus—*male salsus*, "sick joker," a variant on Catullus's *insulsa*—is a similarly grudging compliment to someone who manages to evade unwanted social encounters so gracefully.[53] In all these passages, minor annoyance, as opposed to righteous anger, marks the self-mocking, confiding, vulnerable persona of minor poetry.

Occasionally, though, when irritating people are assimilated to tiny pests and obstacles, it takes us to the edge of something more sinister. Consider Erik Gunderson's telling comment on Cicero's use of *humanus* in the letters to Atticus: "human means 'one of us.'"[54] In *De oratore*, Vargula is swatted on the page because he dared to blow off the Fly brothers. An annoying wife is compared to a pinching shoe because all married men know that feeling, even if they cannot know specifically how it feels to be this one's husband. Both cases involve imaginative relegation of the victims to the subhuman sphere. In Aristophanes's *Plutus*, Poverty sweeps beggars and insects alike in her train, but does the same when she turns on the audience, pitting its overfed, potbellied drones and maggots against its starving wasps. So does Lucian's Gulliver-like Icaromenippus, flying over the nations and seeing them reduced to gnat swarms from above.[55]

As Robert Kaster argues in his discussion of *fastidium* (disgust), conflating human and subhuman was all too quick a Roman reflex in this area. In two passages he considers from Seneca's *De clementia*, treatment of one's fellow humans is sifted into compassionate behavior and the kind of revulsion one feels on touching street people (2.6.2) or insects that are easily crushed and soil one's hands (1.21.4):

> In both cases it is equally clear that the object of *fastidium* (disgust) is not a bug or some other sub-human creature: the object is a person who must first be classified—that is, deliberatively ranked—as no better than a bug, as a precondition for the response to occur. This is a familiar pattern of prejudice-formation: having ranked X as so far inferior a specimen as to be deemed worthy of aversion, you then feel a visceral and reflexive aversion at the sight, smell, touch, or even thought of X. (Kaster 2001, 179)

Here, the socially excluded are assimilated, conceptually and emotionally, to insects and untouchables. This is the thin end of the wedge. It has been argued that in Nazi Germany it was because Jews had long been classed as vermin, parasites, or even bacteria that it was such a short step to press for their extermination (hence Kafka's cockroach and Art Spiegelman's Maus).[56]

Contempt for another person's body that is not quite detachable from one's own, or even functions as synecdochic extension, emerges from two passages in Plautus, both of which compare a slave's physique not to a prosthetic hand, as often, but to a dripping eye.[57] In *Persa*, Toxilus, a slave, says, "I don't serve voluntarily, nor do I satisfy my master according to his orders, but still he can't keep his hands off me, like an infected eye [*lippo oculo*]: he orders me about, puts me in charge of his business."[58] Meanwhile, in *Bacchides*, it is the lecherous master whose voice we hear: "That servant of mine is like an infected eye [*lippi . . . oculi*]; if you don't have one, you don't want it or miss it; but if you do have one, you can't stop touching it."[59] As Amy Norgard puts it: "The 'slave-as-bleary-eye' metaphor deconstructs a human being to a mere body part, which is lowered even further to an *ailing* body part. Slaves already occupied the lowest position in the Roman social hierarchy, and the association with physical ailment only emphasizes the debasement."[60]

## SIGHTS FOR SORE EYES

Dripping eyes and proxy selves bring me to my second case-study: Cicero, again—this time in his *Letters to Atticus*.[61] So far, we have considered what sensitivity to social and cultural irritation does for the construction of a cultivated, specifically Roman self, and conversely, how socially objectionable people can be cruelly excluded by being assimilated to tiny irritants. Let us turn now to a different aspect: how sensitivity to *physical* irritation plays out in the long-term maintenance of a feeling self, a self that tests and records its response to minor sensation—because the alternatives are either excruciating mental pain or deadening numbness.

In her brilliant reading, "Mourning Tulli-a: The Shrine of Letters in *Ad Atticum* 12," Francesca Martelli interprets Cicero's obsession with building a monument for his dead daughter as displacement or compensation for the traumas of civil unrest and Cicero's own political obliteration.[62] Overall, though, across the *Letters to Atticus*, intimate friend and enabler of Cicero's most intimate and personal self-expression, minor annoyance plays just as big a part as serious grief.[63] The vocabulary of feeling switches dizzyingly between large and small disasters in Cicero's fraught life, marking out the epistolary form as apparently minor but with half an eye to major events. Torture, anguish, crucifixion, *o uitam miseram maiusque malum* . . . There is no shortage of agonized words and concepts to describe the heavy stuff: Caesar's rise, the ominous sense of cataclysmic change, fears about individual and family safety.[64] Among these, *molestiae* is the word most often used of political "troubles."[65] But *molestus* (troublesome), *odiosus* (hateful), and *perturbatus* (stirred up) are applied interchangeably to small griefs, too. Among these, I focus on one minor but chronic physical ailment that plagues Cicero in *Ad Atticum* books 7, 8, and 10: *lippitudo*, usually equated with conjunctivitis but covering a whole range of eye irritations that happen to have the capacity to stimulate physiological tears, ones that might mimic (or cover up) the signs of true emotion.[66]

Erik Gunderson's more general diagnosis of Cicero's reports about health and illness in the letters to Terentia and Tiro holds equally for his bulletins about this lesser complaint: "The letters are not so much reporting upon a fact or a relationship as they are negotiating abstract relationships by means of appeals to mundane facts."[67] Just so, Cicero's regular logging of his ophthalmic symptoms reads less as a set of medical records than as a marker of neuroses or emotional states of being. Not only does *lippitudo* supply a practical excuse for writing shorter letters—and sending letters that have to be dictated and then read aloud on arrival (an excuse for transforming a *written* correspondence into a livelier exchange of *voices*, albeit the surrogate ones of secretaries and slaves).[68] It is also a manageable substitute for greater but less expressible pains and fears, daily proof that it is still possible to feel, and to comprehend feeling. Cicero uses the mildly humorous *stomachus* and *stomachari* to register and then suppress his gut reaction to Caesar's rise. Stanley Hoffer therefore concludes as follows: "Someone who says 'let's stop this belly-aching' has already switched from fury to sullen or witty resignation, so the idea of ceasing to be angry is instantiated by the very word *stomachari*."[69]

Unlike emotional dyspepsia, however, Cicero's *lippitudo* is both a metaphor and an actual ailment. His concentration on it evokes the French concept of *abcès de fixation*, a medical term for an abscess artificially stoked to localize a more general infection.[70] It is as if the minute clocking of everyday pains could somehow supplant the numbing horror of global "troubles": "For the troubles have made me numb" (*nam me hebetem molestiae reddiderunt*), as Cicero writes in one letter, reclaiming *molestus* from the mundane sphere.[71] Elsewhere, he suggests, "I am sure you [Atticus] find daily letters boring [*non dubito quin tibi odiosae sint epistulae cottidianae*], especially as I give you no new information, and indeed cannot think of any new theme to write about."[72] Here, conversely, *odiosus* is wrested away from the sickening loathing felt for more traumatic griefs. Cicero's overall claim is that the correspondence guarantees him regular, long-term healing: it gives him peace (*requiesco*), relieves him (*recreare*), and even "pours a restorative infusion" (*restillare*) into a larger wound.[73]

Cicero is not shy when it comes to talking to Atticus about his eyes. The ailment starts small in book 7, but in book 8 two bulletins about *lippitudo* serve as opening salvos. *Att.* 8.12 starts: "My eyes are even more troublesome [*molestior*] than before," and runs with the whole idea of defective vision, first reflecting on the pessimistic prophecies in yesterday's handwritten letter, then inviting Atticus to act as clairvoyant for a blindfolded friend about what the future holds. *Att.* 8.13 begins: "My secretary's hand will serve as an indication of my eye infection and also as an excuse for brevity, not that there is anything to say now." Here, we start to feel a closer affinity between scratchy eyes and the unstoppable compulsion of letter writing—even when there is nothing to say.[74] Now it is Caesar who is as keen-sighted as a lynx: "how sharp, how vigilant, how ready" (*quam acutum, quam uigilantem, quam paratum*). By contrast, Cicero's helpless, medically enforced wakefulness suggests a minor version of the hero Regulus, tortured by having his eyelids forced open and exposed to blinding light.[75]

In book 10, the ailment is back, and the correspondents trade maladies. In Atticus's case, urinary problems, "a damn nuisance" (*ualde molesta*); for Cicero, another bout of *lippitudo*. The letter in question (*Att.* 10.10) opens with an appropriate metaphor: "I've been blind not to see this till now!" (*Me caecum qui haec ante non uiderim!*). Cicero turns out to be longing for a man called, ominously, Ocella, "Little Eye," to arrive with news: now, *lippitudo* is an excuse not just for reducing letters to a shorter minor corpus but also for Cicero's humiliatingly opaque view of politics. In *Att.* 10.14, though, both men's illnesses are upstaged by external events (this is the letter that opens *o uitam miseram maiusque malum!*). A long-awaited potential ally, Servius Sulpicius, finally shows up as a link to the world's greater terrors, a Homeric ghost from the outside who sheds a whole ocean of tears: "I've never seen a man more churned up [*perturbatiorem*] by fear." Meanwhile, Cicero cannot squeeze out a single drop (*ulla lacrima*), despite his ailment being tedious enough to keep him awake: *odiosa propter uigilias*. In due course, *odiosus* is picked up to describe Servius's minor qualms about his son's military posting: "his son's service at Brundisium is an awkward snag [*odiosus scrupulus*]" (Shackleton Bailey's translation). "Snag" attracts the same hyperbolic adjective in this centripetal thrust from outsize woe to finite worries, with their more limited scope for futile, nagging vigilance.[76]

*Lippitudo* appears for the last time in *Att.* 10.17, in the wake of more cheering personal encounters. Cicero underplays his eye pain as something relatively manageable (*per-* and *sub-* prefixes are useful for nuancing the man of feeling's vocabulary, and now there is a new one, *perodiosus*, "super-annoying"):[77]

> My ophthalmia often irritates me, not that it is so very annoying, but it's bad enough to interfere with my writing [*Crebro refricat lippitudo, non illa quidem perodiosa sed tamen quae impediat scriptionem*]. I am glad that your health is re-established, both from your old complaint and your more recent attacks. (*Att.* 10.17.2)

Here, *refricat*, "irritates", conveys the rasping abrasion of the pain and *crebro*, "often", its intermittent stabbing quality. In recognizing the more dramatic shifts of Atticus's symptoms, Cicero pulls back from exaggerating his own. But the eye theme is soon picked up for another check of the barometer: "I wish we had Ocella [the longed-for "Little Eye"] with us, now that things seem to be a little easier [*paulo faciliora*] than I had expected; it's just that the current equinoctial weather is too rough [*perturbatum*] for sailing."

It will be some time before Cicero uses *refricare* again.[78] When it resurfaces in the letters, it is in none other than *Att.* 12.18, where the quest to commemorate Tullia is in full swing. Here, the word underpins the idea that mental pain is best dealt with by being raked over and compressed into another focused abscess.[79] Perhaps, says Cicero, to hallow Tullia with every memorial that Greek and Latin genius can supply will open up my wound again (*quae res forsitan sit refricatura uulnus meum*), stir up grief in order to settle it, and dispel other griefs at the same time.[80] His anguish has reached a new pitch.[81] In 10.17, by contrast, against the backdrop of what is seriously hateful (*perodiosum*) and gravely turbulent (*perturbatum*), yet another exchange of minor aches and weather reports between *amici* scrapes at the pain superficially, returning metaphors that usually govern external troubles—storms, hostility, loathing—to concrete reality and small-scale containability.[82]

If minor ailments are part of what makes Cicero's exchanges with Atticus so compulsive and meaningful, this suggests a more complex function for the correspondence than mere repose or comfort. Could we even see it as a kind of irritant itself, one that demands regular reality checks and stimulates renewed connection with another sentient self—like an eye that goes on being scratched, if only to reassure its owner that sensation, or a response, is still there?[83] In *Att.* 16.6, Cicero assimilates Atticus to his other favorite "eyes," his villas: "Why am I not with you? Why am I not seeing the eyes [we might say "jewels"] of Italy, my pet villas" [*cur ocellos Italiae, uillulas meas, non uideo*]? As Cicero says in the *Tusculan Disputations* of ingrained faults: "A chronic habit [*inueteratio*], as in bodily matters, is harder to get rid of than a sudden mood-change [*perturbatio*], and a sudden swelling in the eye [*repentinus oculorum tumor*] can be cured faster than a chronic eye irritation [*diuturna lippitudo*] can be banished."[84] For better or worse, the correspondence and the ailments are the two things in Cicero's altered life that are still reliably routine. More accurately, they are *imperfectly* reliable, bracingly *irregular*, a source of chronic disquiet in their own right.[85] That is why he needs to keep on rubbing away at them.[86]

## THERE'S THE RUB

Staying with rubbing, my final case study involves a different relationship to irritation. The image of the *scrupulus*, literally a small sharp stone (from *scrupus*, a sharp stone or pebble), is often used by Roman writers to suggest privately felt but nagging sensations. We have seen the word used of the "awkward snag," the *odiosus scrupulus* (a son's posting to Brundisium) that plagued Servius Sulpicius, matching Cicero's eye ailment in its minor "hatefulness." On second thoughts, perhaps "snag" is not quite the right translation when it is not so much the situation that is felt as a little rub as Servius's inner qualms or unease about it. *Scrupulus* has of course settled into a moral sense these days in the concept of *scruple*, a minor but persistent doubt about a belief, claim, or argument. Intriguingly, the stone metaphor was from the beginning confused with another sense of *scrupulus*, sometimes written *scripulus*: a very small weight or measure.

Either way, whether as annoying things inside shoes or external stumbling blocks, stones stand in the way of smooth progress through the world. As we saw, among Pliny the Elder's examples of sudden deaths in *Natural History* 7, two Caesars died while putting on their sandals, Q. Aemilius Lepidus after leaving his bedroom and stubbing his big toe on the doorstep and C. Aufidius when he tripped on the floor of the Comitium.[87] This kind of stumbling was normally seen as ominous because it presaged more serious falls. Together with lightning bolts, oracles, and entrails, Pliny includes omens "trivial to mention" (*parua dictu*), like sneezes (*sternumenta*) and toe stubbings (*offensiones pedum*) at the auguries.[88] Not so trivial, though, to the emperor Augustus, who blamed putting on his left shoe before his right in the morning for the eruption of a military conspiracy, narrowly avoided, later the same day.[89]

People could be stumbling blocks, too, like Socrates the awkward customer portrayed by Dio: "Most of the influential people and professional speakers pretended not even to see him; but whoever of that description did approach him, like those who have struck something with their foot got hurt and speedily departed."[90] Cicero imagines his son-in-law, the Caesarian Dolabella, as an embarrassment, or rather himself as an embarrassment to his own party *because of* Dolabella: *si quid offendimus in genero meo*. "If my son-in-law is a sore point with some," Shackleton Bailey translates.[91] But the idea is more accurately of Cicero as the surrogate obstacle that trips up his sympathizers.

Such external, visible obstacles as these were occasionally replaced by something invisible but no less palpable to the sufferer: a stone in the shoe. This was a private source of irritation and misgiving, harder to share with others. Revealingly, the word *scrupulus* scores most highly otherwise in Terence (always one for sensitivity to "the interface with people") and Apuleius (where it spans physical encounters and moral and philosophical doubts alike). But plenty of *scrupuli* can be found in Cicero—for good reason. A passage in *Pro Roscio Amerino* gives us a useful sense of the metaphorical field of the word, even when it is being used sarcastically. Surely, says Cicero, Chrysogonus, the evil freedman who bought Roscius's *patrimonium* thanks to his friendship with Sulla, cannot sleep at night for gnawing pangs of guilt:

> hunc sibi ex animo scrupulum qui se dies noctesque stimulat ac pungit, ut euellatis postulat. (Cic. *Rosc. Am.* 2.6)
>
> He begs that you will take [literally sweep away] from his mind this uneasiness which day and night is pricking and stinging him.

In other words, Chrysogonus has no conscience at all about the misdeeds that Cicero so gleefully exposes. But we get a fine idea of what the stone metaphor brings with it imaginatively: secret guilt, digging edges, and relentless, repetitive stabbing.[92]

The highest concentration of the word in a single Ciceronian text—four instances in all—is, once again, in the *Letters to Atticus*, which suggests that readiness to spill or at least hint at one's *scrupuli* to a fellow human may be a conscious device in Cicero's literary construction of exceptional intimacy.[93] The most illuminating use of the word is at *Ad Atticum* 1.18, the letter where Cicero idealizes his relationship with his friend for all time. Here is his classic outpouring of what Atticus means to him (even if Cicero never meant the same thing to Atticus)— someone he can speak to without secrecy or fakery:

> I must tell you that what I most badly need at the present time is a confidant—someone with whom I could share all that gives me any anxiety, a wise, affectionate friend to whom I could talk without pretence or evasion or concealment [*nihil fingam, nihil dissimulem, nihil obtegam*] ... And you whose talk and advice has so often lightened my worry and vexation of spirit [*curam et angorem animi mei*], the partner in my public life and intimate of all many private concerns, the sharer of all my talk and plans, where are you? (*Att.* 1.18.1; Loeb, trans. Shackleton Bailey)

Cicero goes on to explain that all his other friendships feel like hollow networking compared with his cozy domestic trio of wife, little daughter, and darling son—but even these ties are outweighed by Atticus's virtual but unique role as distant confidant.

After all the fulsome praise comes the stone in the shoe:

> Of private worries with all their pricks and pains [literally, thorns and pebbles] I shall say nothing [*Ac domesticarum quidem sollicitudinum aculeos omnis et scrupulos occultabo*]. I won't commit them to this letter and an unknown courier. They are not very distressing (I don't want to upset you), but still they are on my mind, nagging away [*sed tamen insident et urgent*], with no friendly talk and advice to set them at rest. (*Att.* 1.18.2; Loeb, trans. Shackleton Bailey)

What's making Cicero so jittery? Thorns (*aculeos*) and pebbles (*scrupulos*) are downplayed with the usual polite restraint. None of this is hugely annoying, just family stuff, but still worth registering, a heavy enough pressure. The elephant in the room? "Family worries," according to Shackleton Bailey, "perhaps refers to Pomponia." This was Atticus's sister, recently wed to Cicero's brother Quintus in a notoriously unhappy marriage, which would end in divorce some fifteen years later (in 55 BCE) but remained a prolonged and uneasy source of shared suffering for Atticus and Cicero, even a family counterpart to the civil war that threatened to fray their perfect *amicitia*.[94] Cicero both parades his distress and conceals it; even the letters are no safe space, he says, for leaked confidences, either to the mailman or the reader. "Between you and me" (*occultabo*) really does hold here. Cicero *will* keep it all hidden, for posterity, will express it only through nudges and winks. Elsewhere, he refers to the small hint (*significatione parua*) that stands in for what he cannot explain in a letter, and urges Atticus to tell him everything, however small (*sed ne tantulum quidem praeterieris*), to tell him the small stuff as well as the big stuff (*quicquid erit non modo magnum sed etiam paruum scribes*), since for his part he will leave nothing out (*equidem nihil intermittam*).[95]

The story with which we began, from Plutarch's *Life of Aemilius Paulus*, concerned the "pinching shoe" of a husband ready to divorce his wife. It may be coincidence, but in four uses of *scrupulus* in *Ad Atticum* (one is Servius Sulpicius's "awkward snag"; another describes an awkward financial situation, also involving Pomponia),[96] the "uncomfortable shoe" image is twice dropped into the larger context of marital strife. It was really up to Pomponia's husband Quintus Cicero to say, "None of you know where the shoe pinches my foot." But Cicero tends to hijack his little brother's suffering along with responsibility for his other actions.[97] His regular checks of the domestic situation chez Quintus and Pomponia give Atticus a vicarious feel of Quintus's shoes: "You write to me of your sister. She will tell you herself how anxious I have been that my brother Quintus should feel towards her as a husband ought"; "My brother Quintus seems to me to feel towards Pomponia as we wish"—this in a letter that ends pointedly by saying that it is Atticus he really loves *fraterne*, "like a brother."[98]

If *Att.* 1.18 suppresses the details of Quintus and Pomponia's problems, the theme of marital strife explodes in the gossip section of the same letter, which leaks names along with allegorical hints about a current scandal or two back at Rome (*skandalon*, as it happens, being another Greek word for stumbling block):[99]

> Now this fine new year is upon us. It has begun with failure to perform the annual rites of the Goddess of Youth, Memmius having initiated M. Lucullus' wife into rites of his own. Menelaus took this hard and divorced the lady—but the shepherd of Ida in olden days only flouted Menelaus, whereas our modern Paris has wiped his boots on Agamemnon as well. (*Att.* 1.18.3; Loeb, trans. Shackleton Bailey)

C. Memmius has run amok, seducing first L. Lucullus's wife, Cato's sister Servilia, later divorced for her "loose behaviour,"[100] and then Lucullus's brother Marcus's wife (also, Shackleton Bailey surmises, subsequently divorced for poor conduct). As Cicero puts it, Paris has cuckolded Agamemnon as well as Menelaus.

This image of two humiliated mythical brothers makes it tempting to read the letter as a double displacement, via Memmius and the Luculli (overt) and Quintus (hinted at), of Cicero's neuroses about his own marriage. True, there are no spoilers yet of the eventual divorce from an increasingly autonomous Terentia, in 47 or 46 BCE.[101] But she has already been put in the shade next to his gushing display of intimacy with Atticus, and Cicero does put it just a little ungenerously when envisaging her in his tableau of hearth and home: "honey son" Cicero junior (*mellito Ciceroni*) and "dear little daughter" Tullia (*filiola*)—but just an unembellished "wife" (*uxore*).[102] With Agamemnon in mind, should we even fastforward with some anxiety to one of Cicero's last letters to Terentia, by which time their connection is wearing thin? Bossy and impersonal, it urges her to have a bathtub ready for him when he gets home—so conducive to life and health![103]

The fourth appearance of *scrupulus* is much briefer, just the vaguest of hints on a longer list. "Back to matters at Rome. First, please, as you're staying in Rome, make sure to build a firmly fortified case for my term of office as governor remaining annual and uninterrupted. And secondly, mind you discharge all my commissions, in particular concerning that domestic worry [*illo domestico scrupulo*], you know what I mean [*quem non ignores*], if anything can be done; and then do something about Caesar."[104] Shackleton Bailey comments shrewdly that *scrupulus* here means "worry," not "hitch"—in other words, that it refers to the internal sensation, not the external source of the rub. He is confident about what lies behind the hint: "C refers to the question of a husband for Tullia (cf. 5.4)." This was another ongoing source of stress, particularly when Tullia and her mother Terentia broke ranks while Cicero was away in Cilicia to engineer a marriage with the pro-Caesarian Dolabella.

That aside, Cicero again embroils Atticus emotionally in his inmost feelings: *quem non ignores* (the point of a stone in one's shoe is that no one else can feel it—unless they are really under one's skin). There are shades here of Emperor Augustus's complaints about disobedient family members (the two Julias and Agrippa Postumus) as his three chronic boils or ulcers: *tris uomicas ac tria carcinomata*.[105] In Cicero's case, this is less a matter of national crisis than an insistent personal or domestic anxiety, which explains why it is woven so meaningfully into the fabric of his epistolary relationship with Atticus, his "second self."

I have only scratched the surface of what minor irritation can bring to the study of Roman emotion and identity—and Cicero, I have conceded, is far from typical. But it can be enlightening to follow one individual so uneasily negotiating the gap between aesthetic and political involvement while so minutely registering the difficulties of his position in and out of various elite communities and calibrating his sensations to match genre, mood, and audience. Paying attention to the role of small and superficial feelings in the construction of this complex personality can deepen our experience of a man who was perhaps never entirely comfortable in his own skin.[106]

# 5

# Diminishing Returns

## *Tales of the Diminutive*

> Little boxes on the hillside
> Little boxes made of ticky-tacky
> Little boxes on the hillside
> Little boxes all the same
> —MALVINA REYNOLDS, "LITTLE BOXES," SONG (1962)

Somewhere in any survey of small Roman things a space needs to be set aside for diminutives, those not so little words that are among the most expressive and inventive in the Latin language. We have seen many of them along the way, even if their appearances have been unobtrusive, even surreptitious: Seneca's split fingernail (*unguiculus*) and irritating little jolts (*punctiunculae*) of nausea; the measured pace of a Ligurian who follows snails and tree in tiny steps (*paulatim* . . . *paulum*) toward a little fort (*castellum*); Caligula, "Bootikins," toddler emperor-in-waiting; Cicero's little stone (*scrupulus*), little eye (*Ocella*), little daughter (*filiola*), and pet villas (*uillulae*). Not to mention the Latin originals of many of the words used to analyze them: "particular," "encapsulate," "oracular," "singular."

In the very amateur, nontechnical exploration that follows, I follow far greater experts before me in considering what diminutives add to Latin literary texts; at the same time, I reflect on what they tell us about relationships between writers and their imaginative worlds. Diminutive words (nouns and adjectives alike) peg themselves with remarkable ease to other "little" themes we have explored so far: minor feelings and discomforts; small things as portable extensions of the human body; not-yetness and not-quiteness; precise calibration; and striving toward points. The word *punctum*, we have already seen, can signify many things: memorable displays of wit; moments of tension; or zeroing in on fine detail. In this context, it will have a further extension: as the unattainable vanishing point to which all diminutives aspire.

Among those scholars who have collected and analyzed diminutives over the last two centuries, a fundamental assumption has always been that the function of these often rather long words is not just to convey relatively small size. Most languages that use them also give them an affective force, so that it is rarely just "little" but instead "dear little," "poor little," "silly little," or even "pathetic little." Edmondo De Amicis once wrote that the diminutive in Italian is like a smile.[1] The problem with this, as Bengt Hasselrot pointed out in his pioneering study of diminutives in modern Romance languages, is that a smile, like a word, can mean many different things.[2] Not surprisingly, C. J. Fordyce, editor of Catullus, expands the possibilities: for him the diminutive is "the counterpart in speech of a smile or a sigh or a shrug"![3]

To reflect these multiple shades of emotion more comprehensively, linguist Daniel Jurafsky has devised an ambitious scheme to cover every possible meaning of diminutives across all cultures and periods of history, based on the proposition that they stem from a core primitive notion of "child."[4] This immediately helps explain some of their bafflingly contradictory senses: how diminutive forms can express precision and intensity but also nuance and vagueness; tenderness for things perceived as adorable or helpless, as well as contempt for things perceived as inadequate, pedantic, or silly. Diminutives can be affectionate or sneering; approximate, softening, hedging ("reddish"; "a little pointed"), or intensifying ("in the very heart"; "right now"); they can suggest both intimacy and distance. Sometimes they fall short of an ideal target; sometimes they zone in on it. All this, it is worth noting, gives them interesting affinities with comparatives and superlatives. In many languages that use superlatives, as Roman Jakobson observed (or at least was quoted as observing by Angelica Pabst in David Lodge's *Small World*), the more intense the degree being expressed, the longer the word.[5] For diminutives, conversely, the smaller the scale, the longer—usually—the word.

Jurafsky also confirms a long-standing connection between the tendency to use diminutive words and the speaker's gender (this applies to augmentatives, too).[6] Again, at the root of this—and most linguists seem to agree—lies the mother-child relationship, which expresses itself cross-culturally in designated language and a distinctive tone of voice that soothes a child's fears by minimizing external threats ("silly little dog") while characterizing the child itself as a little thing, inferior and weak next to the parent but also the object of tender affection and pride. To define external things as small, to see the world in small terms, might look like a gesture of (masculine) power. But to use diminutives is often to embrace vulnerability, femininity, and silliness.

In Latin, which seems to be far more inventive than Greek in this area of language, diminutives are frequently associated with womanly, effeminate, even camp speech.[7] Not only because they tend to reflect the emotions of love and tender appreciation, and so are typical of the language mothers use when talking to children, but also because women were stereotyped as having small outlooks on mostly trivial concerns. As Donatus says of a grumbling mother in Terence's *Adelphoe*:

> For all these [ways of complaining] are feminine when, instead of great hardships, complaints of no importance [*nullius momenti querellae*] are piled up in a kind of heap and itemized. (Don. *ad* Ter. *Ad.* 291)

"Laundry lists of worries" is Dorota Dutsch's apt label.[8] However, given that almost all our surviving Roman writers are male, and diminutives are all over their writing, or at least all over certain kinds of writing, we might more fruitfully ask: what do *men* achieve by using diminutives, and what does it cost them? Does using these words, which register minutiae or minute degrees of difference, allow speakers to display more than just precision: to be weak and sentimental, perhaps, or to forge a special kind of intimacy, or reveal their feminine side? And if so, just how much of a risk is this, when speaking in one's own voice? Are diminutives always a sign of urbanity, which so often trades conventional masculinity for greater sensibility, or are they meant to be heard as ironic in the mouths of men who want to keep a distance from the senses and sentimentality and maintain their manliness?

Some indirect evidence of the sexual, or at least sensual, charge attached to diminutives can be found—somewhat counterintuitively—in the hypermasculine poetry collection *Priapea*, whose primary scenario involves an ithyphallic god's crude threats to intruders in his garden. Priapus taunts the unmanly *cinaedi* who haunt his precinct with their secret desire to feel the full force of his punitive weapon. In addition, as Elizabeth Young argues, he teases those equivalent *cinaedi* in his poetic audience who crave the aural sensuality of diminutive words but who, because of his empty threats, are largely denied them.[9] In one poem, for example, Priapus alludes to the luscious diminutives with which Catullus addresses the *cinaedus* Thallus:

> Cinaede Thalle, mollior cuniculi capillo
> uel anseris medullula uel imula oricilla. (Cat. 25.1–2)
>
> Cinaedus Thallus, softer than rabbit fur
> or the innermost down of a goose or the tip of an earlobe

Only then to ration them for his listeners:

> Quidam mollior anseris medulla
> furatum uenit huc amore poenae:
> furetur licet usque: non uidebo. (*Priap.* 64.1–2)
>
> A certain someone softer than goose down
> comes here to steal because he loves the punishment:
> go on, let him steal and steal: I won't see it.

Young points out how grudgingly Priapus strips away most of Catullus's diminutives, restricting the mellifluous doubled diminutive *medullula* (inmost down) to a single one, *medulla* (down, lit. "marrow").[10]

Indeed, a special respect in which Latin diminutives stand out from their equivalents in many other languages is their common use in connection with body parts—*ocellus* being the standard personalized form of *oculus*, for example.

The sense here may above all be euphemistic—"my own humble little eye" (the one I presume to mention). But there are other possibilities, too: intensified interiority (*auricula*, as opposed to *auris*, means "inner ear";[11] *medulla* means "soft middle part [of the marrow]"); phoniness (*lacrimula* is not just a "little tear" but a "crocodile tear"); and—something touched on earlier—the sense that body parts are miniatures or extensions of the whole individual (*capillus*, hair, for example, comes from *caput*, head; *unguiculus* is the very edge of the nail, as well as a slice of nail). As we will see, this often applies in the case of external diminutive things, as well. In short, diminutives cannot help but express relationships, especially those that span the thin membrane between self and world.

Where genre is concerned, it is no surprise to learn that diminutives feature far more frequently in playful, intimate, small-scale writing; more in comedy than in tragedy; more in satire and the novel than in epic. Everyone knows the famous "scandal" of the only genuine diminutive in the *Aeneid*, one that happens to embody the very notion of tininess, expressed in the abandoned Dido's wish that her lover had left her with a *paruulus Aeneas*. Not just a "little Aeneas," an extension or replica of the original (Dido's dildo?), but "a little baby Aeneas," a formula that combines maternity with affection and longing.[12] It is no coincidence that this word appears in the most feminine and most feminizing book of the *Aeneid*, one unusually focused on a female perspective and female needs.[13] Dido's *paruulus* will duly be picked up in the *Appendix Vergiliana* as a size-appropriate fake signature of Virgil's recessive literary tininess: once in the *Moretum* and the *Ciris*, and twice in the self-consciously miniaturizing *Culex*.

## VANISHING POINTS

Otherwise, I will have little to add here about the metapoetic aspects of diminutives and their relationship to small poetic forms, beyond briefly noting the correlation often implied between small people—women, slaves, children, silly lovers—and the supposed vision of the world that their use of diminutive speech suggests: a pointilliste one of miniature coinages that flower into joyful "contagions" of diminutives and rebloom in the rhyming verse of later antique and medieval Latin. A well-known example is Emperor Hadrian's lovely little poem about his soul:

> Animula, uagula, blandula
> hospes comesque corporis
> quae nunc abibis in loca
> pallidula, rigida, nudula,
> nec, ut soles, dabis iocos. (Hadrian, fr. 3)

> Dear fleeting sweeting little soul,
> My body's comrade and its guest,
> What region now must be its goal,
> Poor little wan, numb, naked soul,
> Unable, as of old, to jest? (Loeb, trans. Duff and Duff)

To which Ronsard's gorgeous translation does more than justice:[14]

> Amelette Ronsardelette,
> Mignonnelette doucelette,
> Tres chere hostesse de mon corps,
> Tu descens là bas foiblelette,
> Pasle, maigrelette, seulette,
> Dans le froid Royaume des mors:
> Toutesfois simple, sans remors
> De meurtre, poison, ou rancune,
> Mesprisant faveurs et tresors
> Tant enviez par la commune.
> Passant, j'ay dit, suy ta fortune
> Ne trouble mon repos, je dors. (Pierre de Ronsard, *Derniers Vers*)

Another poem, from *Carmina Burana*, explores the inevitable consequences of putting two young people of opposite gender into a confined space:

> Si puer cum puellula
> moraretur in cellula,
> felix coniunctio.
> Amore succrescente,
> pariter e medio
> propulso procul taedio,
> fit ludus ineffabilis
> membris, lacertis, labiis. (*Carmina Burana* 19)

> If a boy spends time with a girlie in a little room, a happy union results. As Love increases, and for both boredom goes out of the window, an indescribable game takes place with bodies, arms, lips.

Ultimately, this over-the-top late-antique "contagion" of erotic diminutives is an archaizing device, a legacy of earlier Latin—as in this spectacular example from two hundred years before, a seductive passage in Plautus, supposedly written by a woman in a letter to her lover:

> Ps. teneris labellis molles morsiunculae,
> nostr[or]um orgiorum <osculat>iunculae]
> papillarum horridularum oppressiunculae. (Plaut. *Pseud.* 67–68)

> soft little smooches of tender little lips, the little kisses of our secret rites,
> little pushy squeezes of stubby little nipples.

The pileup here is fantasy on more than one level. It even amounts to a kind of verbal "fondling" of experience, so squeamishly sensitive to small differences of texture that it is uncomfortable and cloying to read—both tender and lubricious at once. In a somewhat different vein, satirist Lucilius imitates the "smooth and agglutinated" style of the orator Albucius:[15]

> Quam lepide lexis conpostae ut tesserulae omnes
> arte pauimento atque emblemate uermiculato! (Lucil. 84–86W)
>
> How charmingly are ses dits put together—artfully like all the little stone dice of mosaic in a paved floor or in an inlay of wriggly wormlike pattern! (Loeb, trans. Warmington)

Once the poet has finished breaking his subject's style down via diminutives (*tesserulae, uermiculato*), it has decomposed into a pixelated design far closer to his *own* satirical worldview, which is above all fragmented and granular.

What interests me more than metapoetics here, though, is the expressive power of diminutives in themselves. How do these "little words" convey nuance and uninhibited emotion, reveal and shape identity, and indicate relationships to body and world? In a comprehensive survey of every diminutive noun and adjective in Catullus, Samuel B. Platner set himself the task of deciding in each case whether a diminutive has significant semantic value or is simply interchangeable with its basic form.[16] In the case of adjectives, for example, Platner judged that in fifteen cases (*albulus, aureolus* [in one of two instances], *frigidulus, languidulus, misellus, molliculus, pallidulus, paruuolus, pusillus, turgidulus, uetulus, aridulus, imulus, lassulus, perlucidulus*), the diminutive form is insignificant; in two cases (*lacteolus, tenellulus*), it is intensifying; in three cases (*turpiculus, eruditulus, mollicellus*), it expresses contempt; in one (*uuidulus*), it conveys the idea of wretchedness. In the remaining three cases (*bimulus, integellus, floridulus*), he concludes that there is no strong evidence either way. What surely matters, though, far more than these gradations is Catullus's overall openness to diminutives as an expressive feature of his poetic worldview: satirical, mocking, intimate, and self-diminishing all at once.

Nor is it hard to see a more than metrical point to using these words. To take just one of Platner's cut-and-dried "insignificant" diminutives—*turgidulus* (a little bit swollen)—from the last line of Catullus 3, describing Lesbia's teary eyes after the death of her pet sparrow:

> tua nunc opera meae puellae
> flendo turgiduli rubent ocelli. (Cat. 3.17–18)
>
> It's your doing now [sparrow] that my girlfriend's sweet eyes are red
> and a little bit swollen with crying.

The diminutives sprout here: *puellae* generates *turgiduli*, followed by the rhyming *ocelli* (*oculis* earlier in the poem).[17] But there is more going on than meets the eye. As Ellen Oliensis has argued in *Freud's Rome*, the choice Catullus makes between *turgidi* and *turgiduli* is far from insignificant.[18] While cosseting nursery language makes the swelling in question superficially guileless—"innocently" transferred to a little girl's sweet little eyes by her tender lover, along with the blush conveyed by *rubent* (or is that another kind of redness?)—it never quite exorcises the phallic phantom that has haunted the poem from its first readers to the present day; indeed, it is what summons it up. Thus, *turgiduli* spares our blushes and provokes them at the same time. In addition to intensifying and falling short, diminutives can drop hints, push limits, and maintain suspense.

A diminutive noun performs a similar function in Catullus 10, a poem we have explored before. In this case, Platner fudges about the word in question, *scortillum* ("a bit of a slut"), used by the poet to convey his first impressions of Varus's female companion: "Here one may suppose that there is a true dim. signification, or one of contempt, or one of endearment. It is impossible to say with certainty." Uncertainty, again, may be the whole point. *Scortillum* is a diminutive of *scortum* (prostitute—literally, "hide" or "skin"—a crude neuter word for something conceived as a marketable, replaceable human commodity). But does this nuance hold for the diminutive as well? This is how William Fitzgerald translates the word in its surrounding passage:[19]

> scortillum, ut mihi tum repente uisum est,
> non sane illepidum neque inuenustum. (Cat. 10.3-4)
>
> a little whore, as I noticed on the spot,
> but not without charm or beauty.

Looked at closely, the lines do not actually include any Latin word for *but* (unless it is the emphatic *sane*: "even so" or "definitely"). Strictly, then, the litotes "not without charm and beauty" (or, more likely, "sex appeal") should be compatible with the sense of the diminutive that comes before it. A possible alternative, then, is to translate *scortillum* more leniently as "a bit slutty"—that is, approvingly or forgivably or indefinably so—nothing so raw as "little whore." There is leeway and curiosity here, despite the snap appraisal, and no hint at this point, given the patronizing tone, that the girl has more autonomy than Catullus gives her credit for. J. N. Adams has it right when he cites *scortillum* as typical of the mixture of "affection and contempt" in the general use that Latin and Greek make of diminutives for prostitutes (and, we might add, in their use of the neuter for the physical "package" they represent).[20] One could compare the blanket plural *amores*, or the innuendo of British English "bit of skirt." None of this implies, though, that Varus's girlfriend *is* a prostitute, only that she has something of a prostitute's availability (and, it turns out, grasping tendency) about her. Catullus sits with his first impressions before finding out that he has grossly underestimated the girl's substance and intelligence. Even so, these first impressions hold after their exchange insofar as he identifies a familiarly transactional flavor to her social interactions.

Along with the diminutive and the double negatives, the poem also includes a striking comparative, *cinaediorem* (technically, "rather like a passive homosexual"; colloquially, "like the little tart she was")—a harsher-seeming judgment:

> hic illa, ut decuit cinaediorem,
> "quaeso" inquit "mihi, mi Catulle, paulum
> istos commoda: nam uolo ad Serapim
> deferri." (Cat. 10.24–27)

> At which she said, like the little tart she was,
> "Please, darling Catullus, lend them to me for a bit:
> I need a ride to the temple of Serapis."

Once again, the word allows Catullus to fall short of open abuse (and accountability for it), hard though it is to bring out either the comparative or the implied queerness in an English translation. As we have seen, he is compromised by the term himself. After all, he has been exposed, however tongue in cheek, as another shameless opportunist, as well as the complicit victim of a "screwing over" by his provincial governor (*irrumator*).[21] Again, there *is* something "cinaedic" in the way the girl softens her request to him with an overfamiliar "darling Catullus" (*mi Catulle*) and another disarming diminutive, "for just a little while" (*paulum*), an example of what Adams elsewhere calls a "polite modifier" typical of feminine speech.[22] Just so, Thetis in Statius's *Achilleid* coaxes Achilles into wearing a dress "for just a little while" (*paulum*).[23] In Catullus 10, all three words—the diminutive *scortillum*, the comparative *cinaediorem*, and the adverb *paulum*—are provisional. They create a lack of definition, an opening of possibility, and a space for flirtation and negotiation (with words as well as with a person).

Some Latin diminutives, of course, are genuinely "lexicalized" in that they have acquired a separate technical identity (for example, *testiculus*, testicle, from *testis*, witness; *musculus*, sea mussel or bodily muscle, from *mus*, mouse; *libellus*, pamphlet, petition, or lampoon, from *liber* book), and so cost their users nothing in loss of masculine dignity. Diminutives often lodged themselves in domestic settings, displacing "larger" words. Pet words, for example, like *porcellus*, piggywig, and *agnellus*, lambkin, came to colonize (and euphemize) the butcher's vocabulary in modern Romance languages. Even so, poets like "shameless" Catullus and "modest" Horace tend to use *libellus* as a genuine diminutive for their urbane little *libri*, thereby seeming to disparage their own productions.

In any case, one could argue that diminutiveness remains a live quality in all these contexts, given the handleable size of all the objects just mentioned. But Latin goes further still. In common with some modern languages, it has free rein to double or multiply its diminutives by reduplicating their syllables, creating in the process a kind of stuttering effect that suggests a failure of precise and complete expression. The distinction in each additional suffix is one of emotional intensification or approximation, not just progressively diminutive size (compare English "small" > "tiny" > "teeny"; or "dear" > "darling" > "little darling" or "darlingest"). Just so, in contemporary Mexican Spanish, the delaying device *ahora* (in a minute) can be whittled (or wheedled?) down into *ahorita, ahoritita,* and even *ahorititita*. Russian, like Italian, boasts many shades of diminutive suffixes, from affectionate to disparaging, and is fond of multiple diminutives: the classic example пирог (*pirog*, pie) can become пирожок (*pirozhok*, small pie, sweetie pie) and пирожочек (*pirozhochek*, very small pie, or little sweetie pie). In the case of Latin, it has been claimed that while it "generally stops creating diminutives at double or triple diminutives [e.g., *rubellulus, agellulus*], there is theoretically no upper limit to the number of diminutive bases that can be added to diminutives to create even more diminutives."[24] For example, *puella* might generate *puellula, puellella, puellilla*—and even, hypothetically, *puellulula, puellellula,* and *puellillula*.

This all seems rather absurd, and indeed most of these forms are never found in classical Latin. Even so, the notion of a limit is thought-provoking. Should "no upper limit" perhaps be no *lower* limit? Or should one be thinking of limits at all? The potential to create ever-more focused diminutives suggests a kind of asymptotic striving toward an imagined vanishing point or unattainable goal of smallness (as in "itsy bitsy teenie weenie yellow polka dot bikini"). It is as though the holy grail were to return to some mystical *punctum* (the word we have seen so often in connection with small things)—here, the concentration of the most intense linguistic precision in the smallest space—or else to recover the tiniest embryonic prototype of a small form (the ultimate diminutive that lies at the other end of the linguistic scale from the basic form, known as its "primitive," *puer*, already turned feminine and diminutive into *puella*).

Put another way, the diminutive form can be conceived as nostalgic, in the sense that approximation or hopeless yearning toward an ideal endpoint entails a kind of loss. In that case, it seems natural that diminutives in Swahili, according to one of Daniel Jurafsky's linguistic maps, include among "handleable little things" a special subcategory for "pointed things/parts."[25] Latin makes a similar connection between diminutives and concentrated pointedness. In Apuleius's *Cupid and Psyche*, for example, Psyche, pregnant but still naïve, marvels that from a tiny pinprick (*de breui punctulo*—the sexual act minimized in proportion to her childish sensations) such a swelling growth from her fertile womb (*tantum incrementum locupletis uteri*) could grow.[26] Conversely, Seneca, as we saw earlier, piles up the most wincingly refined of diminutives to isolate the effects of seasickness on bodily extremities: "the slightest little movement [*leuis . . . motiuncula*] disorients you . . . your feet ache, [the ends of] your limbs feel tiny prickings [*punctiunculas*]."[27]

## LITTLE BOXES

A different but related concept or instinct behind the use of diminutives is that of enclosure.[28] In the first chapter, we saw Tertullian exaggerate the tininess of jewel boxes in his invective against female adornment: "From the smallest boxes [*de breuissimis loculis*] is produced an ample inheritance [*patrimonium grande*]." In

FIGURE 21. Roman basket, Metropolitan Museum, New York, AN 20.2.19.

*De lingua latina*, Varro preserves a rare example of a complete set of multiple diminutives, for different sizes of caskets or baskets:

> magnitudinis uocabula cum possint esse terna, ut cista cistula cistella . . . (Varro, *Ling.* 8.49)
>
> Whereas there can be a set of three words to indicate size, like cista, cistula, cistella . . .

If this is a random choice, it is a very nice one. The tender inward folding of human hands around a felt object suggested by a diminutive is perfectly conveyed by this group of larger containers enfolding smaller ones, nested on the page like matryoshka dolls. Plautus's play named after a little casket, *Cistellaria*, is one of several titles that combine a diminutive object with *-aria* (either an abstract collective neuter plural noun or a feminine adjective qualifying *fabula*, play), as if putting a question mark over the cumulative worth of huddled plurality and smallness combined. Other such titles include *Aulularia* (*The Pot Comedy*), from the diminutive of *olla*, pot; *Mostellaria* (*The Haunted House*), from *mostellum* (little monster or ghost); the lost *Frivolaria* (The One about the Trifles); and the lost and so far unexplained *Nervolaria*, still the subject of a tense standoff between fans of little phalluses and fans of slaves' fetters.[29]

To designate its central object, *Cistellaria* goes one better than Varro by including *cistula*, *cistella*, and *cistellula* among its variants.[30] Mario Telò embraces the charisma and vibrancy of these diminutive containers when he tracks *Cistellaria*'s confusion of its lost heroine Selenium with the frequently mislaid casket that contains the tokens of her birth: "The transference of vitality from person to thing, from *puella* to *cistella*, exposes the characters to affective experiences seen onstage or called forth from the past."[31] He also notes that the girl's lover, once she is in his possession, seems to want to box her up:

> Now that I have this girl, it is my intention not to let her go; for indeed I have decided to glue her entirely onto me. Where are you, slaves? Lock the house with bolts and door-bars [*pessulis, repagulis*] immediately. I will bring this girl inside the threshold. (*Cist.* 647–50)

A similar argument for the inseparability of material containers (for books and other things) from the imaginative concept of containership is made by Lucy Razzall in *Boxes and Books in Early Modern England*. She cites the familiar claim of George Lakoff and Mark Johnson that containment is one of the main "metaphors we live by."[32] Human beings, they explain, as bounded containers in themselves, tend to "project their own in-out orientation onto other physical objects that are bounded by surfaces."[33] Hence Eve Kosofsky Sedgwick's focus on the materiality as well as the *Epistemology of the Closet*, in the context of sexual in-out orientation.[34] Latin diminutives standard for "boxy" spaces, such as *lecticulus*, little couch, and *cubiculum*, little chamber, contain similar notions of cozy (or too cozy) interiority. Andrew Riggsby has identified the Roman *cubiculum* as not a bedchamber so much as a "room for secret activity," from sex to plotting to murder, while Victoria Rimell has shown how interior space can be dangerously *unheimlich*, as well as homey.[35]

In *The Poetics of Space*, Gaston Bachelard had already dreamed up Razzall's book: "An anthology devoted to small boxes, such as chests and caskets, would constitute an important chapter in psychology."[36] He has penetrating remarks of his own to make about the psychology of boxes. When a box is opened:

> The outside has no more meaning . . . even cubic dimensions have no more meaning, for the reason that a new dimension—the dimension of intimacy—has just opened up. (Bachelard 1994, 85)

This state of affairs amounts to a kind of infinite regression, he adds, quoting Jean-Pierre Richard on Edgar Allen Poe's *The Gold Bug*: "We shall never reach the bottom of the casket."[37] The affinity Bachelard perceives between recessive interiors and unsatisfied longing helps clarify the psychological as well as linguistic links

I hinted at earlier between the perfectly tiny version of the diminutive and the extreme form of the superlative. As Bachelard claims, this area of study had itself long been off-limits: "The hidden in men and the hidden in things belong in the same topo-analysis, as soon as we enter into this strange region of the *superlative*, which is a region that has hardly been touched by psychology."[38]

Sometimes a diminutive container word can even set the template for an entire work (and here I do regress briefly to metapoetics). Varro, again, provides an excellent example of "lexicalized" Latin diminutives—that is, words with specific meanings independent of their original noun, when, toward the end of *De re rustica*, he uses this curious analogy to suggest the shape of fishponds divided into fresh and saltwater areas:

> Nam ut Pausias et ceteri pictores eiusdem generis loculatas magnas habent arculas, ubi discolores sint cerae, sic hi loculatas habent piscinas, ubi dispares disclusos habeant pisces. (*Rust.* 3.17.4)

> For just as Pausias and the other painters of the same school have large boxes with compartments for keeping their pigments of different colours, so these people have ponds with compartments for keeping the varieties of fish separate.

The phrase *loculatas magnas . . . arculas* translates literally as "large compartmentalized drawers," the adjective "large" (*magnas*) qualifying the two diminutives on either side. Not only is the "interiority" and miniature size implied by *arculae* ("drawers"—from *arca*, "chest") preserved even when the drawers are outsize (that is, they do not automatically turn into *arcae* but stay "large little containers"), but the idea of subdivision is still conveyed by the participle *loculatus* (made into little places). The word *loculatus* derives from *loculus*, another lexicalized diminutive, from *locus* (place)—a holdall for any number of subdivided or lidded objects: coffins, cells in a beehive, niches of a *columbarium*, library shelves, dogs' kennels, boxes for dried figs, and even school backpacks.[39] In Plautus's *Stichus*, for example, the parasite Gelasimus begs for the tiniest nook (*tantillum loculi*) in his host's house, just big enough for a puppy (*catellus*) to lie in, and expresses very well the hyperbolic connotations of the superdiminutive—in this case, squirming, subhuman compression into an unreasonably narrow space:

> Epignomus: If you can curl up very tightly.
> Gelasimus: Even between two iron wedges, a teeny little slot where a puppy could sleep [*tantillum loculi, ubi catellus cubet*], that's enough space for me. (Plaut. *Stich.* 4.2)

But Varro's divided paintboxes, with their two "lexicalized" diminutives, are more than just miniature versions of the fishponds. They are also building blocks for the larger "places" and containers of *De re rustica*, which make the farm a small-scale analogue for the author's panoramic system for organizing knowledge. At the start of book 3, Varro, like Julius Caesar, breaks down his subject matter to get it under control, distinguishing first between town and country—topographically separate departments (*loco discretae*)—then dividing (*diuiserunt*) country into farmers and herdsmen ("This matter of herding has a twofold division, though no writer has made the distinction clearly, as the feeding around the steading is one thing, and that on the land is another"), then further dividing farming into three subcategories, arable, dairy and pastoral ("three divisions of rural economy which are instituted for gainful ends—one of agriculture, a second of animal husbandry, and a third of the husbandry of the farmstead").[40] This gives a ground map for a final book peppered with other significant *loculi*: the purse or moneybox into which one puts one's meager savings; and the ballot box, symbol of the elections taking place in the city, elections that at one point threaten to interrupt the peace of the dialogue.[41]

It is predictable, then, that Martial, poet par excellence of smallness, has no qualms about reducing *loculus* further still to a double diminutive, *locellus*, in the little epigram where he offers as a party gift some small wooden boxes with nothing inside—apart from a bottom:[42]

> LOCULI LIGNEI
> Si quid adhuc superest in nostri faece locelli,
>     munus erit. nihil est: ipse locellus erit. (Mart. 14.12 (13))
>
> WOODEN BOXES
> If there's anything left in the bottom of my little box you can keep it.
> There's nothing? Well, you can keep the little box.

Curiosity, disappointment, dubious consolation—all in two lines. W. R. Johnson mused on the modernist, even nihilist affinities of this epigram: "Without indulging in a game of faux zen," he wrote, "one could say that the box and its emptiness (a bare, almost abstract object-poem that refuses significance) are about nothing but beauty and the box-poem itself, its own bare beauty: A material object (together with the poem, the mental object which now represents it) is transformed into an aesthetic experience that in turn transforms the experiencer (briefly) into a pure perceiver (of a small and pure beauty)."[43] We are back with the plums in the icebox, which have already vanished but which keep, refrigerated, in poetry, or with Wendy Cope's charming riposte to a neglectful suitor: "But, look, the flowers you nearly brought / Have lasted all this while."[44] In Martial, the subtle turn from plural *loculi* in the title to singular *locellus* in the poem only adds to the impression of a forlorn but endearing emptiness, precariously preserved.

Poets who identify with nothingness and having nothing to offer are especially partial to such diminutive container words, because they function as portable extensions of (some minimal version of) themselves. Repositories of emotions, secrets, and poetry alike, these containers stand in for the compromising intimacy their human owners abundantly promise but ultimately withhold. Catullus

FIGURE 22. Mosaic of doves stealing pearls from a box, House of the Faun, Pompeii, Museo Archeologico, Naples. Photo: Julian Money-Kyrle; Alamy Stock Image.

is relatively uninhibited about delving intimately into his own body or other bodies, whether to invite seduction or tease us with the prospect of deep penetration into the softest interior places, or at least into the narrow passages that lead there: rectum, inner ear, inmost marrow. Diminutives, especially those with liquid sounds, play a large part in forging this intrusive intimacy. As we have seen, Poem 25 starts:

> Thallus you cinaedus softer than rabbit's fur [*mollior cuniculi capillo*] or the plushest down of a goose or the innermost hollow of an earhole [*uel anseris medullula uel imula oricilla*] (Cat. 25.1–2)

This is language that makes the reader's own inmost earholes tingle.

A good example of such a substitute in portable form is the purse in Catullus 13, where Catullus (one diminutive individual: "puppy") invites Fabullus (another: "little bean") to dinner. The joke is that he has precious little to offer:

> You shall have a good dinner [*bonam atque magnam cenam*] at my house, Fabullus, in a few days, please the gods, if you bring with you a good dinner and plenty of it, not forgetting a pretty girl and wine and wit and all kinds of laughter. If, I say, you bring all this, my charming friend, you shall have a good dinner; for the purse of your Catullus is full of cobwebs [*nam tui Catulli | plenus sacculus est aranearum*]. But

on the other hand you shall have from me love's very essence, or what is sweeter or more delicious than love, if sweeter there be; for I will give you some perfume which the Venuses and Loves gave to my lady; and when you snuff its fragrance, you will pray the gods to make you, Fabullus, nothing but nose [*totum . . . nasum*]. (Cat. 13; Loeb, trans. Goold)

The speaker pleads that he cannot afford his own provisions because his purse, *sacculus* (diminutive of *saccus*), is "full of spiders." Not only does Platner rule out the diminutive specificity of *sacculus* here—"This dim. is not uncommon, and other writers seem to use *saccus, sacculus* and *sacellus* oftentimes as synonymous"—he also thinks it a less than ideal choice: "It would seem here—at least from one point of view—that there should be no dim. idea, for the larger the purse, the greater its load of emptiness, and the more forcible the figure. Probably therefore *sacculus = saccus*."[45]

Platner's logic is somewhat hard to follow. He seems deaf to the blend of surprise ("my little purse is full . . . of spiders"), possessiveness, and humble brag all wrapped up in the notion of a small purse full of emptiness, not to mention the fact that a great many cobwebs can still be packed into it, which is all part of the joke; even at the best of times, the entertainment would not have been lavish. More than that, though, the diminutive suggests an analogy with body parts conceived as miniature extensions of an individual. The *sacculus*, in short, can be understood as a surrogate for little Catullus (minor player in the world of social and material exchange), a teasing offering of in-out self-orientation that promises satisfaction but never fully delivers it.

By the end of the poem, another body part is in full view, not detachable so much as consuming its owner. When he smells the one thing Catullus has to offer, his mistress's scent (*unguentum*, whatever that means), he guarantees that Fabullus will dream of becoming "all nose" (*totum nasum*). A modern-day context where such an identification, unusually, is possible is the case of those samplers known in the perfume industry as "noses," whose transformation, Bruno Latour has argued, is more than simply figurative. "It is not by accident," he writes, "that the person is called 'a nose' as if, through practice, she had *acquired* an organ that defined her ability to detect chemical and other differences . . . a nose that allowed her to inhabit a (richly differentiated odoriferous) world."[46] In French, the sample kit with which a trainee parfumier learns to differentiate between scents has a diminutive name: *mallette à odeurs* (from *malle*, a large trunk). This modern-day equivalent of Varro's compartmentalized paintbox presents a miniature version of the "richly differentiated" external world, offering small possibilities for affective responses to it.

For Catullus, by contrast, Fabullus's blown-up nose remains a hypothetical organ that offers neither contact nor possession but only suggestion and frustration, just as his prosthetic *sacculus* fails to deliver even on its limited capacity. Catullus allows interiority without penetration: you can smell but you can't

FIGURE 23. Calliope and Homer with a *capsa* (scrollbox); detail of Roman floor mosaic from Vichten, 240 CE, Musée National d'histoire et de l'art, Luxembourg. Photo: TimeTravel-Rome; Wikimedia Commons.

touch. When fourth-century CE poet Ausonius lewdly invites his friend Axius Paulus to inspect some intimate private musings—in this case a tiny set of poems (*Bissula*) about a favorite adopted former slave (*uirguncula*)—he provides no fewer than three prefaces (one in prose, two in verse) to introduce her charms. But for all the layers of packaging, the German-born Bissula—a name he concedes might seem "hick" (*rusticulum*) and "icky" (*horridulum*) to others but is sexy enough (*uenustum*) to him—remains a mystery: so much wrapping paper, so little inside the box.

Another little container makes its way into Catullus 68, that difficult poem that Denis Feeney has observed is jampacked with comparisons—another form of conceptual yearning that, like its author, leans toward perfect identifications but always stops shy of them.[47] The poem thanks its addressee for supplying Catullus with a love nest in Rome, but even so is drawn back to analogies with tragically separated mythical couple Protesilaus and Laodamia and to continued grief for the brother lost at Troy. Catullus apologizes for his literary inadequacy by pleading that he is a displaced person living out of a suitcase, or rather out of a single book box (a *capsula*, usually cylinder-shaped for holding scrolls):

> For as for my not having plenty of authors at hand, that is because I live at Rome: that is my home, that is my abode, there my life is spent; when I come here only one small box out of many [*una ex multis capsula*] attends me. (Cat. 68.33–36)

Not only is this box a lexicalized smaller entity (than *capsa*, scrollbox): it shows up only to represent scarcity and loss (*una ex multis*). Even so, there is something fond and consoling about the image of the little container as faithful retainer, when neither Catullus nor Laodamia succeeded in following their loved ones to Troy. As Jaś Elsner writes of a prestigious box that has survived from Roman Britain: "We may say ultimately that the Muse Casket evokes an embodied subjectivity in the elite owner—one whose desire is both to see inside the box and to access its tangible contents—who is inevitably directed to a pattern (we may say a materially constituted narrative) of opening and unpacking, of closure and putting away."[48]

A box whose inside contains only a section of an entire poetic corpus fits well among a cluster of images that William Fitzgerald has traced through Catullus 68 and the preceding poems, conveying above all the promise, often deceptive, of "expressing" or "shaking out" things from mysterious interiors.[49] A thread runs from the fruit rolling from a girl's disappearing lap in 65 (a poem that is the "covering letter" to 66 and figures a poet's retentive mind as storehouse and womb) to 68, a poem that is "layered" or "stratified," where Herculean tunnels drilled through the "inmost marrow" of mountains (*fodisse medullis*) are conflated with a mysterious bottomless pit (*barathrum*) and with Lesbia's progress from her husband's lap (*gremium*) to Catullus's.[50] The little *capsula* joins these interiors as another proxy that half serves the futile desires of its abandoned owner for perfect (re)union. This was a versatile word, used of many possible neat containers. It is equivalent to our "bandbox"—for example, in Seneca's *Letters*, where natty (*comptulos*) young men emerge *de capsula*; it is also the name given to the cookie tin placed at the foot of the Flamen Dialis's bed.[51] In late antiquity, *capsula* took on a further specific meaning, as a reliquary for a saint's body parts:[52]

> ac deinde Germanus plenus Spiritu Sancto inuocat Trinitatem et protinus adhaerentem lateri suo capsulam cum sanctorum reliquiis collo auulsam manibus comprehendit. (Constantius, *Vita Germani* 15.5–7)

> And then Germanus, filled with the Holy Spirit, invokes the Trinity and immediately he removes from his neck a small box of saintly relics he kept close to his body and grasps it in his hands.

It is in this context, a saint's sacred biography, that the diminutive's potential to express intimate forms of contact between object and custodian is mostly clearly on show. First, the locket "clings" to Germanus's body; then it is removed from his neck and cradled in his hand. Not only is it a detachable prosthesis in itself: it is even a container of other saints' small, desiccated body parts.

## DILATING PUPILS

An unusual word choice for a body part in another Catullan poem has been similarly underappreciated.[53] In Catullus 63, Attis, formerly a Greek youth, awakens from a trance in the wilds of Phrygia to discover that she has castrated herself under the influence of the goddess Cybele. In a long speech, she mourns the loss of her masculine Greek future and the conventional rites of passage from ephebehood to manhood that she will never experience. It has long been noted that many of the words Attis uses express grammatical paradoxes of gender, above all in the line where she addresses her fatherland, *patria*, a feminine noun with a masculine-sounding root that attracts feminine, maternal adjectives:

> patria o mei creatrix, patria o mea genetrix (Cat. 63.50)
>
> O fatherland that mothered me, o fatherland that bore me

But there is reason to keep these queer combinations in our minds six lines later, when Attis says that her gaze (formerly her "weeping eyes," *lacrimantibus oculis*) is still drawn toward her fatherland. Instead of saying "eye," she now says "pupil," *pupula*:

> cupit ipsa pupula ad te sibi derigere aciem (Cat. 63.56)
>
> My very own eye desires to direct its gaze toward you.

We have seen how Latin tends to use diminutives to refer to one's own or others' body parts, and in a poem already packed full of them (*lassulae, latibula, labellis, corollis*), twin body parts abound: lips, eyes, ears.[54] Still, there is something uncanny about the substituted word here: the singular synecdoche *pupula*. In Latin, as in its English derivative, this word embraced the twin concepts of "eye pupil," and "school pupil." It is well known how one became the other. "Little doll" or "little girl" (from *pupa*, "doll") translates a similar concept in Greek: *kor(e)*, the "maiden" in the eye—that is, the little dolly or mannikin, the tiny image of ourselves, which, as external viewers, we see reflected in another person's iris. The locus classicus for this is Plato's *Alcibiades* 1, later expanded by Cicero, who uses the Latin word *pupula* (rather than *pupilla*), stressing that the iris is deliberately small, so that the organ of viewing will not be easily harmed:[55]

> aciesque ipsa qua cernimus, quae pupula uocatur, ita parua est ut ea quae nocere possint facile uitet. (Cic. *Nat. D.* 2.142)

The actual organ of vision, called the pupil or "little doll," is so small as easily to avoid objects that might injure it.

Pliny the Elder adds further clarification and a gruesome detail:

> The pupil [*pupilla*] has become the window for the horny center of the eye, whose narrowness [*angustiae*] does not allow the vision to wander, uncertain [*non sinunt uagari incertam aciem*], but directs it as though through a channel. So complete a mirror, too, does the eye form [*adeoque his absoluta uis speculi*] that the pupil, small as it is [*tam parua illa pupilla*], is able to reflect the entire image [*totam imaginem*] of a person. This is the reason why most birds, when held in the hand of a person, will peck specifically at his eyes; for seeing their own likeness reflected in the pupils, they are attracted to it by what seem to be the objects of their natural affection [*cognita desideria*]. (Plin. *HN* 11.55.148)

Here, *angustiae* ("narrow straits"), *acies* ("vision," but originally "sharpness"), and *absoluta uis* ("consummate ability") all drive home the idea of a tiny focal point, further illustrating the connection I have claimed between the use of the diminutive and the ideals of precision and perfect accuracy. Cicero normally prefers the form *pupilla* (of course he does: in his sixties, he married his own "little dolly," his fifteen-year-old ward Publilia).

In a poem whose central concern is gender change, the choice of a feminine, diminutive word activates a further possibility. If *pupula* is the name for the diminutive image of our reflected core identity (no pun intended), is Catullus implying that femininity is already innate in all of us, at least when we are looked at by another consciousness? Taken together, the singular noun *pupula*, the verb *cupere*, and the emphatic *ipsa* suggest Attis's psychic loneliness and longing (compare Pliny's *cognita desideria*). If this is how our inner soul always looks to ourselves and other people, perhaps it is not only Attis who can say, "Am I a woman?" (*ego mulier?*) or "Will I be a part of myself?" (*ego mei pars . . . ero?*). Her ability to see herself in the reflections of others recalls, in particular, the response of the slave Sosia in Plautus's *Amphitryo* on first seeing his lost twin:

> By Pollux, surely when I look at him, I recognize my own appearance, in the same way that I am (for I've often seen myself in the mirror); he is even overly similar to me. (*Amph.* 441–42)

As he later explains:

> there is no milk more like milk than that I over there [*ille ego*] is just like me. (*Amph.* 601)

In Maurizio Bettini's words: "When referring to his double, Sosia has no choice but to call him *ego*: 'that *I* over there,' he says: *ille ego*. Faced with this duplicated image of himself, Sosia still calls him *I*."[56] Or could we say "eye," substituting another doublet?[57]

A rare word in Latin, *pupula* attracts puns in its other appearances, too. A fragment from Calvus's *Io* runs: *cum grauis urgenti coniuere pupula somno* ("when the heavy pupil dipped in urgent sleep").[58] According to Edward Courtney, the pupil refers to either Io's weariness or to her guardian Argus's multiple eyes.[59] But the ambiguity holds in any case because Io *is* Argus's *pupula* in the sense of his "charge" or "ward." The double meaning is differently exploited in Ovid's *Amores*, where the lover spies on an old woman instructing his beloved in the art of love for women:

> oculis quoque pupula duplex
> fulminat, et gemino lumen ab orbe uenit. (*Am.* 1.7.15–16)

> From her eyes, too, double pupils dart their lightnings, with rays that issue from twin orbs

A witch with a giveaway double pupil educates her female pupil in erotic duplicity.[60] In the case of Catullus's Attis, *pupula* also signals her new status as wandering devotee of the Magna Mater, permanently fixed in pupillage, or, as she puts it, a handmaiden for the rest of her days (*semper omne uitae spatium famula*), unable to transition from that state.

### END POINT?

So far, we have seen the diminutive used mostly sentimentally or personally. But it can also be used scathingly. Cicero is a master of the invention and acute deployment of diminutives, from the emotionally confiding to the coruscatingly satirical.[61] As Louis Laurand notes, diminutives are unevenly spread across his works, found, not surprisingly, more often in the correspondence and the more conversational speeches than in the more elevated ones. As usual, these words express not just smallness but a range of emotions from tenderness and sympathy to contempt, not to mention "the most delicate forms of Ciceronian irony."[62] We have already seen how Cicero likes to coin words starting with *per-* and *sub-* to add nuance, either to intensify or to downplay—which offers another clue to the quasi-comparative and superlative functions that diminutives perform. He also likes to combine prefixes with diminutive suffixes, overegging the idea of smallness: *perparuolus*, for example.[63] Another group of hybrid adjectives and adverbs is invented by joining comparatives onto diminutive endings: *putidiusculus* (just a little more revolting), *maiusculus* (just a little bigger), *meliuscule* (just a little better).[64]

Such exquisite precision might pass as the height of squeamish but urbane discrimination, as when Cicero claims to rate a "tiny stroll" (*ambulatiuncula*) and a chat with Caelius in Rome worth the entire profits of a province abroad (also the message of Catullus 10), or when *contractiuncula quaedam animi* (a little bit of a downer) registers the slightest dip in mood.[65] Yet the sheer finickyness of the constructions must make them at least partly self-ironizing. J. E. G. Zetzel, who makes a collection of these words, reads Cicero's criticism in *Pro Archia* of an epigram offered to Sulla by a bad Greek poet, *alternis uersiculis longiusculis* (with every other verse just a little too long), as exaggeratedly philistine, since the phrase is "a perfectly accurate, if satirical, description of the elegiac couplet in which an epigram would be written."[66]

Nowhere does Cicero make more colorful use of diminutives than when disparaging Greek philosophy, with its pernickety, overintricate arguments. Gloriously sardonic phrases are used of Zeno's "terse and pointed little syllogisms" (*Zenonisque breuis et acutulas conclusiones*) and of the Stoics' "hair-splitting minutiae" (*interrogatiunculae angustae*), their "fussy syllogisms" (*ratiunculae*), and even "string of involved and pettifogging little syllogisms" (*contortulae quaedam ac minutae conclusiunculae*).[67] Still less mercy is granted to Antony's petits bons mots (*sententiolas*), which are so much less supersharp (*peracutas*) than he thinks they are.[68] Note, again, how the idea of a point recurs in these examples—*acutulas, angustae, peracutas*—enhanced by the diminutives themselves, all straining toward a pinhead or *punctum* of absurd precision while mimicking the overanalytic urges of those satirized: angels dancing on the head of a pin?

Cicero, "chickpea" that his name suggests, has a vested interest in making the Greeks themselves look small and conflating their heroic stature with their minute obsessions. Thus Epicurus is *forticulus* ("little tough man) and Zeno *acriculus senex* ("clever little old man"); the genius Archimedes is a *humilis homunculus*, "humble little human."[69] Tobias Reinhardt has argued that the word *corpusculum*, "little body," which Cicero uses of Epicurus's atoms, must be pejorative in tone because its roots lie in satire, where it is used to belittle the frail and insignificant *human* body.[70] For comparison, he cites Juvenal reducing the *corpusculum* of Alexander the Great to size (*quantula sint hominum corpuscula*, "how small are little human bodies") and Lucilius calling our mortal remains *folliculum* (husk or pod).[71] Cicero must, he argues, be specifically implying "feeble little body," not just "little body," thereby suggesting the absurdity of a world made up of feeble little bodies.[72]

Such newly minted Latin diminutives as these rise admirably to the challenge of dispelling the combined ghosts of Greek celebrity and pedantic distinction while delineating a view of the contemporary world that is both variegated and domestic. This suggests that there is almost a psychological element of self-consolation underpinning their use. Diminutives essentially enable Cicero to break down all human ambition and all potential external threats, including the Greeks, to manageable size. For example, he consistently, patronizingly miniaturizes women, as if reducing them to a known quantity—*aniculae, mulierculae, mimulae, nutriculae*—an attitude that comes back to haunt him when Sulpicius Rufus writes, not without compassion, that it is time for Cicero to man up and snap out of grief for a single daughter: *unius mulierculae animula* ("the frail soul of one dear little [mortal] woman").[73]

We have already seen Cicero pointing out that the Romans have more words for sensibility than the Greeks; we have also seen how the performance of verbal and emotional feebleness is essential to his own construction of an urbane but fragile literary self. A classic example of underplaying with a diminutive is the following coinage in a letter to Atticus, where Cicero bites the bullet and confesses to morally compromising capitulation to Caesar and Pompey, referring to his "palinode" (unspecified, but probably his recent speech *De provinciis consularibus*). To downplay this lapse from principled behavior, he comes up with a novel double diminutive, a "cute" face-saver: *subturpicula*, "just the tiniest bit naughty."[74] As often, his preamble sensitizes us to the nuances of the coinage: "I have spent a long time 'nibbling around' [*iam dudum circumrodo*] at what needs to be swallowed whole [*quod deuorandum est*]." Using the diminutive to indicate a venial sin or peccadillo, straying somewhere shy of gross moral turpitude, sounds almost like an imaginary inner parent petting an inner naughty child; Cicero wants his best friend to witness his weaker self being forgiven by his stronger one. But the sense of evasion or shortcoming is spatialized in advance by *circumrodo*, which prepares us for the way in which the *sub-* prefix, plus the diminutive suffix *-icula*, also beats around the bush of something potentially more serious.

A verb like "gnaw about" suggests little animals—rodents, specifically—which returns us to Cicero's remarks in *De natura deorum* about little houses being built by mice and weasels.[75] It is intriguing to watch him use other engagements with mice to manage and minimize his responses to external pressures.[76] In *Att.* 14.9, for example, looking at problems philosophically as mouse-sized helps him make light of his current misfortunes as a landlord:

> Two of my shops have collapsed and the others are showing cracks, so that even the mice have moved elsewhere, to say nothing of the tenants [*non solum inquilini sed mures etiam migrauerunt*]. Other people call this a disaster [*calamitatem*], I don't call it even a nuisance [*ne incommodum quidem*]. Ah Socrates, Socratics, I can never repay you! Heavens above, how utterly trivial such things appear to me! [*quam mihi ista pro nihilo*].[77] (*Att.* 14.9.1; Loeb, trans. Shackleton Bailey)

In *De divinatione*, similarly, Cicero downplays the gnawing of mice, which some people see as a portent or symptom of something catastrophic, as a purely random or quotidian phenomenon:[78]

> But are we simple and thoughtless enough to think it a portent [*monstrum*] for mice to gnaw something, when gnawing is their one business in life? "But," you say, "the fact that just before the Marsian War mice gnawed the shields at Lanuvium was pronounced by the soothsayers to be a very direful portent [*maximum . . . portentum*]." As if it mattered whether mice, which are always gnawing something day and night, gnawed shields or sieves! By the same token, the fact that, at my house, mice recently gnawed my Plato's *Republic* ought to fill me with alarm for the Roman republic; or if they had gnawed my Epicurus *On Pleasure* I should have expected a rise in the market price of grain! (*Div.* 2.27.59; Loeb, trans. Falconer)

This joking response is a far cry from Virgil's farm pests in *Georgics* 1, initially staged as a minicomedy of little scroungers and parasites—with weevils, moles,

FIGURE 24. Roman leather (toy?) mouse, 12 cm long, Vindolanda Museum. Credit: @Vindolanda Trust.

toads, and an *exiguus mus* (little mouse) among them—but suddenly transformed into a parade of "monsters" (*monstra*, rather than *mostella*, "little monsters"), since they represent, after all, a potentially devastating threat to human livelihoods.[79] Virgil takes small things seriously and humorously at the same time because he is alert to their complexity, in this case to the pests' hard-to-assess identity as companions or competition for human farmers.

If Cicero lightens politics and religion by looking down on mice, and in his more xenophobic or anti-intellectual moods reduces the Greeks to "little people," seeing them, in Susan Stewart's words, "as if it were at the other end of a tunnel, distanced, diminutive, and clearly framed," this brings us back to questions posed at the start of this book.[80] Did the Romans tend to miniaturize their ancestors, genetic or intellectual? Did they make their *maiores* into *minores*, putting them into tiny boxes to make it easier to contain them or cope with them? And if *we* choose to access the Romans and their lives through small daily things, is that choice fueled by a kind of nostalgia that diminishes the past, or does it sharpen our eyes to what seems beneath our notice but is unquestionably, illuminatingly, still there—and still here? In the end, does it all come down to perspective—to shrinking the world, or the past, returning to the language and surroundings of babyhood, in order to manage things and feel safe and in control? Thanks to modern technology, we can look down on a planet reduced to a pinprick (*punctum*) and its populations to ants, just like Seneca in *Natural Questions* or Scipio in his dream: "Now the earth itself seemed to me so small that I felt ashamed of our empire, with which we touch as it were only a pinprick [*punctum*] on the earth's surface."[81]

Coming out of a pandemic, we have learned to embrace smallness, to focus on handling, looking at—and fearing—what lies immediately in front of us. With the loss of the agency, mobility, and sociability we once knew, we even started to blend in with the objects surrounding us. This latest encounter with small things has been one with our own triviality, frailty, animality and mortality (recall Hadrian on his *animula uagula blandula*, or the other Crispus reducing an audience to "not even a fly"). Remember the fly that gained notoriety when it clung so mesmerizingly to

Mike Pence's head during a 2020 vice-presidential debate that it stole his thunder, undermined his authority, and reduced him to an inviting expanse of hair and flesh?[82] Small things cut *us* down to size. But remember, too, the Ukrainian spokesman who proudly declared at the start of a new war: "We are a huge amount of ants." Singly or *en masse*, small things can be an inspiration.

# NOTES

## FOREWORD

1. Pandey 2020.

## 1. THE GOOD OF SMALL THINGS

1. The Latin sculptural metaphor *ad unguem*, "to a T" (lit. "to the nail"), is derived not from a sculptor's perfecting touches but from casting statues from clay molds, which were most carefully worked at the bodily extremities. See D'Angour 1999.

2. Updike anticipates the recent academic turn toward embodied experience and finding the hidden life in inanimate things: the so-called New Materialism, exemplified by Jane Bennett's *Vibrant Materialism* (J. Bennett 2010), Bill Brown's "Thing theory" (B. Brown 2001), and Bruno Latour's attention to the agency of the nonhuman (e.g., Latour 2004). On ancient figurines, their special versality and resistance to categorization, see Elsner 2019; Neer 2020.

3. See the inspirational discussions of Bachelard 1994; Bartman 1992; S. Stewart 1993; Squire 2011, esp. 247–302; Martin and Langin-Hooper 2018; Neer 2020.

4. Discussed by Čulík-Baird 2022; Goldschmidt 2023.

5. Kim et al. (2022) argue for the emotional benefits of taking a limited perspective on life, rather than feeling connected to "the grand scheme of things." Appreciating "the little things" and valuing immediate experiences can bestow "a rich sense of meaning."

6. Cic. *Caecin.* 13.36. At *Att.* 15.26.4 ( = SB 404), Cicero is bothered about a watercourse shared with his neighbor (along with another *parua res*, Tullius's debt). See chapter 4 for Cicero's own focus on small concerns in the *Letters to Atticus*.

7. Bachelard 1994; S. Stewart 1993; Gell 1992; Mack 2007.

8. Squire 2011; Platt 2006; Dolansky 2012; Rimell 2015.

9. Ker 2023; Peirano 2012; Lambert 2020.

10. Padilla Peralta 2020, 33.

11. E.g., Squire 2011, 24: "the objective is to use the *Tabulae Iliacae* to tease out some of the largest and most pressing questions facing the study of classics, classical archaeology, and classical art history—and indeed the humanities at large." See Dolansky 2012, 286: dolls "presented girls with conflicting messages about what being an upper-class woman entailed and what was valued, which potentially had serious implications for girls at a formative stage in their development." See also Platt 2006, 251: seal-rings enabled their owners "to 'make an impression' upon the world itself, to form a causal chain of signs—of 'replications'—which relate the self in its most personal sense to his or her public and social roles; to identify the self as rational, moral agent, and, ultimately, as an authentic being."

12. On eighteenth-century small things, see Rabb 2019; Wigston Smith and Tobin 2022 (especially their introduction, 1–11, "The Scale and Sense of Small Things").

13. Boivin 2008, 232.

14. See Collins 2002–3. On the modernist aesthetic, see Ngai (2012, 3), who identifies "short, compact texts preoccupied with small, easy-to-handle things." See Arendt 1958, 2.

15. Deetz 1977. "Small" for Deetz means modest and unimportant, rather than miniature. See also Wigston Smith and Tobin 2022, 64.

16. Perec 1999.

17. Tim Hitchcock, "Big data, small data, and meaning", *Histryonics* (blog), November 9, 2014, http://historyonics.blogspot.com/2014/11/big-data-small-data-and-meaning_9.html.

18. Ngai 2012, 1–52.

19. K. Stewart 2006, 10; 12.

20. Challenging Seltzer's deflating view of insular academic criticism, H. Love (2016) cites *Citizen*, Claudia Rankine's chronicle of racist microaggressions (Rankine 2014), as a granular project with far-reaching political impact.

21. See Gallagher and Greenblatt 2000, 26: "the ability to keep an object . . . within the high-resolution area of perception" (regarding anthropologist Clifford Geertz's characteristic focus on "a tiny textualized piece of social behavior").

22. See Roy 1997, 165: "And once again, only the Small Things were said. The Big Things lurked unsaid inside."

23. K. Stewart 2006, 40.

24. On the poetic aspects of Virgil's epic juxtaposition of large and small bodies, see Mac Góráin 2009; Young 2013; and Giusti 2014.

25. Martin and Langin-Hooper 2018, 1. Wigston Smith and Tobin 2022, 2 note the haptic challenges presented by small things, which demand "additional scrutiny, nimbleness, and concentration to apprehend and handle."

26. Elsner 2021.

27. See "Think 'Small': Textual Approaches and Practices of Artistic Miniaturization from Antiquity to the Nineteenth Century," *Calenda*, November 5, 2014, https://calenda.org/304651. The organizers, Sophie Duhem, Estelle Galbois, and Anne Perrin Khelissa, list "maniabilité, mobilité, économie, pauvreté, préciosité, minutie, joliesse, étrangeté."

28. Neer 2020.

29. Stewart 1993, 44. Cf. Bachelard 1994, 155: "The tiny things we imagine simply take us back to childhood, to familiarity with toys and *the reality of toys*" (emphasis in the original).

30. The *Eton Latin Grammar* (1758) compiles a list of Latin measures of worthlessness:

*Flocci, nauci, nihili, pili, assis, hujus, teruncii, his verbis, aestimo, pendo, facio, peculiariter adduntur.* On February 21, 2012, one Old Etonian, the Right Honourable Jacob Rees-Mogg, uttered the longest word (now superseded) ever spoken in the UK Parliament: *"floccinaucinihilipilification."*

31. The fate of Sejanus's melted-down commemorative statue, in Juvenal's tenth satire.
32. Fitzgerald 2018, 14–15.
33. Ngai 2012, 103.
34. "I am there and not there," sings the gnat at Ach. Tat. 2.22.3.
35. Lloyd 1966, 15–19: e.g., Alcmaeon D5 Laks-Most = Arist. *Metaph.* 986a34.
36. Anaxag. D24, D25 Laks-Most.
37. Pl. *Phd.* 102d. Lloyd 1966, 127.
38. Pl. *Symp.* 215a–b. Aesop (Perry 108): small men got more intelligence at creation than large ones; Kurke 2010, 267. Cf. Pl. *Tht.* 155b–d.
39. Lloyd 1966.
40. Anaxag. D2, D3 Laks-Most; Lucr. *DRN* 1.830–96.
41. Pl. *Phd.* 110b; 109b.
42. Ar. *Poet.* 1450b.
43. Quint. *Inst.* 10.4.46. See de Angelis 2014 on the similarly head-spinning combination of *megethos* (grandeur) and *akribeia* (precision) in Trajan's Column.
44. Hom. *Il.* 2.799–801. Ford 1992, 79.
45. Ford 1992, 71.
46. On the latter, see S. Stewart 1993, 67.
47. Porter 2011, 286. Already questioned by Cameron 1995, ix: "The notion that [Callimachus] was the uncompromising apostle of the short poem dies hard."
48. Bachelard 1994, 150. On the complexities of scale, see the fine discussion in Squire 2011, 247–302.
49. Radke 2007, cited by Porter 2011, 293–94.
50. Stat. *Achil.* 1.147.
51. Virg. *Aen.* 12.946–47 *furiis accensus et ira | terribilis.*
52. See Fowler 1995, 136–37 on Horace's small-scale allegiances: "Isn't Greatness itself suspect? The polite tones of the *recusatio* . . . conceal a poetic manifesto in which the small-scale genres are actually *preferred* to sublimity on aesthetic grounds: where does that leave the artistic achievement of the Great Leader?"
53. Ngai 2012, 93.
54. Hudson 2019.
55. Hudson 2019, 58.
56. "Tout dépend de l'exécution. L'histoire d'un pou peut être plus belle que celle d'Alexandre." See Gustave Flaubert, Letter 556, to Ernest Feydeau, August 1857 (Flaubert 1926–33, 4.225).
57. In his *Fly*, Lucian is acutely aware of the paradoxes of scale. See *Musca* 1: "The fly is not the smallest of winged things, on a level with gnats, midges, and still tinier creatures; it is as much larger than they are smaller than the bee." In comparing the fly's proboscis to an elephant's, he fulfils the threat at *Musca* 12: "I will stop talking, for fear you may think that, as the saying goes, I am making an elephant out of a fly." See Billerbeck and Zubler 2000; and Pease 1926 on the special challenge to ancient rhetoricians of unimportant things.

58. Plin. *HN* 35.83; 35.112.

59. Writing on bees, Seneca (*Clem.* 1.19.4) describes nature as busying herself in small matters and providing the smallest lessons in great principles: "We should not be ashamed to take lessons from such small creatures."

60. *HN praef.* 1; Wallace-Hadrill 1990, 82.

61. *HN* 10.98.

62. Sen. *Brev. Vit.* 2.1.

63. See Neer 2020, 31 on miniature figurines of Baubo (the flashing goddess) as "managing" disturbing images.

64. I take the metaphor from the satirist Persius and his condensation of his predecessor Horace (*S.* 1.125).

65. Cic. *Somnium* 16 = *Rep.* 6.16.

66. Cf., e.g., Cic. *Fin.* 5.27.80 *integritatem unguiculorum omnium* (soundness of every part from top to toe); cf. *Tusc.* 2.56 *toto corpore atque omnibus ungulis* (with the full force of the body and the tips of the hooves).

67. Sen. *Ep.* 89.2–3.

68. Sen. *Ep.* 89.3.

69. Sen. *Ep.* 49.3, 5.

70. Seneca cites Cicero's equivocal claim (now lost) that were his lifespan doubled he would waste no time in reading the Greek lyric poets.

71. Sen. *Ep. 70.16*. Ker 2009, 270.

72. Livy 3.27.8.

73. The classic essay on the "reality effect" ("l'effet du réel") is Barthes 1986.

74. Gallagher and Greenblatt (2000, 53) credit Auerbach's technique—analyzing a resonant textual fragment to show how it represents both the larger work and the culture in which it was produced and consumed—as a key influence on New Historicism. See ibid., 14–15 for self-reflection on the weaknesses of New Historical methodology: why are certain "luminous details" selected and not others? how to deal with the unrepresented? with leftover traces?

75. Auerbach (1953, 538) notes the contrast "between the brief span of time occupied by the exterior event and the dreamlike wealth of a process of consciousness which traverses a whole subjective universe."

76. Ginzburg 1983. On details in art, see also Hiller et al. (2012); on the overlooked in art, see Bryson 1990.

77. Rowe 2012.

78. Didi-Huberman 1986; Arasse 1992.

79. Pertinent reflections on the latter in Sharrock and Morales 2000.

80. Men. fr. 41 K and 42 K–T; Ter. *An.* 484–85; Gowers 1993, 86; Shipp 1960, 23.

81. Admittedly, he refers later in the same play to "cabbage and little fish" (369 *holera et pisciculos minutos*).

82. Sen. *Controv.* 7 *praef.* 3.

83. Perec 1999, 209: "How should we take account of, question, describe what happens every day and recurs every day: the banal, the quotidian, the obvious, the common, the ordinary, the infra-ordinary, the background noise, the habitual?" My thanks to Daniel Kraus-Vollert for pointing me here.

84. Plin. *HN* 7.180–85.
85. Montaigne, *Essais* 1.19.
86. Horace's *horae momento* (*Sat.* 1.1.7–8).
87. Barthes 1984, 27.
88. Barthes 1984, 45.
89. Plut. *Mor.* 686c.
90. Adams 2021, 17–18: if Plato simply intended to draw attention to the order of speeches, "he could simply have written, 'Next, Eryximachus spoke out of turn.'" Cf. Guthrie 1975, 382n2.
91. Guthrie 1975, 382n2; Plochmann 1963, 10.
92. Adams 2021, 17.
93. Mahoney 2011, 151.
94. Lowenstam 1986, 54.
95. Phillips 1993, 10–11.
96. Foucault 1980, 168. At Pl. *Parm.* 130c, Socrates is reluctant to admit that even things as mean and worthless as mud, hair, and dirt deserve to have an abstract form (*idea*); to do so would, he says, plunge him into a "pit of absurdity." Thanks to Gabriel Bartlett for reminding me of this.
97. Cf. Hunter 2004, 114: "The subject of the *Symposium*, erotic desire, is central to the historical nostalgia which the work has at various times generated."
98. Gallagher and Greenblatt 2001, 53 ("The Touch of the Real").
99. Holmes 2016, 276.
100. See above n. 29.
101. *Aen.* 8.543 *paruos ... penatis*; 9.258 *per magnos ... penatis*; at *Aen.* 3.12, it is unclear whether *penatibus* are being contrasted with or assimilated to *magnis dis*. See Flower 2017, 37: adjectives used of the *lares* include *maximus*, along with *paulus, paruus, paruulus, pauper, exiguus, humilis, gracilis, modicus*, and *tenuis*.
102. Dion. Hal. *Ant. Rom.* 1.69.
103. Cic. *Leg.* 2.42. Cf. Cic. *Dom.* 144; Plut. *Cic.* 31.6.
104. Cic. *Nat. D.* 2.17.
105. Stat. *Silv.* 2.4.11–15; Plin. *HN* 11.16.
106. Bodel 2008, 255.
107. See Bodel 2008, 273–74nn44 and 45 on the contents of emperors' *cubicula* and *lararia*.
108. Robinson 1924.
109. Popkin 2022, 26–27; cf. *Acts of the Apostles* 19:23–27.
110. Pers. 2.69–70; Lact. *Div. Inst.* 2.4.12; ps-Acro *ad* Hor. *Sat.* 1.5.65–66; Ov. *Fast.* 4.133–34.
111. Bettini 1999, 227.
112. Dolansky 2008.
113. Suet. *Aug.* 6.
114. Sen. *Ep.* 86.5.
115. Cic. *Leg.* 2.3.
116. Plut. *Cato Maior* 2.
117. Flor. *Epit.* 1 *praef.* 4–8. A scheme probably derived from the elder Seneca. See Lact. *Inst. Div.* 7.15.4; Facchini Tosi 1990, 29–40.

118. Hudson 2019, 57.

119. Hughes 2018, 63. Susan Stewart (1993, 68) connects the love of miniature things with nostalgia for pre-industrial times.

120. Padilla Peralta 2020, 33.

121. *Fin.* 5.1.2 *quae minor mihi esse uidetur, posteaquam est maior.*

122. Plut. *Ant.* 23.3 *mikron men, sapron de.*

123. Col. *Rust.* 10 *praef.* 4.

## 2. SALLUST'S SALIENT SNAILS

1. See Cranga and Cranga 1991, 1997 on snails as marginal figures in art.

2. Arasse 2013, 19–37.

3. Ettlinger 1978.

4. Arasse 2013, 37.

5. Arasse 2013, 30.

6. Simons 2015, 315–16.

7. Levene 1992.

8. Batstone 2010a, xxvii.

9. Batstone 1988; Batstone 2010b.

10. *Cat.* 3.3–4.2.

11. Gunderson 2000, 112.

12. *Iug.* 6.3.

13. E.g., *Iug.* 38.

14. Brescia 1997.

15. Frontin. *Str.* 3.9.3 (many of these attacks are successfully disguised by distractions like rain, barking dogs, and trumpets).

16. Flor. *Epit.* 1.16.

17. Syme 1964, 150.

18. Batstone 2010b, 36. See Feldherr 2021, 213–67 on Sallust as *brevitatis artifex*. In his manual of British land and freshwater snails, William Turton (Turton 1831, 49) praises Sallust's "elegance of circumstantiality."

19. *Iug.* 19.2 "For concerning Carthage I prefer to remain silent rather than say even a little." For other silences, see 95.4 (Sulla) and 4.9 (contemporary Roman mores).

20. Hor. *Ep.* 2.1.250–54.

21. Arasse 2013, 37.

22. Koestermann 1971, ad loc.

23. Hdt. 1.84.1–5; Brescia 1997, 31.

24. Avery 1967.

25. Philaeni: *Iug.* 79.4–10; Thala: *Iug.* 76.2–6. On the afterlife of the Philaeni in modern Libya, see Agbamu 2019.

26. Kraus 1999, 241. Cf. Feeney 2007, 161 on the disingenuous *forte* (by chance) at Virg. *Aen.* 8.102.

27. *Iug.* 94.7 *forte correcta Mari temeritas.*

28. *Iug.* 41.5.

29. See Feldherr 2021, 70–101 on the Ligurian as proto-Marian *dux*; Brescia 1997, 74: "guida alpina."

30. Cic. *Leg.* 1.1–3, with Dolganov 2008; *Div.* 1.106.
31. Hdt. 1.4.
32. Avery 1967, 327.
33. *Cat.* 1.1 *prona atque uentri oboedentia*; Pl. *Rep.* 586a.
34. Green 1993. Kraus (1999, 236) calls nomadism "the distinguishing feature of the African ethnography."
35. Physical mobility is matched by political fickleness: *Iug.* 56.5 *tanta mobilitate sese Numidae gerunt.*
36. *Iug.* 7.6, 48.1, 67.3, 85.3, 89.3, 89.5; knitted with the *asperitas* of the region (*Iug.* 17.2, 37.2, 50.6, 75.2, 89.4, 92.4, 94.2), its inhabitants (*Iug.* 18.1), and its king (*Iug.* 29.1); See also Scanlon 1988.
37. Feldherr (2021, 191) reads the sandstorm at *Iug.* 79.6 as "a cause and a symbol of the limits of historical vision." Jugurtha's agile movements and inaccessibility add to the disordered feeling of the narrative. See Kraus 1999.
38. Plin. *HN* 9.82.173.
39. Lubell 2004, 78, 88.
40. *Iug.* 17.5 *arbori infecundus*; 79.6 *nuda gignentium.*
41. As it does for the Bandusine ilex at Hor. *Carm.* 3.13.14–15.
42. *Iug.* 18.2; 44.5. See Koestermann, ad loc.; Wiedemann 1993, 54.
43. Tac. *Germ.* 89.7; Sall. *Iug.* 85.39.
44. *Bellum Africum* 8.3.1.
45. Ngai 2012, 93.
46. See Yarrow 2018. Her fig. 13 shows RRC 426/1, a coin with King Bocchus holding out an olive branch while supplicating to Sulla and presenting the captured Jugurtha. The tradition continues on contemporary labels for South African Zalze wine: "Rooted firmly on a hillside, this majestic tree guards the valley where wine has been made for centuries."
47. Virg. *Aen.* 1.701; Cato, *Orig.* fr. 34 Cornell. Virg. *Aen.* 10.185–97 is more positive about Ligurian bravery.
48. E.g., *Rep.* 2.359c.
49. Sen. *Thy.* 889–90.
50. See Pacini 2014 on the significance of trees in the novel. Calvino was a vigorous spokesman for Ligurian regional identity, describing the terrain as "magra e ossuta" (thin and bony).
51. Calvino 2021, 13. In particular, "the pleasure of overcoming difficult protuberances and forks, and getting as high as possible [il piacere di superare difficili bugne del tronco e inforcature, e arrivare più in alto che si poteva]" feels like a reminiscence of Sallust's *cupido difficilia faciundi* ("desire to do difficult things", *Iug.* 93.3).
52. Calvino 2021, 288.
53. Feldherr 2021, 200–201.
54. As quoted in Theoph. *De Caus. Plant.* 2.11.7–8; cited by Zatta 2016, 116. Ahmed (2006) connects queerness with orientation—sexual and otherwise.
55. Reynolds in his Oxford Classical Text prefers *animum inuadit* to *animum alio uortit.*
56. *Iug.* 104.2.
57. Letter to Robert Bridges, February 15, 1915 (Abbott 1935, 66). Ovid (*AA* 2.649) uses *coalescere* in a grafting image for the birth of the hermaphrodite; Sallust uses it of the

unlikely union of diverse peoples in the newly formed Roman polity (*Cat.* 6.2) and of the speedy assimilation of raw recruits and hardened soldiers (*Iug.* 87.3).

58. *Silv.* 2.3.2–4, 77; Hardie 2006.

59. *Carm.* 1.12.45–46 *crescit occulto uelut arbor aeuo | fama Marcelli*; Giusti 2022, 98 observes "ramifications that lie well beyond the poet's control."

60. Ahlgren et al., 2015.

61. Polyb. 12.13. Rehm 1937 suggests a cart concealing a treadmill, to move it at a slow pace.

62. *Poen.* 264.

63. Stewart 1993, 65–67. In *The Sound of a Wild Snail Eating*, a memoir of slow convalescence in the company of a snail, Elizabeth Tova Bailey recalls writing to her doctor: "Watching another creature go about its life . . . somehow gave me, the watcher, purpose too. If life mattered to the snail and the snail mattered to me, it meant something in my life mattered, so I kept on . . . Snails may seem like tiny, even insignificant things compared to the wars going on around the world or a million other human problems, but they may well outlive our own species" (Bailey 2010, 154).

64. It used to be thought, wrongly, that the spirals on a snail's shell revealed its age, like the rings of a tree.

65. Feldherr 2021, 196; cf. ibid., 210: "pointillist."

66. Brecher 1937, 205 quotes Von Baer: "Die Zeit, die wir brauchen, um uns seines Eindruckes auf unsere Sinnesorgane bewusst zu werden" (the time that we need in order to make known its impression on our sensory organs).

67. Brecher 1937. On Brecher and the idea of "the moment," see Fischer 1965.

68. Kubler 1967, 850.

69. Scott 2008.

70. Cited by Feldherr (2021, 202); Riggsby 2009. See Feldherr 2021, 197 on "the divergent ways in which Sallust uses spatial descriptions to convey time."

71. Batstone 2010a, 102 (with "bitter" changed to "great").

72. Cf. Feldherr 2021, 210. In antiquity, desert was conceived as the inverse of civilized, temperate, and habitable space. See Ségalas 2015, 237–39.

73. Plin. *HN* 7.32 *in Africae solitudinibus hominum species obuiae subinde fiunt momentoque euanescunt.*

74. Feldherr 2021, 184–97. Ségalas (2015, 231n2) points to two meanings of *uastus*, "immense" and "desolate": desert as enormous not-space. Catiline's mind is famously compared to desert, no-man-fathomed, at *Cat.* 5.5: *uastus animus inmoderata, incredibilia, nimis alta semper cupiebat*; see Krebs 2008.

75. As Anna Uhlig has pointed out to me.

76. The disingenuously quotidian features of this scene are not lost on Quintilian: "Cicero achieved this effect not just by including the details but also by his everyday and common language and well-concealed art" (4.2.57–59).

77. Koselleck 2000.

78. Grethlein 2014, 324; See Koselleck 2000, introduction.

79. General Erhard Raus coined the term "snail offensive" to describe the Sixth Panzer division's improvised but dogged pushback of Soviet forces in the winter of 1942 (through a combination of careful preparation and surprise attacks from the rear and at night). An Allied Forces propaganda poster of 1944 shows a snail bearing the Allies' flags

slowly advancing up Italy to liberate Rome; it is claimed that a snail moving at 0.8 m per minute could have advanced 320 km (actually 220 km) by April 1, whereas the Allies had only advanced 180 km. See Victoria and Albert Museum, "It's a Long Way to Rome," accessed June 30, 2024, https://collections.vam.ac.uk/item/O118146/its-a-long-way-to-poster-unknown/.

80. There may have been other soldiers, too. Frontin. (*Str.* 3.9.3) records "a few choice centurions", along with fast-moving foot-soldiers and brass-players.

81. Hor. *Sat.* 2.4.59; Sall. *Iug.* 107.1 *nudum et caecum corpus*; 88.4 *ita Iugurtham aut praesidiis nudatum iri*; 79.6 *loca nuda gignentium*. Cf. Shakespeare, *King Lear* (1.5.24–6): Fool: "I can tell why a snail has a house." Lear: "Why?" Fool: "Why to put's head in; not to give it away to his daughters, and leave his horns without a case." As "poor Tom," Edgar will play houseless snail by emerging naked from his hovel.

82. Cf. Shakespeare, *As You Like It* (4.1.57): the snail "brings his destiny with him." Bachelard (1994, 105–35) discusses snail shells and their fascination for architects, dreamers, and lovers of solitude.

83. *Iug.* 18.5–8.

84. Hes. *Op.* 571; Hdt. 4.46.3: Scythian nomads carry their dwellings on wagons.

85. Philemon fr. 104. Cf. Symphosius, *Anth. Lat.* 286.18. Cicero quotes an obscure kenning (*Div.* 2.64.133): *terrigenam, herbigradam, domiportam, sanguine cassam* ("earth-born, grass-creeping, house-carrying, bloodless thing"), followed by another riddle whose answer is *testudo*, tortoise.

86. *Iug.* 94.3. Bachelard (1994, 129) contrasts Bernard Palissy's vision of a snail-shaped fortress with more practical nature-inspired devices: "when military men build 'hedgehog' defenses, they know that they are not in the domain of the image, but in that of simple metaphor." In Latin, *aries* (battering ram), *uinea* (movable arbour or shelter), and even *cochlea* (snail = screw) were all strategic tools.

87. Plut. *Ant.* 45. Cf. Isidore 12.6.5: the *testudo* is so called because it is protected by a roof (*tegmine testae*), like a vaulted chamber; Dio Cass. 49.30.

88. Plin. *HN* 9.12.38; cf. *HN* 6.28.109.

89. Cranga and Cranga 1997, 73n9.

90. Plin. *HN* 11.45.125; cf. 11.52.140.

91. See Feldherr 2021, 230–31 on *carptim*.

92. Gunderson 2000, 99.

93. Kubler 1967, 849.

94. *Iug.* 4.3.

95. Baraz 2012, 35.

96. E.g., *Iug.* 30.3 (Memmius) *inter dubitationem et moras*; 45.1 (Metellus) *inter ambitionem saeuitiamque*; 101.10 (Jugurtha) *inter tela hostium*.

97. On a visit to Roman Volubilis in Morocco in December 2022, I noticed a fallen column base depicting a palm tree together with three spiral shapes (fig. 18). The ground nearby was strewn with empty snail shells.

## 3. BRIEF LIVES: THE CASE OF CRISPUS

1. Lec 1962, 110.

2. Carter 2019; Stephen 1956, 131–32.

3. On "little lives," see Johnston 2003. The genre was revived by Leslie Stephen's daughter Virginia Woolf in her novella about the Brownings' spaniel, *Flush* (1933).

4. Laite 2020.

5. Hitchcock 2014.

6. Ginzburg 1980, xxvi: "a dispersed fragment, reaching us by chance, of an obscure and shadowy world."

7. Andrade 2010, 575; cited by Laite 2020, 965.

8. Laite (2020, 965) counters this with Ghobrial 2014, 58–59: "In our rush to populate global history with human faces . . . we risk finding ourselves in a world populated by faceless globetrotters, colourless chameleons and invisible boundary crossers, individuals stretched so far out of any local, confessional or personal context as to make them little more than panes of glass through which to view the worlds in which they lived."

9. Andrade 2010, 591.

10. Mouritsen (2011, 290) identifies conformity and integration as features of freedman inscriptions.

11. Henderson 1998.

12. Plaut. *Pseud.* 767–89; 783. This common closural formula to mark the entry of other characters (also voiced by the super-confident Pseudolus at *Pseud.* 409) is in this instance no less a badge of silencing, a breach in the play's illusion of an all-powerful slave hero. Richlin (2017, 229–31) registers "the ugly truth" of the passage.

13. Aldine text, 510.

14. Butler 1998, 250.

15. Butler 1998, 252.

16. John Aubrey *F*39, f.340 (writing to Anthony Wood); quoted Bennett 2015, vol 1, xci.

17. Bennett 2015, 1.365.

18. The ultimate example of a compressed but productive life is that of the medieval infant Saint Rumwold, who lived for only three days, during which he managed to profess his faith, get baptized, and preach a precocious sermon (R. Love 1996; thanks to Rebecca Laemmle for introducing me to this text).

19. For sparkling parody of the unremarkable life, see Stephen Leacock's short "biography," "The Life of John Smith" (Leacock 1911; thanks to Julia Griffin for pointing me here). It ends: "At sixty-five Smith was taken ill, and, receiving proper treatment, he died. There was a tombstone put up over him, with a hand pointing north-north-east. But I doubt if he ever got there. He was too like us."

20. Dryden (1683–86) 1971, 274; Bennett 2015.

21. Bodleian MS Aubrey 9, fol. 29r ( = Aubrey, "Hobbes," 1.18).

22. Bodleian Library, MS Aubrey 7, fol. 3, cited by Bennett, "John Aubrey's Brief Lives and Life-Writing," Oxford Handbooks Online, accessed June 30, 2024, https://www.oxfordhandbooks.com/view/10.1093/oxfordhb/9780199935338.001.0001/oxfordhb-9780199935338-e-14?.

23. K. Stewart 2006, 41.

24. Kaster 1995, xxiii.

25. Quintilian (*Inst.* 10.1.23) also includes him in a list of distinguished orators. Piso's life, too, survives in a Juvenalian scholion (5.109). See Jones 1986.

26. Juv. 4.81.

27. Appended to his edition of Juvenal (1486). Vibius Crispus Placentinus is described as a skilled courtier (*et manu promptus et lingua*), who lost many children and was poisoned by his attractive wife (unnamed). Nor does Jerome name Agrippina as the perpetrator (*Chron. Euseb. Ol.* 1.204.2, 260; Fotheringham: *Passienus filius fraude heredis suae necatur*).

28. Cf. Suet. *Nero* 6.3: "In fact, when Claudius took power, not only did he inherit his father's wealth, but he was enriched by a legacy from his stepson Crispus Passienus."

29. La Penna 1976.

30. Sen. *Ben.* 6.32.4.

31. Diog. Laert. 17.135.

32. Thanks to Carole Newlands for the reminder.

33. Suetonius' analysis sounds like the quickfire version of Tacitus' twin accounts of staying afloat via evasion and dissimulation: first at the start of the *Histories*, about how he survived a series of regimes by being tactful, and then at the start of the *Annals*, about how to negotiate writing history by avoiding passion and bias.

34. Fineman 1989, 56.

35. Gallagher and Greenblatt 2000, 49.

36. Fineman 1989, 56: "The anecdote ... as the narration of a singular event, is the literary form or genre that uniquely refers to the real."

37. Dryden, "Life of Plutarch" (Dryden 1971, 275).

38. Deutsch 2009.

39. Quoted by Fadiman 1985, xix.

40. Barthes 1964, 189.

41. He continues: "The anecdote produces the effect of the real, the occurrence of contingency, by establishing an event within and yet without the framing context of historical successivity."

42. Gallagher and Greenblatt 2000, 57, quoting Israel D'Israeli. They offer (49–74) a genial riposte to Fineman 1989 (whose playful essay challenged New Historicism's creed of "touching the real", his subtitle "Fiction and Fiction" alluding to Greenblatt's earlier essay "Fiction and Friction"). In their view, not only do anecdotes—the stranger the better—disrupt historical narrative, but the fissures they produce in its conventional barriers reveal exhilarating "counterhistories" in the process (51–52).

43. Plass 1988, 13.

44. Cf. Rigney 2001, 108: subjects "can only incidentally be revealed, in a negative way, by anecdotes or faits divers in which the normally hidden routine is for some reason disrupted and hence recorded. The 'glimpse' becomes a methodological principle."

45. Plass 1988, 123.

46. Tac. *Hist.* 1.45.2.

47. Plass 1988, 13.

48. Van de Hout 1999, 30; Dickey 2007, 284.

49. Ferri 2008 deduces that Crispus's faux pas was to reverse the expected order of emperor and senate (citing Tac. *Ann.* 6.8 *idem finis et te, Caesar, et nos absoluerit* and 16.31 *tu, Caesar, et uos, patres conscripti*).

50. Compare the laconic formula with which Tacitus launches *Hist.* 1.1, a record of imperialism masquerading as republicanism: *Initium mihi operis Seruius Galba iterum*

*Titus Vinius consules erunt* (I begin my work with the consulships of Servius Galba [i.e., the emperor], for the second time, and Titus Vinius).

51. Power 2021.

52. Power 2021: 72–73. In a review of Power, David Woods suggests an alternative interlocutor for Crispus: Nero's similarly named father, Gn. Domitius Ahenobarbus, who had been charged by Tiberius with treason and other crimes, including incest with his own sister (Suet. *Nero* 5.2). The question was thus "simply an ironical way of asking whether he had been charged with treason yet. The conversation was not really about incest at all" (Woods 2022, 63). He notes that in any case Nero's own subsequent marriage to his stepsister/adopted sister Octavia is more pertinent than incest with his mother (62–63).

53. Power (2021, 73), who notes another similarity (at 74–77): just as it is moot whether Crispus ever committed incest with the "sister" he and an emperor shared, so the jury is out over whether Nero himself ever slept with Agrippina. According to salacious historian Cluvius Rufus, Agrippina's attempts to seduce Nero were sidelined by a prostitute lookalike, who sometimes stood in for her as his love-interest (Suet. *Nero* 28). The point in any Neronian scenario may be that Crispus also slept with only a distant, affinal version of a "sister", whereas in a Gaian scenario he had "sisters" aplenty but never made it to committing incest with them.

54. Freud 2002, 155.

55. Freud 2002, 172.

56. Murdoch 1999, 182. This is discussed by Beard (2015, 131, 214). Earlier versions of the joke are found at Val. Max. 9.14.3; Macrob *Sat.* 2.4.19–20.

57. Max Beerbohm makes himself just such a fly on the wall in his essay, "A Clergyman" (Beerbohm 1921); thanks to William Fitzgerald and Julia Griffin for directing me here. Beerbohm imagines the fateful aftermath to which Boswell is oblivious in his brusque account of a young cleric whose timid query about Dodd's sermons was crushed by Samuel Johnson: "Nothing is told of him but that once, abruptly, he asked a question, and received an answer."

58. Thanks to Sarah Morris for this example. As the classically inflected names suggest, Christopher Nolan was influenced by the magic squares of Pompeii.

59. Juv. 4.90–1; Sen. *De ira* 2.33.2.

60. Bettini 1991: 10–11; Gowers 2011.

61. Hunt 2016: 91; cf. Beagon 1996: 302.

62. Macrob. *Sat.* 3.13.3.

63. Probus's life of (Vibius) Crispus does mention several deceased children; see n. 27 above.

64. Suet. *Aug.* 43; Dio Cass. 63.29.3. Cf. Dio Cass. 48.52.3–4; Suet. *Galba* 1; Suet. *Aug.* 43.1; Pliny, *HN* 15.136–37. On the grove, see Flory 1989, 345.

65. I owe this insight to Juliet Mitchell.

66. Ov. *Am.* 1.5.3; 1.8.22; 1.6.3–4.

67. On the autonomy of doors, see Latour 1992.

68. Isid. *Etym.* 9.7.18. Cf. 9.7.12: brides "avoid stepping on the thresholds [of their new houses], because at that place the doors both come together and separate."

69. Diog. Laert. 17.135.

70. Onians (1988, 332–33) traces *necessitudo* qua relationship back to Sanskrit words for *bond*. See ibid. n. 9: "there is no obvious relation between compulsion or necessity and

kinship, but . . . both have a natural point of contact in binding which implies not only constraint but also union and proximity. Thus we say, 'It is bound to happen.'"

71. Quint. *Inst.* 6.3.74.

72. Hdt. 1.119 (Harpagus); Sen. *De ira* 3.15 (a situation Seneca likens to servitude for the modern courtier, from which suicide is the only honorable escape: *ostendemus in omni seruitute apertam libertati uiam*); cf. ibid. 2.33.3–4 (Gaius and Pastor).

73. Lipps 1898, 90.

74. Fischer 1899, 51.

75. Suet. *Gaius* 30; *Tib.* 59. On the republican and imperial political afterlife of the phrase, see Leigh 1996.

76. Freud 2002, 155.

77. Sen. *Ben.* 3.27.9.

78. On *Nondum*, the opening word of Calpurnius Siculus's *Eclogues*, in relation to imperial decline, see Gowers 1994.

79. Foucault 2000, 162. Discussed by Gallagher and Greenblatt (2000, 66–70) as an expression of Foucault's "counterhistorical ardor" (66), the collection is introduced by its author as "Brief lives, chanced upon in books and documents . . . Singular lives, those which have become, through I know not what accidents, strange poems: that is what I wanted to gather together into a sort of herbarium."

80. Didi-Huberman 1989, 140.

81. After excusing himself from one of Vitellius's marathon feasts, Vibius Crispus made a "very witty remark": "If I hadn't been taken ill, I would surely have perished" (Dio Cass. 64.2.3). Tacitus (*Hist.* 4.43) records Vibius smiling (*renidens*) while he and another *delator*, Marcellus, were being attacked in the Senate by Curtius Montanus and Helvidius Priscus. Quintilian (*Inst.* 10.1.119) calls him *delectationi natus* ("born to charm"). Cf. other witticisms at Quint. *Inst.* 8.5.15; 8.5.17. Tacitus makes an aphorism out of Vibius himself, in the context of his petty and hypocritical vendetta against informers: "In money, status and talent Vibius Crispus ranked more among the notable (*claros*) than among the noble (*bonos*)" (*Hist.* 2.10.1). See also Plass 1988, 53.

82. Deleuze (1995, 108) writes of Foucault's essay: "The infamous man's a particle caught in a shaft of light and a wave of sound." Cf. Tac. *Dial.* 20.4 on the brief "flash" of an epigram: *sensus aliquis arguta et breui sententia effulsit*.

## 4. TINY IRRITANTS: ITCHING EYES, STONES IN SHOES, AND OTHER ANNOYANCES

1. Mack 2007, 163.
2. Theoc. *Id.* 4.55.
3. Sen. *QNat.* 6.2.5.
4. *Ep.* 53.6.
5. *Ep.* 24.14.
6. J. Buchan 1929, 19–20, cited by Gossman 2003, 161. Recent studies of the emotions in antiquity include Kaster 2005; Braund and Gill 1997; Cairns and Nelis 2016; Chaniotis 2012. On *fastidium*, see Kaster 2001; Lateiner and Spatharas 2017.
7. Hor. *Sat.* 1.5.7–9, 14–15; Sidon. *Ep.* 8.11.42–44.

8. Rhick Samadder, "Got the Ick? When a Sudden Pang of Disgust Ruins Your Romance," *Guardian*, July 31, 2022, https://www.theguardian.com/lifeandstyle/2022/jul/31/got-the-ick-when-a-pang-of-disgust-ruins-your-romance.

9. There are similar, if more hopeful, conclusions in H. Love 2016.

10. Kaster 2001.

11. Chaucer, The Merchant's Tale, *The Canterbury Tales*, line 1553: "I woot best where wryngeth me my sho"; Trollope, *The Warden*, ch. 13: Mr Harding to his daughter: "There is an old saying, Nelly: 'Everyone knows where his own shoe pinches!'"; see also chapters 16 and 17; Watt 2016. See Dewey 2016, 153–4: "The man who wears the shoe knows best that it pinches and where it pinches, even if the expert shoemaker is the best judge of how the trouble is to be remedied." Compare Hor. *Ep.* 1.10.42–3, and an unplaceable aphorism attributed to John Locke: "Our incomes are like our shoes; if too small, they gall and pinch us; but if too large, they cause us to stumble and to trip."

12. At Cic. *De or.* 1.54.231, Antonius quotes Socrates comparing Lysias's oratory to a pair of Sicyonian shoes—too womanish, even if comfortable and well-fitting.

13. Pl. *Poen.* 34–35. See above p. 45 on the scene in Cicero's *Pro Milone* where Milo, after changing his shoes, is irked, as men always are, by his wife's slow preparations.

14. The Routledge series *Senses in Antiquity* leads the way: Butler and Purves 2013 (synesthesia); Bradley 2014 (smell); Squire 2015 (sight); Purves 2017 (touch); Rudolph 2017 (taste); Butler and Nooter 2018 (sound). See also Toner 2014; Betts 2017.

15. See Rimell 2015, 163–78 for a virtuoso reading of the "auditory hissings" (167) of this "letter-as-bathhouse-as-noise" (168).

16. *Ep.* 56.5.

17. Gurd 2016, 18. Massumi 2005, 85.

18. Ngai 2005, 184.

19. Ngai 2005, 184 further notes: "Conversely, one of the synonyms for 'irritation' qua 'mild anger'—namely, 'aggravation'—carries the implication of worsening or worrying a wound or sore, with 'sore' itself signifying both a condition of the skin or body (an ulcer, abrasion, or inflammation) and, in twentieth-century slang, a state of indignation or resentment."

20. Ngai 2005, 184.

21. Hoffer 2007.

22. Leeman, Pinkster and Nelson 1985, 202–3 and 207–8; Becker 1938, 18.

23. Hall 2008, 14–15. I use his translation here.

24. Virg. *Aen.* 1.33.

25. The first word of *De oratore*, *Cogitanti* ([to me] thinking), sets the contemplative tone.

26. Cic. *De or.* 2.29.

27. See Hall 2008, 14–15 and 15n67: "One of Cicero's aims in this scene is to present a model of sophisticated manners." See Leeman, Pinkster and Nelson 1985, 202–203 and 207–208. Kaster 2001, 13–27 is an excellent discussion of *uerecundia*, restraint, or rather the ingrained inhibition against producing *molestia* in others ("not dread or gut-wrenching anxiety" but "a mild and strategic fear"). On not giving offense, see also Cic. *Off.* 1.99; Barrios-Lech 2016, 276–79 (in Roman comedy).

28. Ngai 2005, 184.

29. Beard 2015, 107.
30. *De or.* 2.247.
31. Corbeill 1996, 90.
32. *De or.* 2.244. The word *acumen* is used of a mosquito's sting at *Culex* 184.
33. *De or.* 2.244. Also deplored is the courtroom joke on brevity (rhetorical and physical) which follows at 2.245: "A tiny witness [*pusillus testis*] came forward. 'May I question him?' asked Philippus. The presiding judge, who was in a hurry, said: 'Yes, only if you are short [*modo breuiter*]'. 'No problem,' replied Philippus, 'for I will be just as short as that man there.' This was quite funny. But the presiding judge was L. Aurifex, who was even shorter than the witness; so the humor was directed against him; it all became a joke in poor taste [*uisum est totum scurrile ridiculum*]." On the social and cultural associations of *praecones*, see Lowe 2018.
34. In Cicero's *Brutus*, Granio is commended for blowing a rival out of the water with his unique brand of robust Roman humor (172: *nescio quo sapore uernaculo*).
35. *De or.* 2.243–44.
36. *De or.* 2.259.
37. Beard 2015, 112.
38. Macrob. *Sat.* 2.1.12; Kish 2021.
39. *De or.* 2.18.
40. Beard 2015, 110. At *De or.* 2.217, the Athenians are singled out for their silly theories of humor: "those who have attempted to deliver rules and principles on that topic have shown themselves so silly [*insulsi*] that there ends up being nothing to laugh at but their silliness [*insulsitas*]." Antonius has in fact sent up the whole project of *De oratore* as silly in itself: "For what is sillier [*ineptius*] than talking about talking when talking is always silly [*ineptum*], except when it is necessary?" (*De or.* 1.112).
41. Cf. Dutsch 2008, 195.
42. Theophr. *Char.* 22.12; 7.7; 19.4; 25.5.
43. Ar. *Plut.* 537–39; Loeb, trans. Henderson.
44. Conti Bizzarro 2009.
45. Aesch. *Ag.* 887–94. See also Freud 2002, 456: "But when we sleep, and the unconscious wish has shown its power to form a dream, and with it to awaken the foreconscious, why, then, does this power become exhausted after the dream has been taken cognisance of? Would it not seem more probable that the dream should continually renew itself, like the troublesome fly which, when driven away, takes pleasure in returning again and again?" On Freud's and other psychic flies, see Knapp 2021, 28.
46. Apologies for the lexical inadequacy of Latin in relation to Greek were by now familiar: e.g., Lucr. *DRN* 1.830–33; and in this very poem, *Sat.* 1.10.20–35. Lucretius's apology (*DRN* 1.830–32) is incidentally followed by his grassroots explanation of Anaxagorean *homoeomeria*, where "mini"-words are used to explain false analogies between atoms and whole organisms: 835 *e pauxillis atque minutis*, 836 *de pauxillis atque minutis*.
47. Hor. *Sat.* 1.10.78–80.
48. See the penetrating readings of Fitzgerald 1995, 169–79 and McCarthy 2013.
49. E.g., McCarthy 2013, 66: "*unambiguously aggressive* sexual slur" (emphasis mine).
50. Fitzgerald 1995, 177. I discuss another aspect of the poem in chapter 5.
51. *Sat.* 1.9.9–12.

52. See Henderson 1999, 224–25 on the exquisite choreography of these encounters.

53. Gowers 2003, 86: "Aristius Fuscus is a portrait of the ideal satirist for the new regime: smooth, humble, and above all elusive.... The friend's satirical performance is Horace's *esprit d'escalier*, his memo to himself to do better next time."

54. Gunderson 2000b, 196.

55. Luc. *Icarom.* 12: "Just now you were searching for the Earth, it was so diminished by distance, and if the Colossus had not betrayed it, you would have taken it for something else; and now you develop suddenly into a Lynceus, and distinguish everything upon it, the men, the beasts, one might almost say the gnat-swarms." Compare the lofty maneuver of Emperor Tiberius when he uses the parable of a man tolerating the flies that buzz around him to justify his own strategy of keeping in place corrupt but reassuringly familiar provincial governors (Joseph. *AJ* 18.6).

56. Dawidowicz (1990, 60) quotes Paul Lagarde: "With trichinae and bacilli one does not negotiate, nor are trichinae and bacilli to be educated; they are exterminated as quickly and thoroughly as possible."

57. Slave as hand: Reay 2003, Blake 2012; Fitzgerald 2021. Cf. Robbins 1993 on English fictional servants.

58. Plaut. *Persa* 1012.

59. Plaut. *Bacch.* 913–15.

60. Norgard 2015, 44.

61. I have often been indebted here to D. R. Shackleton Bailey's Cambridge edition of the Letters (1965–71) and his Loeb translation (1999) but have kept the conventional numbering of the Letters.

62. Martelli 2016. Cf. Gunderson 2007, 14 on *Fam.* 14.2.2, *tantis tuis miseriis meae miseriae subleuentur*: "We can say that Terentia displaces and replaces Cicero's misery."

63. See Cappello 2016, 481 on "the specular gaze as a key characteristic of the relation" constructed by Cicero.

64. E.g. *Att.* 10.14.1; 8.14.1 *torqueor*; 8.14.2 *pestiferum*; 8.15.2 *cruciari*; 8.15a.1 *me ... conscindi*. 9.1.1 *angebar*; 9.6.4 *angebar*; 9.6.5 *dolorem*, 9.5.7 *dolorem*; 10.15.2 *torqueor*.

65. E.g. *Att.* 7.11.2: "even in these grim times, I enjoy giving lectures with you as my audience" (*libenter enim in his molestiis ἐνσχολάζω σοι* [enscholazo soi]; Cappello 2016, 485n33. Cf. *incommoda* (inconveniences), at *Att.* 9.19.2, 10.2.2.

66. According to Fortson (2008, 55), *lippus* is connected more with liquid than lipid (from the Indo-European root *uleik "liquid, flowing") and with water rather than mucus.

67. Gunderson 2007, 1. Cf. also 9.

68. *Att.* 7.13a.3: "If I had written it myself, the letter would have been longer, but I dictated it because of my eye infection"; *Att.* 7.14.1 "since I had a mild eye infection." Cf. *QFr.* 2.2.1: "I was forced by a tiny eye irritation (*paruula lippitudine*) to dictate this letter".

69. Hoffer 2007, 95.

70. John Ma first introduced me to this useful concept. See Gowers 2002, 146 on Hor. *Sat.* 1.7 as an abscess (figured in the poem by a side-reference to *lippitudo*); ibid. 152 for a different medical model in Horace: "black eye ointment" (*Sat.* 1.5.30 *nigra collyria*) works as "homeopathic remedy" for a satirist's *lippitudo* (or blindness to political events).

71. *Att.* 9.17.2. Gunderson 2007, 7: "The banal, the commonplace, and the obvious conceal as much as they reveal."

72. *Att.* 8.14.1.

73. *Att.* 8.14.1; 9.4.1 *requiesco*; 9.6.5 *recreant*; 9.7.1 *restillarunt*; 10.1.1: Cicero "breathes a little more easily" on reading a letter from Atticus (*paulum lectis respiraui*). In *Att.* 9.4, he frames writing political philosophy for Atticus as displacement activity.

74. Cf. Martelli 2016, 419–20 on "no news" as an epistolary stimulus (e.g. *Att.* 12.42.1). The brevity of a letter and its frenzied composition have functioned as "signs" before, when Cicero guesses correctly that Atticus wrote to him in the middle of a fever (*Att.* 6.9), effectively staging a divination scene to diagnose the physical and mental state of his distant correspondent; Cappello 2016, 474.

75. Regulus: Cic. *Pis.* 43 (*resectis palpebris*); cf. Diod. 23.16; Val. Max. 9.2.ext.1; Gell. *NA* 7.4 (citing Tuditanus and Tubero). Perhaps imitating the opthalmic condition of trachoma? Cels. 6.6.27A: "Sometimes inflammation also occurs due to trachoma [*aspritudine*]. . . . In this type of condition, some people scrape the inflamed and rough eyelids with a fig leaf, a sharp probe, or sometimes with a scalpel; and every day they rub [*suffricant*] ointments on the inside of their eyelids." At *Fam.* 14.4 Cicero reports dismissing a faithful freedman on the grounds of an eye impairment.

76. Cf. Dixon 1984, 83: in the letters to Terentia, Cicero uses "the nagging tone of the powerless."

77. Haury 1955, 73: compounds in *per-* express "comical excess": e.g., *peracutus* (*Phil.* 3.21), *perlitteratus* (*Pro Gallio*, fr. 2 Klotz-Schoell), *perparuola* (*Verr.* 5.95), *perparuolum* (*Verr.* 5.96); *Fam.* 7.11.2 (to Trebatius) *perfer, permane, pertimesco, perferas, perlibenter, perdiscere*; *sub*-words are very rare in the speeches; e.g., *Pis.* 67 *subrancida*. See also Laurand 1940. In *Ad Atticum*, see, e.g., 1.5.4 *subodiosum*; 1.18.2 *permolesti*; 4.5.1 *subturpicula* (see below, chapter 5).

78. *Perfricare* (rub all over) appears in the speeches, always used of other people's excess or effrontery (e.g., Verres's or Piso's).

79. Cf. Martelli 2016, 420: "As ever, correspondence with Atticus will be Cicero's talking cure . . . to submit the confusion of his grief to the very processes of dialecticization that a good analysand knows to be an essential preliminary to overcoming a trauma."

80. *Att.* 12.18.1; cf. *Att.* 12.45.1 *nec haec quae refricant <non> hic me magis angunt* (a letter that also registers Atticus' mirroring dysphoria, *akedia*); *Att.* 5.15.3 *Appi uulnera non refrico*. At *Att.* 12.19.2, numbness to political machinations has returned: "I want you to realize that this news did not alarm me [*me neque . . . perturbatum*] and that no news will ever alarm me any more [*nec . . . perturbatum iri*]." This is also the case of Quintus's disloyalty. See *Att.* 11.22 (whether Quintus is harmed by or cleared of blame for his treatment of his men), "I'm not bothered" (*mihi molestum non est*); Claassen 1996, 222.

81. E.g., *Att.* 12.45.1.

82. See Martelli 2016, 421–22 on *Att.* 12.18.1 ("while I flee memories that cause pain like a kind of gnawing" [*dum recordationes fugio quae quasi morsu quodam dolorem efficient*]): "the adverb *quasi* . . . spells out the figurative nature of the metaphors through which Cicero describes his emotional pain."

83. See above n. 73 for *re-* prefixes that indicate the repetitive, quasi-remedial relief of Atticus's letters. At *Att.* 10.18.3, Cicero desists from writing more to avoid involving Atticus in his personal torment: *ne te quoque excruciem*.

84. *Tusc.* 4.37.81.

138   NOTES

85. E.g., in *Att.* 8.15, Atticus's letters have arrived late, all in a confusing bunch; at *Att.* 12.42.1, Cicero actively resists Atticus's suggestion of regular "letter-days" (which Shackleton Bailey notes would reduce the supply).

86. At *Att.* 6.1.2, a long medical simile captures the difference between Appius, former governor of Cilicia, who put the province on a reducing regime, and Cicero, who is fattening it up again. At *Att.* 12.21.5, Cicero is a robust patient (*fortis aegroti*), for whom philosophy ingested in solitude is medicine (*medicinam . . . remediis*).

87. *HN* 7.181. See chapter 1.

88. *HN* 2.6.24.

89. Cf. Suet. *Aug.* 92.

90. Dio Chrys. *Or.* 54.3.

91. *Att.* 7.14.3.

92. Cf. *Fin.* 4.80: a parting shot, a challenge to another debate: *scrupulum, inquam, abeunti; sed uidebimus*; *Clu.* 28: a doubt or scruple; cf. *De Ag.* 3.2.

93. For Cicero's influence on later ideals of intimacy between friends, see Eden 2012.

94. Henderson 2016, 440: "This marvelously absent but never distant 'soul brother' was wound into the family as securely as affinal relations could contrive, but even his sister's marriage to Quintus could never make a brother-in-law a *Cicero*." Cf. Henderson 2007.

95. *Att.* 1.17.10; 15.27.3; 14.1.2.

96. *Att.* 2.4.1: "But since I have mentioned money, do please get things settled with Titinius any way you can. If he doesn't keep his word, the best thing in my opinion is to return the bad bargain, if Pomponia can be brought to agree. If even that won't do, better pay the money than have any awkwardness [*scrupulus*]." (Loeb, trans. Shackleton Bailey).

97. Henderson 2016.

98. *Att.* 1.5.2; *Att.* 1.6.2.

99. As David Friedman reminds me.

100. Plut. *Cat. Min.* 24: "She was the wife of Lucullus, a man of the highest repute in Rome, and had borne him a child, and yet she was banished from his house for unchastity". See also Plut. *Luc.* 38: "In all other respects, Servilia was as vile and abandoned [as Clodia, his first wife], and yet Lucullus forced himself to tolerate her, out of regard for Cato. At last, however, he put her away."

101. See the minute analysis of the marriage from the letters by Claassen 1996, e.g., 212: "In the often mentioned *Att.* 5.1.3–4, May 50, Cicero details one such scene of marital strife, in terms which suggest that he was unused to similar wrangling within his own household." Cf. Hallett 1984, 230, and Richlin 2013 for an imaginative reconstruction of the "fragments" of Terentia's replies (*Fam.* 14), positing a woman "at the home front" far more politically active than her husband. Cf. Gunderson 2007, 7: "In Terentia we find a too-healthy wife and her effeminizing effect on Cicero."

102. Gunderson (2007, 8n33) critiques Claassen 1996 (222–23) for seeing "the painful relationship with Quintus as the unexpressed root of the troubles with Terentia. This is an interesting solution to the problem of Terentia letters: look *hors du texte*." By contrast, he sees the "drone" of routine "Be well" salutations in increasingly content-free letters as covert clues to the end of the marriage (ibid. 45).

103. *Fam.* 14.20.

104. *Att.* 5.13.33.

105. Suet. *Aug.* 65.4.

106. Sen. *Brev. Vit.* 5.1–2 singles Cicero out for eloquently vocalizing his feelings of stress in a letter to Atticus (now unknown): "How tearful his expression in a letter to Atticus, when Pompey the elder had been conquered, and his son was still trying to restore his shattered arms in Spain! 'Do you ask,' he said, 'what I am doing here? I am lingering in my Tusculan villa half a prisoner.' He then proceeds to other statements, bewailing his former life and complaining of the present and despairing of the future." (Loeb, trans. Basore).

## 5. DIMINISHING RETURNS: TALES OF THE DIMINUTIVE

1. De Amicis 1910, 219.
2. Hasselrot 1957, 319.
3. See Fordyce 1961, 95: "Catullus makes free use of them . . . to enhance the emotional colour which is characteristic of his writing; with him they express a whole range of feelings—endearment . . . tenderness . . . pathos . . . playfulness . . . scorn . . . " (then, sentimentally, in n. 1: "Those who are familiar with Northern Scots know the warmth which that speech gains from its characteristic diminutives; its ability to give a nuance of personal feeling even to the most casual and prosaic utterance by adding a diminutive suffix to almost any noun—and on occasion doubling it—offers a close parallel to the Latin idiom"). Thanks to John Henderson for this reference.
4. Jurafsky 1996.
5. See Lodge 1985, 23: "Jakobson cites the gradation of positive, comparative and superlative forms of the adjective as evidence that language is not a totally arbitrary system. For instance: *blank, blanker, blankest.* The more phonemes the more emphasis. The same is true of other Indo-European languages, for instance Latin: *vacuus, vacuior, vacuissimus.* There does seem to be some iconic correlation between sound and sense across the boundaries of natural languages."
6. Jurafsky 1996, 535.
7. See Adams 1984, 53: the eunuch priests at Apul. *Met.* 8.26 use *palumbulus, pulchellus,* and *pullulus,* "no doubt intended to be feminine in tone."
8. Dutsch 2008, 30.
9. Young 2015.
10. Young 2015, 199–200.
11. Cf. Lucilius 298W: *ne auriculam obsidat canes, ne uermiculi qui* (where *uermiculus* is a small worm that affects the inner ear).
12. Virgil is assumed to be alluding to Catullus 61, where *paruulus* is used of the bouncing baby whose face is so reassuring a miniature of his father's (212 *Torquatus uolo paruolus Matris e gremio*). The lyric book that, oddly enough, contains the most occurrences of *paruus* is *Carm.* 3, the one where Horace becomes a lofty spokesman for Roman morals. This suggests the intriguing possibility that *paruus* is not associated so much with kneejerk metapoetic labelling as with periodically anchoring increasing grandeur to the frugal or rural past (the small contained inside the large: see chapter 1 and Fowler 1995).
13. Hinds 2000, 230.
14. Thanks to Julia Griffin for introducing me to this delightful version.
15. *Coagmentatus et leuis,* "glued together and smooth."

16. Platner 1895.
17. Fordyce's innocent comments on the diminutive (see above n. 3) are attached to this word.
18. Oliensis 2009, 122–24.
19. Fitzgerald 1995, 174.
20. Adams 1983, 153: "A good example of an affectionate diminutive is at Catull. 10.3 ... The woman had wit and sophistication, and the diminutive was 'weniger derb als *scortum*' [less coarse than *scortum*] (Kroll). It does not occur elsewhere."
21. See Braund 1996: if Catullus's "reveal" of his penniless return contrives preemptive self-acquittal in the context of imperial embezzlement (*de repetundis*), then this insult to "sad sack" incorruptible Memmius turns out to be a compliment. Thanks to Ingo Gildenhard for pointing me here. Cf. Hinds 2001, 234: "banter."
22. Adams 1995. See also Clackson 2023, 599: *quaeso* (please), far from being peremptory or imperious, is commonly used by those at a disadvantage when they make requests. For Hoffman (1951, 139), the diminutive evokes sympathy and affection, while *mi* in polite requests in comedy suggests concern for the addressee. See in general on the language of politeness Brown and Levinson 1987; and Barrios-Lech 2016, 108–109, 276–79 for "politeness phenomena" in Roman comedy, including *paulum/paullulum, paucis/pauca, paullisper, parumper, si tibi molestum non est* (and variants).
23. Stat. *Achil.* 1.260.
24. Miller 2012, 6.
25. Jurafsky 1996, 540.
26. Apul. *Met.* 5.12.
27. Sen. *Ep.* 53.6.
28. See Bobaljik 2012, 31–36 on languages that "nest", "contain", or "embed" comparatives within superlatives.
29. Matzilas 2015.
30. At Plaut. *Amph.* 773, *cistula* mutates into *cistellula* at a moment of great suspense, when the contents of a box are slowly being revealed.
31. Telò 2016, 299–300.
32. Razzall 2021, 14; Lakoff and Johnson 1980.
33. Lakoff and Johnson 1980, 29.
34. Sedgwick 1990.
35. Riggsby 1997; Rimell 2015.
36. Bachelard 1994, 81 (as Razzall [2021, 28–29] acknowledges).
37. Bachelard 1994, 86.
38. Bachelard 1994, 89.
39. *OLD* s.v. *loculus*.
40. *Rust.* 3.1.1–9.
41. *Rust.* 3.7.7; *Rust.* 3.5.18.
42. The poem has a deluxe counterpart in the shape of ivory boxes which are judged worthy of holding only gold coins: 14.11 (12) *Loculi eborei*.
43. Johnson 2005, 145.
44. Cope 1992, 4.
45. Platner 1895, 198–99. He compares Mart. 5.39, from a legacy-hunter: "I have ransacked my moneyboxes and my purse" (*excussi loculosque sacculumque*); and Sen.

*Ep.* 87.18: "Whoever sets a price on a full purse except for the price established by the sum of money deposited in it?" (*Quis pleno sacculo ullum pretium ponit nisi quod pecuniae in eo conditae numerus effecit?*) But in both these cases *sacculus* has a fully diminishing force: the legacy-hunter is indigent and desperate; Seneca's purse is worthless aside from its contents.

46. See Latour 2004, 207: "Thus body parts are progressively acquired at the same time as 'world counter-parts' are being registered in a new way. Acquiring a body is thus a progressive enterprise that produces at once a sensory medium *and* a sensitive world."

47. Feeney 1992.

48. Elsner 2019, 77.

49. Fitzgerald 1995, 189–211.

50. See Fitzgerald 1995, 192 (on 65): "These alternative models for the poetic mind, storehouse and womb, are fused in the image of the of the virgin from which the apple falls in the final simile." Cf. 66.72–74: "for I will not cover up truth for any fear, not even if the constellations tear me apart with their carping will it prevent me from rolling out what's stored in a true heart (*condita quin ueri pectoris euoluam*)."

51. Sen. *Ep.* 115.2; Gell. *NA* 10.15.14.

52. Bezzone 2012.

53. See Oliensis 2009, 121 on the phallic connotations of the many "foot" words in the poem.

54. Cat. 63.75: *geminas . . . aures*.

55. Pl. *Alc.* 1 132d–133c.

56. See Bettini 1991, 232. He continues: "Neither the mirror nor the double can create anything other than the *ego*, the *I*: when I look at my reflected image, I cannot help but call it *I*."

57. Ellis (1889, ad 63.56) calls up an unfortunate parallel for Attis: "So Byron of a passionate weeper, *The very balls Of her black eyes seem'd turned to tears, Don Juan* iv.33."

58. Fr. 11 Courtney.

59. Courtney 2003, ad loc.

60. See M. Buchan 1995, 72: "as the poet-lover watches, what he sees in the eyeball of the woman he constructs is the turning of the tables: for through her eyes, there isn't just a single, faithful suitor, but two, from her doubled pupil!"

61. Choice coinages to sneer at others or deprecate himself include: *cauponula* ([mean] little tavern) (*Phil.* 2.77); *praediola* (little farm) (*Att.* 13.9.2, his own); *gloriola* (little glory) (*Fam.* 7.5.3, of Trebatius; *Fam.* 5.12.9, of himself); *togula* (little toga) (*Att.* 1.18.6, Pompey's).

62. See Laurand 1965, 3.265: "les formes les plus délicates de l'ironie cicéronienne." This is quoted by Haury (1955, 70), who supplements (p. 71) Laurand's blanket "affective" theory of Ciceronian diminutives with the more "rational" flavor of Cicero's parodic words for Greek philosophical subtlety.

63. *Verr.* 5.95, *Verr.* 5.96. Haury 1955, 72: "même quand la valeur en paraît affaiblie" (even when its force seems weakened).

64. *Fam.* 7.5.3; *Fam.* 9.10.3; *Fam.* 16.5.1, *Att.* 4.6.2.

65. *Fam.* 2.12.2; *Tusc.* 3.83.

66. *Arch.* 25. Zetzel 2003, 124.

67. *Nat. D.* 3.18; *Fin.* 4.7; *Tusc.* 2.29; *Tusc.* 2.42.

68. *Phil.* 3.21. Compare Seneca, *Ep.* 49.8 on syllogisms (*quaestiunculae*), which he considers concoctions of *acuta deliratio*, "acute craziness."

69. *Tusc.* 2.45; *Tusc.* 3.38; *Tusc.* 5.64.
70. E.g. *Tusc.* 1.22; *Nat. D.* 1.66.
71. Juv. 10.173; Lucil. 691W.
72. Reinhardt 2005, 158–62.
73. *Fam.* 4.5.4. The context is Servius's Scipio-like epiphany, as the result of a stay in Greece, about the tiny and transient role of human beings: "Ah! How can we manikins (*nos homunculi*) wax indignant if one of us dies or is killed, ephemeral creatures as we are, when the corpses of so many towns lie abandoned in a single spot?"
74. *Att.* 4.5.1.
75. See chapter 1.
76. Somewhat differently, a little mouse (*breuis . . . mus*) scuttles under the floorboards in Ovid's description of the ritual of goddess Tacita Muta (*Fast.* 2.574), its inarticulate squeaks suggesting the goddess's ability to disarm hostile human mutterings.
77. Cf. *Fam.* 7.18.3: Cicero writes of "the great din of little frogs" (*uim maximam ranunculorum*), mobbing him like human clients in the marshes of Ulubrae.
78. Cf. Sen. *Apocol.* 7 *ubi mures ferrum rodunt*. Similarly philistine (*opici*) mice gnaw "divine poems" at Juv. 3.207.
79. *Georg.* 1.181–86.
80. Stewart 1993, 44.
81. Cic. *Somn.* 16.
82. See Scott 2008, 13: "The early modern fly is an irritant to notions of anthropocentrism, as it is simultaneously able to contaminate and celebrate humankind. . . . The fly theatrically and symbolically recognizes both the potential for and the absence of a value system."

ACKNOWLEDGMENTS

I would like to thank Gary Turchin for allowing me to reprint his poem "A thousand little irritants" and Dale Copeland for her kind permission to reproduce her artwork "Lares et Penates" (fig. 6). Thanks are also due to Cristina D'Alessandro of Scala Archives, Florence (cover photo); Barbara Birley of the Vindolanda Trust (fig. 24); Ruth Pohlman, representing the estate of Malvina Reynolds (epigraph to chapter 5); the Ashmolean Museum, Oxford (fig. 1); Kate Gallagher of the Johns Hopkins Archaeological Museum, Baltimore (fig. 7); St James's Ancient Art, London (fig. 20); and Tommaso Bernardini, the original designer of Crispus's family tree (fig. 19). Nandini Pandey generously allowed me to quote from and discuss her Society for Classical Studies blogpost (Pandey, 2020).

I thank the efficient team at the University of California Press who have worked tirelessly to produce this book at speed: Eric Schmidt, Jyoti Arvey, Gabriel Bartlett, Sylvie Bower, Cindy Fulton, and Paige MacKay. I also thank Roberta Engleman for creating the index. I am profoundly grateful to the two positive and attentive readers of my submitted manuscript and to all those friends (acknowledged individually in the endnotes) who have helped to improve it. All remaining mistakes are my own.

# REFERENCES

Abbott, Claude C. 1935. *The Letters of Gerard Manley Hopkins to Robert Bridges*. London: Oxford University Press.
Adams, Don. 2021. "Aristophanes's Hiccups and Erotic Impotence." *Philosophy and Literature* 45:17–33.
Adams, James N. 1983. "Words for Prostitutes." *Rheinisches Museum* 126:321–58.
———. 1984. "Female Speech in Latin Comedy." *Antichthon* 18:43–77.
———. 1995. "Neglected Evidence for Female Speech in Latin." *Classical Quarterly* 55:582–96.
Agbamu, Samuel. 2019. "The Arco dei Fileni: A Fascist Reading of Sallust's *Bellum Jugurthinum*." *Classical Receptions Journal* 11:157–77.
Ahlgren, J., B. B. Chapman, P. A. Nilsson, and C. Brönmark. 2015. "Individual Boldness is Linked to Protective Shell Shape in Aquatic Snails." *Biol. Lett.* 11:20150029. http://dx.doi.org/10.1098/rsbl.2015.0029.
Ahmed, Sarah. 2006. *Queer Phenomenology: Orientations, Objects, Others*. Durham, NC: Duke University Press.
Andrade, Tonio. 2010. "A Chinese Farmer, Two African Boys, and a Warlord: Toward a Global Microhistory." *Journal of World History* 21:573–91.
Arasse, Daniel. 1992. *Le détail: Pour une histoire rapprochée de la peinture*. Paris: Flammarion.
———. 2013. *Take Another Look*. Translated by A. Waters. Princeton, NJ: Princeton University Press. Originally *On n'y voit rien: Descriptions*. Paris: Éditions Denoël: 2000.
Arendt, Hannah. 1958. *The Human Condition*. Chicago: University of Chicago Press.
Auerbach, Erich. 1953. *Mimesis*. Translated by W. R. Trask. Princeton, NJ: Princeton University Press. Originally *Mimesis. Dargestellte Wirklichkeit in abendländischen Literatur*. Bern: A Francke Verlag: 1946.
Avery, Harry C. 1967. "Marius Felix Sallust, *Jug.* 92–94." *Hermes* 95:324–30.
Bachelard, Gaston. 1927. *Essai sur la connaissance approchée*. Paris: Vrin.

——. 1994. *The Poetics of Space*. Translated by M. Jolas. Boston: Beacon Press. Originally *La poétique de l'espace*. Paris: Presses Universitaires de France: 1958.

Bailey, Elisabeth Tova. 2010. *The Sound of a Wild Snail Eating*. Chapel Hill, NC: Algonquin Books.

Baraz, Yelena. 2012. *A Written Republic: Cicero's Philosophical Politics*. Princeton, NJ: Princeton University Press.

Barney, Stephen A., W. J. Lewis, J. A. Beach, O. Berghof, eds. and trans. 2009. *The Etymologies of Isidore of Seville*. Cambridge: Cambridge University Press.

Barthes, Roland. 1964. "Structure du fait divers." *Essais critiques*. Paris: Éditions du Seuil, 188–97.

——. 1986. "The Reality Effect." In *The Rustle of Language*. Translated by R. Howard, 141–48. Berkeley: University of California Press. Originally "L'effet de reél." *Communications* 11:84–89: 1968.

——. 1984. *Camera Lucida*. Translated by R. Howard. London: Flamingo. Originally *La chambre claire: note sur la photographie*. Paris: Seuil: 1980.

Bartman, Elizabeth. 1992. *Ancient Sculptural Copies in Miniature*. Leiden: Brill.

Batstone, William. 1988. "The Antithesis of Virtue: Sallust's Synkrisis and the Crisis of the Late Republic." *Classical Antiquity* 7:1–29.

——. 2010a. *Catiline's Conspiracy, The Jugurthine War, Histories*. Oxford: Oxford University Press.

——. 2010b. "Postmodern Theory and Roman Historians." In *Cambridge Companion to Ancient Historians*, edited by A. Feldherr, 24–40. Cambridge: Cambridge University Press.

Beagon, Mary. 1996. "Nature and Views of Her Landscapes in Pliny the Elder." In *Human Landscapes in Classical Antiquity: Environment and Culture*, edited by G. Shipley and J. Salmon, 284–329. London: Routledge.

Beard, Mary. 2015. *Laughter in Ancient Rome: On Joking, Tickling, and Cracking Up*. Berkeley: University of California Press.

Beerbohm, Max. 1921. "A Clergyman." In *Modern Essays*, ed. C. Morley. New York: Harcourt, Brace, and Company.

Bennett, Jane. 2010. *Vibrant Matter: A Political Ecology of Things*. Durham, NC: Duke University Press.

Bennett, Kate. 2015. *John Aubrey, Brief Lives with An Apparatus for the Lives of our English Mathematical Writers*. 2 vols. Oxford: Oxford University Press.

——. 2024. "John Aubrey's *Brief Lives* and Life-Writing." Oxford Handbooks Online. Accessed June 30. https://www.oxfordhandbooks.com/view/10.1093/oxfordhb/9780199935338.001.0001/oxfordhb-9780199935338-e-14?.

Bettini, Maurizio. 1991. *Anthropology and Roman Culture: Kinship, Time, Images of the Soul*. Translated by J. Van Sickle. Baltimore: Johns Hopkins University Press.

——. 1999. *The Portrait of the Lover*. Berkeley: University of California Press.

Bezzone, Francesca. 2012. "Relics and Reliquaries in the *Vita Germani Auctore Constantio*: The *Capsula*." *The Heroic Age* 15, https://www.heroicage.org/issues/15/bezzone.php.

Billerbeck, Margarethe, and Christian Zubler. 2000. *Das Lob der Fliege von Lukian bis L.B. Alberti. Gattungsgeschichte, Texte, Übersetzungen und Kommentar*. Bern: P. Lang.

Blake, Sarah. 2012. "*In Manus*: Pliny's Letters and the Art of Mastery." In *Roman Literary Cultures: Domestic Politics, Revolutionary Poetics, Civic Spectacle*, edited by A. Keith and J. Edmondson, 89–108. Toronto: University of Toronto Press.

Bobaljik, Jonathan. 2012. *Universals in Comparative Morphology: Suppletion, Superlatives, and the Structure of Words*. Cambridge, MA: MIT Press.
Bodel, John. 2008. "Cicero's Minerva, Penates, and the Mother of the Lares: An Outline of Roman Domestic Religion." In *Household and Family in Antiquity*, edited by J. Bodel and S. M. Olyan, 248–74. Cambridge: Cambridge University Press.
Boivin, Nicole. 2008. *Material Cultures, Material Minds: The Impact of Things on Human Thought, Society, and Evolution*. Cambridge: Cambridge University Press.
Bowles, Paul. 2009. *The Sheltering Sky*. Harmondsworth: Penguin Books. Originally published in 1949.
Bradley, Mark, ed. 2014. *Smell and the Ancient Senses*. Milton Park: Routledge.
Braund, David. 1996. "The Politics of Catullus 10: Memmius, Caesar and the Bithynians." *Hermathena* 160:45–57.
Braund, Susanna M., and Christopher Gill, eds. 1997. *The Passions in Roman Thought and Literature*. Cambridge: Cambridge University Press.
Brecher, Gerhard. 1937. "Die Entstehung und biologische Bedeutung der subjektiven Zeiteinheit." *Zeitschrift für vergleichende Physiologie* 18:204–43.
Brescia, Graziana. 1997. *La scalata del Ligure: Saggio di commento a Sallustio, Bellum Jugurthinum 92–94*. Bari: Edipuglia.
Brown, Bill. 2001. "Thing Theory." *Critical Inquiry* 28:1–22.
Brown, Penelope, and Stephen Levinson. 1987. *Politeness. Some Universals in Language Usage*. Cambridge: Cambridge University Press.
Bryson, Norman. 1990. *Looking at the Overlooked: Four Essays on Still Life Painting*. London: Reaktion Books.
Buchan, John. 1929. *The Causal and the Casual in History*. Cambridge: Cambridge University Press.
Buchan, Mark. 1995. "Ovid *Imperamator*: Beginnings and Endings of Love Poems and Empire in the *Amores*." *Arethusa* 28:53–85.
Butler, Shane. 1998. "Notes on a *Membrum Disiectum*." In *Women and Slaves in Greco-Roman Culture: Differential Equations*, edited by S. R. Joshel and S. Murnaghan, 236–55. London: Routledge.
Butler, Shane, and Alex Purves, eds. 2013. *Synaesthesia and the Ancient Senses*. Durham: Acumen.
Butler, Shane, and Sarah Nooter, eds. 2018. *Sound and the Ancient Senses*. London: Routledge.
Cairns, Douglas L., and Damien Nelis, eds. 2016. *Emotions in the Classical World: Methods, Approaches, and Directions*. Stuttgart: Franz Steiner Verlag.
Calvino, Italo. 2021. *The Baron in the Trees*. Translated by Ann Goldstein. London: Vintage Classics. Originally *Il barone rampante*. Turin: Einaudi: 1957.
Cameron, Alan. 1995. *Callimachus and his Critics*. Princeton, NJ: Princeton University Press.
Cappello, Orazio. 2016. "Everything You Ever Wanted to Know About Atticus But Were Afraid to Ask: Looking for Atticus in Cicero's *Ad Atticum*." *Arethusa* 49:463–87.
Carter, Philip. 2019. "Can a Short Life Be a Good Life? Brevity in Historical Biography." *On History* (blog), July 18, 2019, https://blog.history.ac.uk/2019/07/can-a-short-life-be-a-good-life-brevity-in-historical-biography/.
Chaniotis, Angelos, ed. 2012. *Unveiling Emotions: Sources and Methods for the Study of Emotions in the Greek World*. Stuttgart: Franz Steiner Verlag.
Claassen, Jo-Marie. 1996. "Documents of a Crumbling Marriage: The Case of Cicero and Terentia." *Phoenix* 50:208–32.

Clackson, James. 2023. "Latin Literature and Linguistics." In *Cambridge Critical Guide to Latin Literature*, edited by R. Gibson and C. Whitton, 563–612. Cambridge: Cambridge University Press.
Collins, Douglas. 2002-3. "The Great Effects of Small Things: Insignificance with Immanence in Critical Theory." *Anthropoetics* 8: https://anthropoetics.ucla.edu/ap0802/collins-2/.
Conti Bizzarro, Ferruccio. 2009. *Comici entomologici*. Alessandria: Edizioni dell'orso.
Cope, Wendy. 1992. *Serious Concerns*. London: Faber.
Corbeill, Anthony. 1996. *Controlling Laughter: Political Humor in the Late Roman Republic*. Princeton, NJ: Princeton University Press.
Corbin, Alain. 2001. *The Life of an Unknown: The Rediscovered World of a Clog Maker in Nineteenth-Century France*, trans. A. Goldhammer. New York: Columbia University Press. Originally *Le monde retrouvé de Louis-François Pinagot: sur les traces d'un inconnu*. Paris: Flammarion: 1998.
Courtney, Edward. 2003. *The Fragmentary Latin Poets*. 2nd ed. Oxford: Oxford University Press.
Cranga, Françoise, and Yves Cranga. 1991. *L'escargot. Zoologie, symbolique, imaginaire, médecine, gastronomie*. Dijon: Éditions du bien public.
———. 1997. "L'escargot dans le midi de la France: approche iconographique." *Mémoires de la societé archéologique du midi de la France* 57:71–90.
Čulík-Baird, Hannah. 2022. *Cicero and the Early Latin Poets*. Cambridge: Cambridge University Press.
D'Angour, Armand. 1999. "Ad unguem." *American Journal of Philology* 120:411–27.
Dawidowicz, Lucy S. 1990. *The War Against the Jews 1933–45*. Harmondsworth: Penguin Books.
De Angelis, Francesco. 2014. "Sublime Histories, Exceptional Viewers: Trajan's Column and its Visibility." In *Art and Rhetoric in Roman Culture*, edited by J. Elsner and M. Meyer, 89–114. Cambridge: Cambridge University Press.
Deetz, James. 1977. *In Small Things Forgotten: An Archaeology of Early American Life*. Garden City, NY: Anchor Press/Doubleday.
Deleuze, Gilles. 1995. *Negotiations, 1972–1990*. Translated by M. Joughin. New York: Columbia University Press.
Deutsch, Helen. 2009. "Oranges, Anecdote, and the Nature of Things." *SubStance* 118:31–55.
Dewey, John. 2016. *The Public and its Problems: An Essay in Political Enquiry*. Edited by M. L. Rogers. Athens, OH: Swallow Press. Originally published in 1927.
Dickey, Eleanor. 2002. *Latin Forms of Address: From Plautus to Apuleius*. Oxford: Oxford University Press.
Didi-Huberman, Georges. 1989. "The Art of Not Describing: Vermeer—the Detail and the Patch." *History of the Human Sciences* 2:135–69. Originally "L'art de ne pas décrire: Une aporie du détail chez Vermeer." *La Part de l'Oeil* 2:102–19: 1986.
Dixon, Suzanne. 1984. "Family Finances: Tullia and Terentia." *Antichthon* 18:87–101.
Dolansky, Fanny. 2012. "Playing with Gender: Girls, Dolls, and Adult Ideals in the Roman World." *Classical Antiquity* 31:256–92.
Dolganov, Anya. 2008. "Constructing Author and Authority: Generic Discourse in Cicero's 'De Legibus.'" *Greece and Rome* 55:23–38.
Dow, Sterling. 1965. *Fifty Years of Sathers: The Sather Professorship of Classical Literature in the University of California, Berkeley, 1913/4–1963/4*. Berkeley: University of California Press.

Dutsch, Dorota. 2008. *Feminine Discourse in Roman Comedy: On Echoes and Voices.* Oxford: Oxford University Press.
Dryden, John. 1971. "Life of Plutarch." In *Works of John Dryden*, edited by E. N. Hooker and H. T. Swedenberg, 270–77. Vol. 17. Berkeley: University of California Press. Originally published in 1683–86.
Eden, Kathy. 2012. *The Renaissance Rediscovery of Intimacy.* Chicago: University of Chicago Press.
Ellis, Robinson. 1889. *A Commentary on Catullus.* 2nd ed. Oxford: Oxford University Press.
Elsner, Jaś. 2019. "A Roman Vessel for Cosmetics: Form, Decoration, and Subjectivity in the Muse Casket." In *Vessels: The Object as Container*, edited by C. Brittenham. Oxford: Oxford University Press, 50–80.
———. 2020. "Introduction." In *Figurines: Figuration and the Sense of Scale*, edited by J. Elsner, 1–10. Oxford: Oxford University Press.
———. 2021. Review of Martin and Langin-Hooper 2018. *Critical Inquiry* 47:410.
Ettlinger, Helen. 1978. "The Virgin Snail." *Journal of the Warburg and Courtauld Institutes* 41:316.
Facchini Tosi, Claudia. 1990. *Il proemio di Floro: la struttura concettuale e formale.* Bologna: Pàtron.
Fadiman, Clifton. 1985. *The Little, Brown Book of Anecdotes.* New York: Little, Brown.
Feeney, Denis. 1992. "'Shall I Compare Thee . . . ?: Catullus 68B and the Limits of Analogy." In *Author and Audience in Latin Literature*, edited by T. Woodman and A. Powell, 33–44. Cambridge: Cambridge University Press.
———. 2007. *Caesar's Calendar.* Berkeley: University of California Press.
Feldherr, Andrew. 2021. *After the Past: Sallust on History and Writing History.* Chichester: Wiley.
Ferri, Rolando. 2008. BMCR 2008.07.10, Review of Andrea Balbo 2007. *I frammenti degli oratori romani dell'età augustea e tiberiana. Parte seconda, Età tiberiana. Minima philologica.* 2 vols. Alessandria: Edizioni dell'orso.
Fineman, Joel. 1989. "The History of the Anecdote: Fiction and Fiction." In *The New Historicism*, edited by H. A. Veeser, 49–76. New York: Routledge.
Fischer, Kuno. 1871. *Über die Entstehung und die Entwickelungsformen des Witzes.* Heidelberg: F. Bassermann.
Fischer, Roland. 1965. "Aesthetics and the Biology of the Fleeting Moment." *Perspectives in Biology and Medicine* 8:210–17.
Fitzgerald, William. 1995. *Catullan Provocations: Lyric Poetry and the Drama of Position.* Berkeley: University of California Press.
———. 2018. "Claiming Inferiority: Weakness into Strength." In *Complex Inferiorities: The Poetics of the Weaker Voice in Latin Literature*, edited by S. Matzner and S. Harrison, 13–28. Oxford: Oxford University Press.
———. 2021. "The Slave, Between Absence and Presence." In *Unspoken Rome: Absence in Latin Literature and its Reception*, edited by T. Geue and E. Giusti. Cambridge: Cambridge University Press, 239–49.
Flory, Marleen B. 1989. "Octavian and the Omen of the 'Gallina Alba.'" *Classical Journal* 84:343–56.
Flower, Harriet. 2017. *The Dancing Lares and the Serpent in the Garden: Religion at the Roman Street Corner.* Princeton, NJ: Princeton University Press.

Fordyce, Christian J. 1961. *Catullus: A Commentary*. Oxford: Clarendon Press.
Fortson, Benjamin. 2008. "Bleary Eyes and Ladles of Clay: Two Liquid Sabellicisms in Latin." *Glotta* 84:52–71.
Foucault, Michel. 1980. "Theatrum Philosophicum." *Language, Counter-Memory, Practice: Selected Essays and Interviews*. Ithaca, 165–96. Originally *Critique* 282:885–908: 1970.
———. 2000. "Lives of Infamous Men." In *Power*, edited by J. D. Faubion, 156–75. Translated by R. Hurley. London: Penguin Books. Originally "La vie des hommes l'infâmes." *Les cahiers du chemin* 29, 25 (January 1977).
Fowler, Don. 1995. "Horace and the Aesthetics of Politics." In *Homage to Horace: A Bimillenary Celebration*, edited by S. J. Harrison, 248–66. Reprint in *Oxford Readings in Horace's Odes and Epodes*, edited by M. Lowrie, 249–70. Oxford: Oxford University Press: 2009.
Freud, Sigmund. 2002. *The Joke and Its Relation to the Unconscious*. Translated by J. Crick. London: Penguin Books. Originally *Der Witz und seine Beziehung zum Unbewussten*. Leipzig: F. Deuticke: 1905.
Gallagher, Catherine, and Stephen Greenblatt. 2000. *Practicing New Historicism*. Chicago: University of Chicago Press.
Gell, Alfred. 1992. "The Technology of Enchantment and the Enchantment of Technology." In *Anthropology, Art and Aesthetics*, edited by J. Coote and A. Shelton, 40–63. Oxford: Oxford University Press.
Ghobrial, John-Paul A. 2014. "The Secret Life of Elias of Babylon and the Uses of Global Microhistory," *Past and Present* 222:51–93.
Gibson, Roy. 2014. "Suetonius and the *Viri Illustres* of Pliny the Younger." In *Suetonius the Biographer*, edited by T. Power and R. K. Gibson, 199–230. Oxford: Oxford University Press.
Ginzburg, Carlo. 1980. *The Cheese and the Worms: The Cosmos of a Sixteenth-Century Miller*. Translated by J. and A. Tedeschi. Baltimore: Johns Hopkins University Press. Originally *Il formaggio e i vermi: il cosmo di un mugnaio del '500*. Turin: Einaudi: 1976.
———. 1983. "Morelli, Freud, and Sherlock Holmes: Clues and Scientific Method." In *The Sign of Three: Dupin, Holmes, Peirce*, edited by U. Eco and T. Sebeok, 81–118. Bloomington: Indiana University Press.
———. 2012. Contribution to Hiller et al. 2012, 49.
Giusti, Elena. 2014. "Virgil's Carthaginians at *Aen.* 1.430–6: Cyclopes in Bees' Clothing." *Cambridge Classical Journal* 60:37–58.
———. 2022. "Horace's *Ode* 1.12: Subterranean Lyrics." *American Journal of Philology* 143:75–107.
Goldschmidt, Nora. 2023. *Fragmentary Modernism: The Classical Fragment in Literary and Visual Cultures, c. 1896–c. 1936*. Oxford: Oxford University Press.
Gossman, Lionel. 2003. "Anecdote and History." *History and Theory* 42:143–68.
Gowers, Emily. 1993. *The Loaded Table: Representations of Food in Roman Literature*. Oxford: Oxford University Press.
———. 1994. "Persius and the Decoction of Nero." In *Reflections of Nero*. London, edited by J. Elsner and J. Masters, 199–230. Reprint in *Oxford Readings in Persius and Juvenal*, edited by M. Plaza, 173–98. Oxford: Oxford University Press: 2009.
———. 2002. "Blind Eyes and Cut Throats: Amnesia and Silence in Horace, *Satires* 1.7." *Classical Philology* 97:145–61.
———. 2003. "Fragments of Autobiography in Horace *Satires* 1." *Classical Antiquity* 22:55–91.
———. 2011. "Trees and Family Trees in the *Aeneid*." *Classical Antiquity* 30:87–118.

Green, Carol M. C. 1993. "*De Africa et Eius Incolis*: "The Function of Geography and Ethnography in Sallust's History of the Jugurthine War (*BJ* 17–19)." *Ancient World* 24:185–97.

Grethlein, Jonas. 2014. "Future Past: Time and Teleology in Ancient Historiography." *History and Theory* 53:309–30.

Gunderson, Erik. 2000a. "The History of Mind and the Philosophy of History in Sallust's *Bellum Catilinae*." *Ramus* 29:85–126.

———. 2000b. *Staging Masculinity: The Rhetoric of Performance in the Roman World*. Ann Arbor: University of Michigan Press.

———. 2007. "S.V.B.; E.V." *Classical Antiquity* 26:1–48.

Gurd, Sean. 2016. *Dissonance: Auditory Aesthetics in Ancient Greece*. New York: Fordham University Press.

Guthrie, W. Keith C. 1975. *History of Greek Philosophy*. Vol. 4. Cambridge: Cambridge University Press.

Hall, Jon. 2008. *Politeness and Politics in Cicero's Letters*. Oxford: Oxford University Press.

Hallett, Judith. 1984. *Fathers and Daughters in Roman Society*. Princeton, NJ: Princeton University Press.

Hardie, Philip. 2006. "Statius' Ovidian Poetics and the Tree of Atedius Melior (*Silvae* 2.3)." In *Flavian Poetics*, edited by R. R. Nauta, J. J. L. Smolenaars, and H.-J. van Dam, 207–21. Leiden: Brill.

Hasselrot, Bengt. 1957. *Études sur la formation diminutive dans les langues romaines*. Uppsala: Lundequistska Bokhandlen.

Haury, Auguste. 1955. *L'ironie et l'humour chez Cicéron*. Leiden: Brill.

Henderson, John. 1998. *A Roman Life: Rutilius Gallus on Paper and in Stone*. Exeter: University of Exeter Press.

———. 1999. *Writing Down Rome: Satire, Comedy, and Other Offences in Latin Poetry*. Oxford: Oxford University Press.

———. 2007. "' . . . When Who Should Walk into the Room but . . . ': Epistoliterarity in Cicero, *Ad Qfr*. 3.1." In *Ancient Letters: Classical and Late Antique Epistolography*, edited by R. Morello and A. D. Morrison, 37–85. Oxford: Oxford University Press.

———. 2016. "Cicero's Letters to Cicero, *ad QFr*: Big Brothers Keepers." *Arethusa* 49:439–61.

Hiller, Susan, Spike Bucklow, Johannes Endres, Carlo Ginzburg, Joan Kee, Spyros Papapetros, Adrian Rifkin, Joanna Roche, Nina Rowe, Alain Schnapp et al. 2012. "Notes from the Field: Detail." *Art Bulletin* 94:490–514.

Hinds, Stephen. 2000. "Essential Epic: Genre and Gender from Macer to Statius." In *Matrices of Genre: Authors, Canons, and Society*, edited by M. Depew and D. Obbink, 221–44. Cambridge, MA: Harvard University Press.

———. 2001. "Cinna, Statius, and Immanent Literary History." In *L'histoire littéraire immanente dans la poésie latine*, edited by E. Schmidt, 221–65. Geneva: Fondation Hardt.

Hine, Harry M. 2006. "Rome, the Cosmos, and the Emperor in Seneca's *Natural Questions*." *Journal of Roman Studies* 96:42–72.

Hitchcock, Tim. 2014. "Big Data, Small Data and Meaning. *Historyonics* (blog). Accessed June 30, 2024. http://historyonics.blogspot.com/2014/11/big-data-small-data-and-meaning_9.html.

Hoffer, Stanley. 2007. "Cicero's 'Stomach': Political Indignation and the Use of Repeated Allusive Expressions in Cicero's Correspondence." In *Ancient Letters: Classical and*

*Late Antique Epistolography*, edited by R. Morello and A.D. Morrison, 87–106. Oxford: Oxford University Press.

Hoffman, Johann Baptist. 1951. *Lateinische Umgangsprache*. 3rd ed. Heidelberg: Winter.

Holmes, Brooke. 2016. "Cosmopoiesis in the Field of 'The Classical.'" In *Deep Classics: Rethinking Classical Reception*, edited by S. Butler, 269–90. Oxford: Oxford University Press.

House, Humphry, ed. 1937. *The Notebooks and Papers of Gerard Manley Hopkins*. London: Oxford University Press.

Huber, Sonya. 2021. *Supremely Tiny Acts: A Memoir of a Day*. Columbus: Ohio State University Press.

Hudson, Jared. 2019. "The Empire in the Epitome: Florus and the Conquest of Historiography." *Ramus* 48:54–81.

Hughes, Jessica. 2018. "Tiny and Fragmented Votive Offerings from Classical Antiquity." In Martin and Langin-Hooper 2018, 47–71.

Hunt, Ailsa. 2016. *Reviving Roman Religion: Sacred Trees in the Roman World*. Cambridge: Cambridge University Press.

Leeman, Anton D., Harm Pinkster, and Hein L. W. Nelson, eds. 1985. *M. Tullius Cicero, De Oratore Libri III*. Vol. 2. Heidelberg: Winter.

Hunter, Richard. 2004. *Plato's Symposium*. Oxford: Oxford University Press.

Johnson, W. Ralph. 2005. "Small Wonders: The Poetics of Martial, Book Fourteen." In *Defining Genre and Gender in Latin Literature*, edited by W. W. Batstone and G. Tissol, 139–50. New York: Lang.

Johnston, Freya. 2003. "Little Lives: An Eighteenth-Century Sub-Genre." *Cambridge Quarterly* 32:143–60.

Jones, Christopher P. 1986. "Suetonius in the Probus of Giorgio Valla." *Harvard Studies in Classical Philology* 90:245–51.

Jurafsky, Daniel. 1996. "Universal Tendencies in the Semantics of the Diminutive." *Language* 72:533–78.

Kaster, Robert A. 2001. "Dynamics of *Fastidium* and the Ideology of Disgust." *American Journal of Philology* 147:143–89.

Kim, Jinhyung, Patricia N. Holte, Frank Martela, Colin Shanahan, Zhanhong Li, Hong Zhang, Nikolett Eisenbeck, David F. Carreno, Rebecca J. Schlegel, and Joshua A. Hicks. 2022. "Experiential Appreciation as a Pathway to Meaning in Life." *Nature Human Behaviour* 6:677–90.

Kish, Nathan. 2021. "Comic Invective, Decorum and Ars in Cicero's *De Oratore*." In *Comic Invective in Ancient Greek and Roman Oratory*, edited by S. Papaioannou and A. Serafim, 191–210. Berlin: De Gruyter.

Knapp, Ivan. 2021. *Meme-Work: Psychoanalysis and the Alt-Right*. Unpublished PhD thesis, University of London.

Koestermann, Erich. 1971. *C. Sallustius Crispus: Bellum Iugurthinum*. Heidelberg: Winter.

Koselleck, Reinhardt 2000. *Zeitschichten: Studien zur Historik*. Frankfurt: Suhrkamp.

Kraus, Christina S. 1999. "Jugurthine Disorder." In *Limits of Historiography: Genre and Narrative in Ancient Historical Texts*, edited by C. S. Kraus, 217–47. Leiden: Brill.

Krebs, Christopher. 2008a. "Catiline's Ravaged Mind: *Vastus Animus* (Sall. *BC* 5.5)." *Classical Quarterly* 58:682–86.

──. 2008b. "The Imagery of 'The Way' in the Proem to Sallust's 'Bellum Catilinae' 1–4." *American Journal of Philology* 129:581–94.
Kubler, George. 1967. "Style and the Representation of Historical Time." *Annals of the New York Academy of Sciences* 138:849–55.
Kurke, Leslie. 2010. *Aesopic Conversations: Popular Tradition, Cultural Dialogue, and the Invention of Greek Prose*. Princeton, NJ: Princeton University Press.
Lakoff, George, and Mark Johnson. 1980. *Metaphors We Live By*. Chicago: University of Chicago Press.
Lambert, Cat. 2020. "The Ancient Entomological Bookworm." *Arethusa* 53:1–24.
Latour, Bruno. 2004. "How to Talk About the Body: The Normative Dimension of Science Studies." *Body and Society* 10:205–29.
Laite, Julia. 2020. "The Emmet's Inch: Small History in a Digital Age." *Journal of Social History* 53:963–89.
La Penna, Antonio. 1976. "Il ritratto paradossale da Silla a Petronio." *RFIC* 104:270–79. Reprint in *Aspetti del pensiero storico latino*, 193–221. Turin: Einaudi: 1978.
Laurand, Louis. 1940. *Études sur le style des discours de Cicéron*. 3rd ed. Paris: Belles Lettres.
Leacock, Stephen. 1911. "The Life of John Smith." In *Literary Lapses*, 138–44. London: Lane.
Lec, Stanislaw J. 1962. *Unkempt Thoughts*. Translated by J. Galaska. New York: St Martin's Press.
Leigh, Matthew. 1996. "Varius Rufus, Thyestes and the Appetites of Antony." *Proceedings of the Cambridge Philological Society* 42:171–97.
Levene, David S. 1992. "Sallust's *Jugurtha*: An 'Historical Fragment.'" *Journal of Roman Studies* 82:53–70.
Lipps, Theodor. 1898. *Komik und Humor*. Hamburg: Voss.
Lloyd, Geoffrey. 1966. *Polarity and Analogy: Two Types of Argumentation in Early Greek Thought*. Cambridge: Cambridge University Press.
Lodge, David. 1985. *Small World: An Academic Romance*. Harmondsworth: Penguin Books.
Love, Heather. 2016. "Small Change: Realism, Immanence, and the Politics of the Micro." *Modern Language Quarterly* 77:419–45.
Love, Rosalind. 1996. *Three Eleventh-Century Anglo-Latin Saints' Lives: Vita S. Birini, Vita et Miracula S. Kenelmi, and Vita S. Rumwoldi*. Oxford: Oxford University Press.
Lowenstam, Steven. 1986. "Aristophanes' Hiccups." *Greek, Roman and Byzantine Studies* 27:43–56.
Lubell, David. 2004. "Prehistoric Edible Land Snails in the Circum-Mediterranean: The Archaeological Evidence." In *Petits animaux et societés humaines. Du complément alimentaire aux ressources utilitaires. XXIVe rencontres internationales d'archéologie et d'histoire d'Antibes*, edited by J.-P. Brugal and J. Desse, 77–98. Antibes: Éditions APDCA.
Mac Góráin, Fiachra. 2017. "Microcosm and the Virgilian Persona." *Camenae* 7.
Mack, John. 2007. *The Art of Small Things*. London: British Museum.
Mahoney, Paul. 2011. "On the 'Hiccuping Episode' in Plato's 'Symposium.'" *Classical World* 104:143–59.
Martelli, Francesca. 2016. "Mourning Tulli-a: The Shrine of Letters in *Ad Atticum* 12." *Arethusa* 49:415–37.
Martin, S. Rebecca, and Stephanie Langin-Hooper, eds. 2018. *The Tiny and the Fragmented: Miniature, Broken, or Otherwise Incomplete Objects from the Ancient World*. New York: Oxford University Press.

Massumi, Brian. 2005. "The Autonomy of Affect." *Cultural Critique* 31:83–109.
Matzilas, Dimitris. 2015. "Plautus' *Nervolaria*: What Could it Mean?" *Bollettino di studi latini* 46:144–49.
McCarthy, Kathleen. 2013. "Secrets and Lies: Horace *Carm.* 1.27 and Catullus 10." *Materiali e discussioni* 71:45–74.
Miller, Ian. 2012. "The Formation of Latin Diminutives of Nouns and Adjectives." Research Gate. January 2012. https://www.researchgate.net/publication/323534846_The_Formation_of_Latin_Diminutives_of_Nouns_and_Adjectives.
Mouritsen, Henrik. 2011. *The Freedman in the Roman World*. Cambridge: Cambridge University Press.
Murdoch, Iris. 1999. *The Sea, the Sea*. London: Vintage. Originally published in 1978.
Neer, Richard. 2020. "Small Wonders: Figurines, Puppets, and the Aesthetics of Scale in Archaic and Classical Greece." In Elsner 2020, 11–50.
Ngai, Sianne. 2005. *Ugly Feelings*. Cambridge, MA: Harvard University Press.
———. 2012. *Our Aesthetic Categories: Zany, Cute, Interesting*. Cambridge, MA: Harvard University Press.
Norgard, Amy. 2015. "The Senses and Synaesthesia in Horace's *Satires*." PhD diss., University of Illinois at Urbana-Champaign.
Ondaatje, Michael. 1992. *The English Patient*. London: Bloomsbury.
Oliensis, Ellen. 2009. *Freud's Rome: Psychoanalysis and Latin Poetry*. Cambridge: Cambridge University Press.
Onians, Richard B. 1988. *The Origins of European Thought: About the Body, the Mind, the Soul, the World, Time and Fate*. Cambridge: Cambridge University Press.
Pacini, Giulia. 2014. "Arboreal and Historical Perspectives from Calvino's *Il barone rampante*." *Romance Studies* 32:57–68.
Padilla Peralta, Dan-el. 2020. *Divine Institutions: Religions and Community in the Middle Roman Republic*. Princeton, NJ: Princeton University Press.
Pandey, Nandini. 2020. "What Parts of Classics Would We Choose to Preserve for the Future?" (blog), https://classicalstudies.org/scs-blog/pandey/blog-what-parts-classics-would-we-choose-preserve-future.
Pease, Arthur S. 1926. "Things Without Honor." *Classical Philology* 21:27–42.
Peirano, Irene. 2012. *The Rhetoric of the Roman Fake: Latin Pseudepigrapha in Context*. Cambridge: Cambridge University Press.
Perec, Georges. 1999. "Approaches to What?" In *Species of Space and Other Pieces*, trans. J. Sturrock, 209–11. London: Penguin Books. Originally published in 1973.
Phillips, Adam. 1993. *On Kissing, Tickling, and Being Bored: Psychoanalytic Essays on the Unexamined Life*. Cambridge, MA: Harvard University Press.
Plass, Paul. 1988. *Wit and the Writing of History: The Rhetoric of Historiography in Ancient Rome*. Madison: University of Wisconsin Press.
Platner, Samuel B. 1895. "Diminutives in Catullus." *American Journal of Philology* 16:186–202.
Platt, Verity. 2006. "Making an Impression: Replication and the Ontology of the Greco-Roman Seal Stone." *Art History* 29:233–57.
Plochmann, George K. 1963. "Hiccups and Hangovers in the Symposium." *Bucknell Review* 11:1–18.
Popkin, Maggie. 2022. *Souvenirs and the Experience of Empire*. Cambridge: Cambridge University Press.

Porter, James I. 2011. "Against λεπτότης: Rethinking Hellenistic Aesthetics." In *Creating a Hellenistic World*, edited by A. Erskine and Ll. Llewellyn-Jones, 271–312. Swansea: Classical Press of Wales.
Power, Tristan. 2021. "The Sister of Passienus Crispus." In *Collected Papers on Suetonius*, edited by T. Power, 70–77. London: Routledge.
Purves, Alex, ed. 2017. *Touch and the Ancient Senses*. Abingdon: Routledge.
Rabb, Melissa Alliker. 2019. *Miniature and the English Imagination: Literature, Cognition, and Small-Scale Culture, 1650–1765*. Cambridge: Cambridge University Press.
Radke, Gyburg. 2007. *Die Kindheit des Mythos—die Erfindung der Literaturgeschichte in der Antike*. Munich: Beck.
Rankine, Claudia. 2014. *Citizen: An American Lyric*. Minneapolis: Graywolf Press.
Raus, Erhard. 2003. *Panzer Operations: The Eastern Front Memoir of General Raus, 1941–1945*. Edited and translated by S. H. Newton. Cambridge, MA: Da Capo Press.
Razzall, Lucy. 2021. *Books and Boxes in Early Modern England: Materiality, Metaphor, Containment*. Cambridge: Cambridge University Press.
Reay, Brendon. 2003. "Some Addressees of Vergil's *Georgics* and their Audience." *Vergilius* 49: 17–41.
Reinhardt, Tobias. 2005. "The Language of Epicureanism in Cicero: The Case of Atomism." In *Aspects of the Language of Latin Prose*, edited by T. Reinhardt, M. Lapidge, and J. N. Adams, 151–77. Oxford: Oxford University Press.
Rehm, Albert. 1937. "Antike Automobile." *Philologus* 92:317–30.
Richlin, Amy. 2013. "The Fragments of Terentia." In *Roman Literature, Gender, and Reception: Domina Illustris*, edited by D. Lateiner, B. K. Gold, and J. Perkins, 93–118. New York: Routledge.
———. 2017. *Slave Theater in the Roman Republic: Plautus and Popular Comedy*. Cambridge: Cambridge University Press.
Riggsby, Andrew. 1997. "'Public' and 'Private' in Roman Culture: The Case of the *Cubiculum*." *JRA* 10:36–56.
———. 2009. "Space." In *The Cambridge Companion to the Roman Historians*, edited by A. Feldherr, 152–65. Cambridge: Cambridge University Press.
Rigney, Ann. 2001. *Imperfect Histories: The Elusive Past and the Legacy of Romantic Historicism*. Ithaca: Cornell University Press.
Rimell, Victoria. 2015. *The Closure of Space in Roman Poetics: Empire's Inward Turn*. Cambridge: Cambridge University Press.
Robbins, Bruce. 1993. *The Servant's Hand: English Fiction from Below*. Durham, NC: Duke University Press.
Robinson, David M. 1924. "Some Roman Terra-Cotta Savings-Banks." *American Journal of Archaeology* 28:239–50.
Rowe, Nina. 2012. Contribution to Hiller et al. 2012, 508–9.
Roy, Arundhati. 1997. *The God of Small Things*. London: Flamingo.
Rudolph, Kelli, ed. 2017. *Taste and the Ancient Senses*. Abingdon: Routledge.
Scanlon, Thomas F. 1988. "Textual Geography in Sallust's *The War with Jugurtha*." *Ramus* 17: 138–75.
Scott, Charlotte. 2008. "Still Life? Anthropocentrism and the Fly in *Titus Andronicus* and *Volpone*." In *Shakespeare Survey* 61, edited by P. Holland, 256–68. Cambridge: Cambridge University Press.

Sedgwick, Eve Kosofsky. 1990. *The Epistemology of the Closet*. Berkeley: University of California Press.

Ségalas, Robin. 2015. "L'espace désertique africain: un exemple des perceptions romaines du monde et de l'humanité." In *L'espace dans l'Antiquité*, edited by P. Voisin and M. de Béchillon, 227–53. Paris: L'Harmattan.

Seltzer, Mark. 2011. "The Official World." *Critical Inquiry* 37:724–53.

Sharrock, Alison, and Helen Morales, eds. 2000. *Intratextuality: Greek and Roman Textual Relations*. Oxford: Oxford University Press.

Shipp, George P. 1960. *Terence Andria*. Oxford: Oxford University Press.

Simons, Patricia. 2015. "Salience and the Snail: Liminality and Incarnation in Francesco del Cossa's *Annunciation* (c. 1470)." In *Religion, the Supernatural and Visual Culture in Early Modern Europe*, edited by J. Spinks and D. Eichberger, 305–29. Leiden: Brill.

Shackleton Bailey, David R. 1965–71. *Cicero's Letters to Atticus*. 7 vols. Cambridge: Cambridge University Press.

———. 1999. *Cicero: Letters to Atticus*. 3 vols. Cambridge, MA: Harvard University Press.

Squire, Michael. 2011. *The Iliad in a Nutshell*. Oxford: Oxford University Press.

———, ed. 2015. *Sight and the Ancient Senses*. London: Routledge.

Stephen, Leslie. 1956. *Men, Books, and Mountains. Essays by Leslie Stephen*. London: Hogarth Press. Originally published in 1893.

Stewart, Kathleen. 2007. *Ordinary Affects*. Durham, NC: Duke University Press.

Stewart, Susan. 1993. *On Longing: Narratives of the Miniature, the Gigantic, the Souvenir, the Collection*. Durham, NC: Duke University Press.

Kaster, Robert A. 2005. *Emotion, Restraint, and Community in Ancient Rome*. Oxford: Oxford University Press.

Syme, Ronald. 1964. *Sallust*. Berkeley: University of California Press.

Telò, Mario. 2016. "Basket Case: Material Girl and Animate Object in Plautus's *Cistellaria*." In *Roman Drama and its Contexts*, edited by S. Frangoulidis, S. J. Harrison, and G. Manuwald, 299–316. Berlin: De Gruyter.

Turton, William. 1831. *A Manual of the Land and Fresh-Water Shells of the British Isles*. London: Longman, Rees, Orme, Brown, and Green.

Updike, John. 1972. *Museums and Women, and Other Stories*. New York: Alfred A. Knopf. Short story originally published in 1967.

Van de Hout, Michel P. J. 1999. *A Commentary on the Letters of M. Aurelius Fronto*. Leiden: Brill.

Wallace-Hadrill, Andrew. 1990. "Pliny the Elder and Man's Unnatural History." *Greece and Rome* 37:80–96.

Wiedemann, Thomas. 1993. "Sallust's *Jugurtha*: Concord, Discord, and the Digressions." *Greece and Rome* 40:48–57.

Wigston Smith, Chloe, and Beth Fowkes Tobin, eds. 2022. *Small Things in the Eighteenth Century: The Political and Personal Value of the Miniature*. Cambridge: Cambridge University Press.

Yarrow, Liv M. 2018. "The Tree and Sunset Motif: The Long Shadow of Roman Imperialism on Representations of Africa." *Classical Receptions Journal* 10:275–311.

Watt, Garry. 2016. "'Where the Shoe Pinches': True Equity in Trollope's *The Warden*." *Polemos* 10:293–309.

Woolf, Virginia. 1968. *The Waves*. Harmondsworth: Penguin Books. First published in 1931.
Woods, David. 2022. Review of Power 2021, *Histos* 16:56–64.
Young, Elizabeth. 2013. "Homer in a Nutshell: Vergilian Miniaturization and the Sublime." *Publications of the Modern Language Association* 128:57–72.
———. 2015. "The Touch of the *Cinaedus*: Unmanly Sensations in the *Carmina Priapea*." *Classical Antiquity* 34:183–208.
Zatta, Claudia. 2016. "Plants' Interconnected Lives: From Ovid's Myths to Presocratic Thought and Beyond." *Arion* 24:101–26.
Zetzel, James E. G. 2003. "Plato with Pillows: Cicero on the Uses of Greek Culture." In *Myth, History and Culture in Republican Rome: Studies in Honour of T .P. Wiseman*, edited by E. Gee, D. Braund, and C. Gill, 119–38. Exeter: University of Exeter Press.

# INDEX

Achilles Tatius, gnat of, 123n34
Adams, J. N., 102
*ad unguem* ("to the nail") metaphor, 121n1
Aelian, on Xerxes, 64
Aeneas: "little Aeneas," 99; sacrifice to Penates, 21, *fig.* 5
Aeschylus, *Agamemnon*, 83
Aesop, 10; on small men, 123n38
aesthetics: of cuteness, 11–12, 39; of smallness, 4, 10, 122n14
affect: of diminutives, 97; gradations of, 76; manifestation in skin, 78
Africa: colonial, 39; in *Jugurtha*, 37–38, 42, 43–44, 47, 49, 127n37; natural history of, 37–38, 45; pre-Herculean inhabitants of, 38
Africa Nova, Sallust's governorship of, 32
agriculture: gardening as miniature of, 27; subdivisions of, 108
Agrippina (mother of Nero): *adfines* of, 60–61; incest with son, 60, 64, 132nn52,53; marriage to Passienus Crispus, 56, 63, 68
Ahenobarbus, Gnaeus Domitius, 61, 62, 132n52; Domitia's suit against, 68
Ahmed, Sarah, 127n54
*ahora* (Mexican Spanish), diminutives of, 103–4
Alexander the Great, 12; anecdotes of, 54; *corpusculum* of, 116
Allied forces, snail's pace of, 128n79
Anaxagoras: *homoeomeria* theory, 10, 135n46; small-large oppositions of, 9

ancestors, Roman, 26; miniaturization of, 26, 118. *See also* Penates
Andrade, Tonio, 53
anecdotes, 58–60; of ancient lives, 54, 55; authenticity of, 59; as interruptions, 59; larger contexts of, 59; in New Historicism, 59, 131n42; *nondum* in, 59–60; postmodern appeal of, 59; purpose of, 58–59; the real in, 131nn36,41; revealing of subjects, 131n44; urban legends from, 59
the Anthropocene, 46
antiquity: countercultural values of, 9; as cultural childhood, 7; emotions in, 133n6; incompleteness of, 3; large/small dialectic of, 11; laughter in, 80; "little," 3; senses in, 77; size/power relationships of, 6; size/value relationships of, 7, 9, 12–13; trope of rescue, 21, 55
Antonius, Marcus: in *De oratore*, 79–80, 135n40
Antony, Mark, 27; Cicero's diminutives for, 116
ants, 10, 14–15, 118, 119
*Appendix Vergiliana*: *Ciris*, 99; *Culex*, 11, 99, 135n33; diminutives of, 99
Apuleius: *Cupid and Psyche*, 104; diminutives of, 139n7; use of *scrupulus*, 91–92
Ara Pacis Augustae (Rome), sacrifice to Penates in, *fig.* 5
Arasse, Daniel, 16, 43; "The Snail's Gaze," 30, 35; on transhistorical contact, 18
Archimedes, Cicero's diminutives for, 116

159

## INDEX

Arendt, Hannah: *The Human Condition*, 4
Aristophanes: depiction of Socrates, 20; hiccups attack in Plato's *Symposium*, 19–20, 28, 30; insects in, 86–87; *Plutus*, 86–87
Aristotle, *Poetics*: on large and small, 10
art, visual: Pliny the Elder on, 12; smallness in, 12, 16
Athenaeus, comic details of, 17
Atticus: ailments of, 89–90, 137n74; Cicero's correspondence with, 74, 87–91, 92–93, 117, 136nn65,68, 138n85; Cicero's dependence on, 88, 92–94, 137nn73,79,83; mirroring of Cicero's dysphoria, 137n80
Aubrey, John: *Brief Lives*, 54–55; *Life of Hobbes*, 55
Auerbach, Erich, 124nn74,75; *Mimesis*, 16
Augustus, Emperor: childhood home of, 26; family difficulties of, 93; shoe superstition of, 91
Aulus Gellius, *Attic Nights*: minutiae of, 27
Ausonius, *Bissula*: diminutives of, 111

baby figurine (1600 BCE–700 BCE), 2, *fig.* 2
Bachelard, Gaston, 3; on defense metaphors, 129n86; on nostalgia, 21; on snail shells, 129n82. Works: *Essai sur la connaissance approchée*, 16; *The Poetics of Space*, 10–11, 106–7
Bacon, Francis: on details, 55
Bailey, Elizabeth Tova: *The Sound of a Wild Snail Eating*, 128n63
Baker, Nicholson, 5
banality, concealment through, 136n71
Baraz, Yelena, 50
Barthes, Roland: on *faits divers*, 59; on the *punctum*, 18–19; "reality effect" of, 124n73
baskets, Roman, 105, *fig.* 21; snails in, *fig.* 11
Bassus, Junius: joke on Domitia, 68–69
Batstone, William, 32, 34
*Battle of the Frogs and Mice*, 11
Baubo (goddess), miniature figurines of, 124n63
Beard, Mary, 132n56; on *De oratore*, 80, 82; on laughter, 80
Beerbohm, Max: "A Clergyman," 132n57
Bennett, Jane: *Vibrant Materialism*, 121n2
Bettini, Maurizio: on doubles, 114, 141n56; on Roman dolls, 24–25
biographies, Roman: court life in, 57; epigraphic, 53; reconstructed, 53
biographies, short: Bacon on, 55; details in, 58; Dryden on, 54–55; political aspects of, 52; reversing of injustice, 52
Blessed, Brian, 58
Bodel, John, 23

body parts, human: diminutives for, 98, 110, 113; noses, 110; world counterparts of, 141n46
Boivin, Nicole: on the unnoticed, 4
Boswell, James, 132n57
boxes: *capsae*, 112, *fig.* 23; compartments of, 105, 107, 108, 110; containerism and, 106; doves stealing from, *fig.* 22; embodied subjectivity of, 112; empty, 108; jewelry, 12–13, 104; Muse Casket, 112; reliquary, 112–13. *See also* enclosures, small
Branagh, Kenneth, 63
Brecher, Gerhard: snail experiment, 42, *fig.* 13
Brescia, Graziana, 34
Bridges, Robert, 40–41
Brown, Bill: "Thing Theory," 121n2
Brueghel, Pieter: *Fall of Icarus*, 71
Buchan, John: "The Causal and the Casual in History," 74
Buchan, Mark, 141n60
Butler, Shane, 53
Byron, Lord: *Don Juan*, 141n57

Caesar, Julius, 107; Cicero's capitulation to, 117; as keen-sighted, 89; last breath of, 74
Caligula, Emperor: dual identity of, 70; incest with sisters, 61–62; Passienus Crispus's relationship with, 56, 57, 63, 69; relationship with Tiberius, 69
Callimachus, 123n47; *Hymn to Zeus*, x
Calpurnius Siculus: *Eclogues*, 133n78
Calvino, Italo: *Il barone rampante*, 39–40, 49; knowledge of Sallust, 40; on Ligurian identity, 127n50; tree imagery of, 39–40, 127n51
Cameron, Alan, 123n47
*capsae* (scrollboxes), 112; Calliope and Homer with, *fig.* 23. *See also* boxes
*capsulae* (little boxes), as reliquaries, 112–13
*Carmina Burana*, diminutives of, 100
Cassander of Macedon, 42
cataclysm sentences, x
Cato the Elder, 26
Catullus: belittling terms of, 85, 101, 135n50; *cinaedi* in, 98, 102; diminutives of, 85, 99, 101–3, 109–11, 113, 139nn3,12, 140nn17,20; as displaced person, 111; on his trifles, 13; interiority of, 109, 110–11; leisure of, 80; microaggression in, 85; *molestiae* in, 83–86; *neglegentia* of, 85; poetic worldview of, 100–101; poverty of, 109–10, 140n21; use of *insulsus*, 85, 86; use of litotes, 102; Works: Poem **1**, 13; Poem **3**, 101; Poem **4**, 49; Poem **10**, 83–86, 102–3, 115; Poem **13**, 109–10; Poem **25**, 98, 109; Poem **61**, 139n12; Poem **63**, 113,

114, 115; Poems **65–66**, 112, 141n50; Poem **68**, 111–12
Catulus, Q. Lutatius: in *De oratore*, 78–79, 80, 82
Chaucer, Geoffrey: small irritants in, 76, 134n11
childhood: antiquity as, 7; of the gods, 11; as miniature, 7
children: baby figurine (1600 BCE–700 BCE), 2, *fig.* 2; nurseries of, 26; toys of, 122n29, *fig.* 1
Chin, Mike, 4
Cicero, Marcus Tullius: annoyingness in, 78; Atticus's support for, 88, 92–94, 137nn73,79,83; belief in the divine, 21; capitulation to Caesar, 117; "chickpea" name, 116; as *consularis scurra*, 82; diminutives of, 115–18, 141n61, 142n77; disparagement of Greek philosophy, 116; divorce from Terentia, 94; emotional pain metaphors, 137n82; on emotional restraint, 74; governorship of Cilicia, 94, 138n86; on Greek lyric poets, 124n70; healing through correspondence, 89; on his birthplace, 26; on his villas, 90; on intimacy between friends, 138n93; kenning terms of, 129n85; letters to Terentia, 88, 137n76, 138nn101,102; *lippitudo* (eye ailment) of, 87–91, 136n68; literary self of, 117; on loathing, 89; loathing for Caesar, 88; marital strife of, 94, 138n101; monument to Tullia, 88, 90; neuroses of, 88; on numbing troubles, 88–89; rescue of Minerva, 21; retreat from politics, 79, 88, 90–91, 139n106; small irritants of, 2, 88, 121n6; spatiotemporal markers of, 45, 128n76; on the super annoying, 90; use of *humanus*, 86; use of *pupula*, 113; use of *scrupulus*, 92–95; wakefulness of, 89. Works: *Brutus*, 135n34; *De divinatione*, 117; *De finibus*, 26–27; *De natura deorum*, 21, 117; *De provinciis consularibus*, 117; *De republica*, 14; *Dream of Scipio*, 14, 118; *Letters to Atticus*, 74, 87–93, 117, 136nn65,68, 138n85; *Marius*, 36; *Pro Archia*, 116; *Pro Milone*, 45, 134n13; *Pro Roscio Amerino*, 92
—*De oratore*, 78–82; contemplative tone of, 134n25; date of, 79; Greek humor in, 135n40; Greek tactlessness in, 82; the inept in, 82; jokes in, 80–82; *molestia* in, 78–80, 82; negative emotions in, 80; participants in, 78–79, 80; "redressive politeness" in, 80; refinement in, 79; sophisticated manners in, 134n27; types of humor in, 81
Cicero, Marcus Tullius (the younger), 94
Cicero, Quintus Tullius, 138n102; disloyalty of, 137n80; divorce of, 93
*cinaedi*: in Catullus, 102; in Latin poetry, 98, 109

Claassen, Jo-Marie, 138nn101,102
Claudius, Emperor, 62; legacy from Passienus Crispus, 131n28
Cluvius Rufus, 132n53
Columella, apologia for his work, 27
comedy, Greek: irritants in, 83
comedy, Roman: politeness terms in, 140n22
*commentarii*, versus histories, 34
Constantius, *Vita Germani*, 112–13
containment, metaphors of, 106. *See also* boxes; enclosures, small
Cope, Wendy, 108
Copeland, Dale: "Lares et Penates," *fig.* 6
Corbeill, Anthony, 81
Corbin, Alain: *Life of an Unknown*, 53
*cornua* (horns), 48–49
cosmology, ancient: insignificant things in, 9
courtiers: charades with emperors, 63, 65; contract with rulers, 70–71; Domitian's, 56; fear among, 60; ideal, 69; tact of, 58, 63, 68
court life, Roman: Passienus Crispus's negotiation of, 57, 62–63, 67
Courtney, Edward, 115
Crassus, L. Licinius: in *De oratore*, 78, 80, 81–82
Crispus, Passienus: adaptability of, 70; artificial rhetoric of, 64; bon mots of, 55–56; brief life of, 55–58; Caligula and, 56, 57, 63, 69; career of, 56, 62; currying emperors' favor, 69; death of, 56, 57; as dissimulator, 55, 57–58; door imagery of, 66, 67; as emperors' doorkeeper, 67; emulation of Maecenas, 57; encounters with power, 71; family of origin, 57; fortune of, 56, 57, 62; infertility of, 65; in Julio-Claudian family, 56, 57, 60–62, 63, 65, 67; Juvenalian scholion on, 56, 60; in lawsuit against Ahenobarbus, 68; legacy to Claudius, 131n28; literary record of, 56; marriage to Agrippina, 56, 63, 68; marriage to Domitia, 56, 61, 67, 68; mildness of, 68; negotiation of court life, 57, 62–63, 67; *nondum* joke of, 56, 59–63, 67, 70; as orator, 55; passion for tree, 63–65, 66; on resisting flattery, 66; Sallust's adoption of, 57; Suetonius on, 56, 60, 70, 131n33; Tacitus on, 69; Tiberius and, 56, 60, 131n49
Crispus, Passienus, the elder: Tacitus on, 57, 58
Crispus, Vibius, 56, 118; bon mots on emperors, 71, 133n81; Juvenal on, 56, 71; Probus's life of, 132n63; Quintilian on, 133n81; self-preservation by, 63; skill as courtier, 131n27; Tacitus on, 133n81
*cubicula*: Roman emperors', 23, 125n107; secret activity in, 106
Čulík-Baird, Hannah, xii, 121n4

Curius Dentatus, Sabine farm of, 26
cuteness, modern aesthetic of, 11–12, 39
Cyrus, Sardis campaign of, 35, 48

Dawe, Roger, x
De Amicis, Edmondo, 97
death: accidental, 53; falling and, 18; randomness of, 17–18; by stumbling, 91; subalterns', 53; sudden, 17, 75, 91
Deetz, James: *In Small Things Forgotten*, 4, 122n15
deities, childhood of, 11
deities, Roman: domestic, 24; miniatures, 22–23, 24. *See also* Penates
del Cossa, Francesco: Annunciation, *fig*. 10; emergence of the invisible, 30; past/present continuity in, 43; scale of, 30, 32; snail figure, 30, 35, *fig*. 9
Deleuze, Gilles: on Foucault, 133n82; on smallness, 20
Demetrius of Phaleron, mechanical snail of, 42
Demochares, on snails, 42
Democritus, on twisted plants, 40
deserts: conception in antiquity, 128n72; protraction of warfare, 43; time/space relationships of, 44–45; tracking devices of, 44
details, 16–21; Bacon on, 55; causal, 18, 19, 20; empirical reality of, 18; function of, 16–17; of Greco-Roman reality, 17–21; in Homer, 9, 10; intertextual, 17; literary, 16–21; quick shocks from, 18; in small lives, 58; sordid, 17; in Vermeer, 16; vitality of, 18; the whole and, 32. *See also* small things
details, visual: image/viewer separation in, 19
devotional objects, Roman: miniature, 21, 23. *See also* Penates
Dewey, John, 76
Didi-Huberman, Georges, 16, 71
diminutives: affective force of, 97; comparatives and, 97, 139n5; double, 108, 117; function of, 96–97; gender and, 97; for minor emotions, 96; in modern Romance language, 97; in mother-child relationships, 97; multiplication of, 103; Northern Scots', 139n3; nuances of, 97; Ronsard's, 100; suffixes, 104, 139n3; superlatives and, 97, 107, 115; Swahili, 104
diminutives, ancient, 7, 9. *See also* smallness, ancient
diminutives, Latin, 28, 96–119; Apuleius's, 139n7; asymptotic, 104; Ausonius's, 111; bases of, 104; for body parts, 98, 110, 113; of *Carmina Burana*, 100; Catullus's, 85, 99, 101–3, 109–11, 113, 139nn3,12, 140nn17,20; Cicero's use of, 115–18, 141n61, 142n77; comparatives and, 103, 115; "contagions" of, 99, 100; container words, 108; disparaging, 103; domestic, 103; emotional range of, 115, 140n22; erotic, 98, 100, 101–2; expression of precision, 97, 104, 114–15; expressive power of, 101; external, 99; feminine, 139n7; as focal points, 114; for Greeks, 118; Hadrian's, 99–100, 118; hybrids, 115; interiority of, 99; lexicalized, 103, 107, 112; Lucilius's, 100–101, 116, 139n11; male use of, 98; Martial's, 108; metapoetics of, 99, 107; perspective through, 118; Plautus's, 100, 105–6, 107, 140n30; pointedness of, 104; prefixes, 115, 117; self-ironizing, 115; Seneca's, 73, 104, 141n45; the sensual in, 98; suffixes, 103–4, 115, 117; Virgil's, 99, 139n12; for women, 97–98. *See also* Latin language; literature, Latin
Diodorus Siculus, on Ligurians, 39
Diogenes, anecdotes of, 54
Dionysius of Sicily, death of, 17
D'Israeli, Israel, 131n42
dissonance, in Greek soundscape, 78
Dodd, William: Johnson's joke on, 132n57
Dolabella: as sore point, 91; marriage to Tullia, 94
Dolansky, Fanny, 3; on dolls, 24–25
dolls: as aspirational objects, 25; as forlorn, 24–25; messages conveyed by, 122n11
dolls, Roman: Crepereia Tryphaena's, 24–25, *fig*. 8; of late third century CE, *fig*. 3. *See also* toys
Domitia (wife of Passienus Crispus), 56, 61; Bassus's joke on, 68–69; Nero's murder of, 67–68; suit against Ahenobarbus, 68
Domitian, Emperor: torture of flies, 71; Vibius Crispus's joke on, 71
Donatus, on feminine worries, 97–98
doubles, 114; diminutive, 108, 117; in nature of jokes, 62–63; in Ovid, 115; reflected, 113–14, 141n56
Dow, Sterling, ix
Dryden, John: on biographical details, 58; "Life of Plutarch," 54–55
Dutsch, Dorota, 98

Ellis, Robinson, 141n57
Elsner, Jaś, 112
emotions: grand, 74; orators' stimulation of, 79–80
emotions, minor, 28; enclosures for, 108; expressed by diminutives, 115; expression of powerlessness, 76; in Latin literature, 74–76; outward orientation of, 75; representational

## INDEX 163

space for, 75; in Roman identity, 94; shared community of, 77; validation of, 75–76. *See also* irritants, small
emperors, Roman: courtiers' charades with, 63, 65; *cubicula* of, 23, 125n107; *lararia* of, 125n101; statuette collections of, 23; stoic response to, 69
enclosures, small, 104–13; for emotions, 108; for humans, 106; infinite regression in, 106; psychological aspects of, 106–7; subdivision of, 107. *See also* boxes
encyclopedists, Greco-Roman: on small things, 2–3
environment, man's intervention in, 45–46
epic, pastoral subsumed in, 11. *See also* Homer; Virgil
Epicurus, Cicero's diminutives for, 116
Eros, fullness/emptiness of, 20
*escargotières* (snail shell deposits), 38, *fig.* 12
*Eton Latin Grammar* (1768), worthlessness in, 122n30
Extinction Rebellion protest (New York, 2019), 5
eye inflammations: Cicero's, 87–91; in Horace, 136n70; rubbing at, 91, 137n75
eyes, likenesses reflected in, 113–14, 141n60. See also *pupulae*

Fanon, Franz, 78
*fastidium* (disgust), 76, 87
Feeney, Denis, 111
Feldherr, Andrew, 36, 40; on Sallust's landscapes, 42, 127n37; on space/time relationships, 44
Ferri, Rolando, 131n49
Feynman, Richard, x
Fineman, Joel: on anecdotes, 58–59, 131nn36,41; on historemes, 58
fingernails, 2, 15, 19, 20, 73, 96, 99, 121n1
Fischer, Kuno, 70
Fitzgerald, William, 102, 112, 141n50; on Roman imperialism, 85
"Flash Histories" conference (University of Bristol, 2019), 52
Flaubert, Gustave, 12
flies, 9, 12, 118–19; Domitian's torture of, 71; in early modern era, 137n82; Freudian interpretation of, 83; jokes about, 81, 86. See also insects
Flores, Samuel Ortencio, x
Florus: epitome of Jugurthine War, 34; epitome of Livy, 12, 26
Fordyce, C. J., 97; on Catullus, 139n3, 140n17

Fortson, Benjamin, 136n66
Foucault, Michel: "counterhistorical ardor" of, 133n79; on the everyday, 5; "Lives of Infamous Men," 71, 72, 133n82; on Platonism, 20
fragments, confrontation with incompleteness, 3
freedmen, Roman: epigraphic records of, 53, 130n10
Freud, Sigmund: on dreams, 135n45; *The Interpretation of Dreams*, 83; on jokes, 62, 69–70
Frontinus, *Strategemata*, 34, 126n15, 129n80
Fuscus, Aristius: in Horace's *Satires* 1.9, 86, 136n53
Gaius Caesar. *See* Caligula, Emperor
Gallagher, Catherine, 124n74, 133n79; on anecdotes, 59, 131n42
gardening, as miniature of agriculture, 27

Geertz, Clifford, 122n21
Gell, Alfred, 3
Ghobrial, John-Paul, 130n8
Ginzburg, Carlo: *The Cheese and the Worms*, 53, 130n6
Giusti, Elena, 128n59
gnats, 12, 13, 83, 87, 123n34. See also insects; mosquitoes
Gossman, Lionel, 59
Graves, Robert: *I, Claudius*, 58
Greek language, vocabulary of smallness, 7, 9, 97
Greeks, tactlessness of, 82
Greenblatt, Stephen, 124n74, 133n79; on anecdotes, 59, 131n42; on "foveation," 6
Grethlein, Jonas, 45
Gunderson, Erik, 86; on Cicero's ailments, 88; on *humanus* in Cicero, 86; on marriage of Cicero and Terentia, 138nn101,102
Gurd, Sean, 78
Guthrie, W. Keith: on the *Symposium*, 19

Hadrian, Emperor: diminutives of, 99–100, 118
Hall, Jon, 79, 134n27
Hasselrot, Bengt, 97
*Helix pomatia* (Burgundian snail), 35
Henderson, John, x; on Rutilius Gallicus, 53
Herodotus: on Harpagus, 69; parallels with *Jugurtha* in, 35, 36, 48
Hesiod, on snails, 47
hierarchies: of ancient values, 13; Platonic, 7
historemes (small facts), 58
historiography, Roman: "not-words" in, 59
history, *Annales* school of, 5, 36
Hitchcock, Tim: on small things, 4–5

Hoffer, Stanley, 78, 88
Hoffman, Johann Baptist, 140n22
Homer: *Odyssey*, 16; small details in, 9, 10, 123n52; with Calliope, *fig.* 23
Hopkins, Gerard Manley: on "inscape," 40–41
Hopkinson, Neil, x
Horace: insect imagery of, 83; Persius's condensation of, 124n64; "Pest" of, 86; on small irritants, 75, 77; on snails, 47; on tact, 83; tree imagery of, 41; trope of humility, 34, 123n52, 139n12. Works: *Epistle to Augustus* (*Ep.* **2.1**), 34; *Epistles* **1**, 69; *Satires* **1.3**, 83; *Satires* **1.5**, 91, 136n70; *Satires* **1.9**, 86; *Satires* **1.10**, 83, 136n70
horn players: in *Jugurtha*, 48–49; on limestone relief (Amiternum), *fig.* 16
Hortensius (orator), 64
houses, Roman: miniature, 21–23; penetralia of, 21
Huber, Sonya: *Supremely Tiny Acts*, 5, 7, 21
Hudson, Jared, 12
Hughes, Jessica, 3; on votives, 26
human beings: diminutive surrogates for, 110; embodied experiences of, 78, 121n2; object relations of, 2. *See also* body parts, human
human life: limited perspective on, 121n5
humor, Cicero's: in *Brutus*, 135n34; in *De oratore*, 81, 135n40. *See also* jokes
Hunter, Richard: "The Morning After," 20

*I, Claudius* (BBC TV series), 58
identity, personal: diminutives' reflection of, 114; displacement of, 6–7
images, reflected, 113–14
imperialism, Roman: macroagression of, 85; Sallust on, 33, 36, 39; Tacitus on, 131n50; virtue/vice in, 33
incest, Julio-Claudians', 60–62, 65, 68, 70, 132nn52,53
the individual, tension with the plural, 6
the infinitesimal, in Greek philosophy, 15
insects: on intaglio of ring, *fig.* 20; irritating, 83, 86–87; in Pliny's *Natural History*, 13–14; the socially excluded as, 87; in Theophrastus's *Characters*, 82–83. *See also* ants; flies; gnats; lice; mosquitoes
interiority: dangerous, 106; in Catullus, 109, 110–11; of Latin diminutives, 99; recessive, 106; without penetration, 110–11
irritants, physical: Latin imagery of, 75; sensation of, 78, 134n19; sensitivity to, 87–88
irritants, small, 73; Cicero's, 2, 88, 121n6; in divorce, 76, 77; in English literature, 76, 134n11; in great grief, 88; in Greek comedy, 83; insects, 81, 83; involuntary responses to, 74; noise, 77; pests as, 83, 86, 87; physical sensation of, 78; Roman sensitivity to, 83; rubbing at, 91, 94, 137n75; Stoicism and, 77; stumbling blocks, 77; supplanting of global troubles, 88; Theophrastus on, 82–83; Varro on, 76–77. *See also* emotions, minor; *molestiae*; small things
Isidore of Seville: on door terminology, 66–67; *testudo* etymology, 129n87; on thresholds, 132n68
"Islanders" (exhibit, Fitzwilliam Museum, Cambridge), 2

Jakobson, Roman, 97
Johnson, Mark, 106
Johnson, Samuel: hoarding anecdote concerning, 58; joke on Dodd, 132n57
Johnson, W. R., 108
jokes: on brevity, 135n33; concealment in, 70; in *De oratore*, 80–82; double-headed quality, 62–63; Freud on, 62, 69–70; scurrilous, 81; witnesses to, 63. *See also* humor, Cicero's; *nondum* (not yet)
Jonson, Ben: *Volpone*, 81
Joyce, James, 5
Jugurtha: as treacherous, 32, 33; capture of, 127n46; as erratic, 127n37; growth of, 36
Jugurthine War: effect on Roman Republic, 32; Florus's epitome of, 34; siege of Capsa, 34. *See also* Sallust, *Jugurtha*
Julio-Claudian family: childlessness of, 65; family tree of, 60, *fig.* 19; incestuous relationships of, 60–62, 65, 68, 70, 132nn52,53; litigation within, 68; Passienus Crispus's place in, 56, 60–62, 63, 67; ruler-courtier relationships, 69–71
Julius Obsequens, *Prodigies*, 53–54
jumpiness, in the mundane, 5
Jurafsky, Daniel, 97, 104
Juvenal: small things of, 9, 116; on Vibius Crispus, 56, 71. Works: *Satire* **4**, 56, 71; *Satire* **10**, 123n31

Kafka, Franz: cockroach of, 87
Kant, Immanuel: on anecdotes, 59; "mathematical sublime" of, 10
Kaster, Robert, 134n27; on *fastidium*, 76, 87
Ker, James, 4; on the *punctum*, 16
knowledge, subdivisions of, 107–8

Koestermann, Erich, 35
Koselleck, Reinhard: on *Zeitschichten*, 45
Kubler, George, 50; "Style and the Representation of Historical Time," 42–43

Laelius, Gaius, 27, 58
Lagarde, Paul, 136n56
Laite, Julia, 130n8
Lakoff, George, 106
Lambert, Cat, 4
landscapes: African, 37–38; fractal representation of, 42. *See also* deserts
Langin-Hooper, Stephanie: *The Tiny and the Fragmented*, 6–7
*lararia*, emperors', 125n101
largeness, compressed into smallness, 11–12
Larsen, Nella: *Quicksand*, 78
Latin language: irritation in, 75, 78, 83; lexical inadequacies of, 135n46; phonemes of, 139n5; politeness terms, 140n22; terms for worthlessness, 122n30; vocabulary of smallness, 7, 9; words for sensibility, 116. *See also* diminutives, Latin
Latour, Bruno, 110; on the nonhuman, 121n2
laughter, in antiquity, 80. *See also* humor; jokes
Laurand, Louis, 141n62
Leacock, Stephen: "The Life of John Smith," 130n19
Lec, Stanisław, 63; *Unkempt Thoughts*, 52
lice, 12, 83
Lichtenberg, Georg Christoph: apothegms of, 63
Ligurians: in the *Aeneid*, 127n47; Calvino on, 127n50; deceitfulness of, 39; in *Jugurtha*, 33–42, 45–47, 49, 96, 126n29; topography of, 39
*lippitudo*. *See* eye inflammations
Lipps, Theodor, 69–70
literature, Latin: markers of disingenuity, 36; the ordinary in, 6; size/importance dialectic of, 12–13. *See also* diminutives, Latin; Latin language; poetry, Latin
Livy: Florus's epitome of, 12; on *punctum temporis*, 16
Locke, John: on small troubles, 134n11
*loculi* (little containers): Martial's, 108, 140nn42,45; subdivision of, 108
Lodge, David: *Small World*, 97
love: barriers to, 66, 67; as physiological process, 19. *See also* Eros
Love, Heather, 122n20
Love, Rachel, 4

Lucian: encomia to small things, 12; *Fly*, 12, 123n57; *Icaromenippus*, 87, 136n55
Lucilius, diminutives of, 100–101, 116, 139n11
Lucretius, 135n46; small things in, 9
Lucullus, M.: wife's adultery, 93–94, 138n100

Ma, John, 136n70
Mack, John, 3; *The Art of Small Things*, 73
Maecenas: as archetype of friendship, 57; experience of small irritants, 77, 83
Mago the Carthaginian, 39
*mallettes à odeurs* (perfume samples), 110
Mandell, Alice, x, xii
Mardians (Persian nomads), 48
Martelli, Francesca: "Mourning Tulli-a," 88
Martial: diminutives of, 108; *loculi* of, 108, 140nn42,45; modernist interpretation of, 108; small things of, 9; on snails, 35
Martin, S. Rebecca: *The Tiny and the Fragmented*, 6–7
martyrs, Libyan: parallels with Jugurtha, 35, 36
Massumi, Brian, 78
Memmius, C.: seduction of Servilia, 93–94, 138n100
Menedemus, prevarication of, 58, 67
mice: on cameo, *fig.* 4; in Cicero, *De divinatione*, 117; in Cicero, *De natura deorum*, 21, 117; gnawing, 117, 142n78; in Ovid, 142n76; toy, *fig.* 24; in Virgil, 118
Michals, Duane: Warhol photograph of, 19
microaggression, 28; in Catullus 10, 85; as protest, 5; racist, 122n20
microanalysis, scholarly debate over, 4
microhistory, global history and, 52, 130n8
miniature objects, Roman, 21–25; keepsakes, 23; moneyboxes, 23, 24, *fig.* 7; rooms, 26. *See also* dolls, Roman; small things; toys
miniaturization: of agriculture, 27; archaism and, 26; nostalgia and, 21–27; of Roman ancestors, 26, 118
*molestiae* (annoyances), 76; avoidance of, 78; in Catullus, 83–86; continual feeling of, 80; cultural capital of, 82; in *De oratore*, 78–80; ineptness and, 82; interior/exterior, 80; leisure as, 80; Plautus on, 77; of political trouble, 88; restraint against, 134n27. *See also* emotions, minor; irritants, small
momentariness, caught in perpetuity, 43
moneyboxes, Roman, 23, 24, *fig.* 7
Montaigne, Michel de: on death, 18
mosquitoes: in *Agamemnon*, 83; in *Culex*, 135n32

Mouritsen, Henrik, 130n10
Murdoch, Iris: *The Sea, the Sea*, 62

Nazis, vermin imagery of, 87
*necessitudo*, as relationship, 68, 132n70
Neer, Richard, 7
negatives, Tacitus's use of, 59–60
Nero, Emperor, 56; dissembling with Seneca, 65, 70; incest with Agrippina, 60, 64, 132nn52,53; murder of Domitia, 67–68; Tacitus on, 65
New Historicism, 5; anecdotes in, 59, 131n42
New Materialism, 121n2
Ngai, Sianne: on cuteness, 11–12; on hypersensitivity, 80; on irritation, 134n19; *Our Aesthetic Categories*, 127n45; *Ugly Feelings*, 75–76, 78
noise, as irritant, 77
Nolan, Christopher: classical influences on, 132n58; *Tenet*, 63
nomadism: in African ethnography, 127n34; in *Jugurtha*, 37, 38; Scythian, 129n84
*nondum* (not yet), 65; Crispus Passienus's joke using, 56, 59–63, 67, 70; function in anecdotes, 59–60
Norgard, Amy, 87
noses, whole persons as, 110
nostalgia: miniaturization and, 21–27; for pre-industrial times, 126n118; for small daily things, 118; *Symposium*'s generation of, 20, 125n97
Numidians, of *Jugurtha*, 38, 46–47, 48

Ocella (acquaintance of Cicero), 89, 90
*ocellus* (personalized form of *oculus*), 98, 101
Ofilius Hilarus, M.: death of, 18
Oliensis, Ellen: *Freud's Rome*, 101
Ollier, Edmund: "An Incident in the Jugurthine War," *fig.* 17
Ondaatje, Michael: *The English Patient*, 44
Onians, Richard B.: on *necessitudo*, 132n70
the ordinary, intensities of, 5
*ostia* (doorways): brides' crossing of, 132n68; etymology of, 66; reversibility of, 66–67
Otho, Emperor: use of *nondum*, 59
Ovid: doubles in, 115; grafting imagery of, 127n57; mice in, 142n76. Works: *Amores*, 67, 115; *Remedia amoris*, 75; *Tristia*, 66
*Oxford Dictionary of National Biography*, 52

Pabst, Angelica, 97
Padilla Peralta, Dan-el, xi, 55; on temples, 4
Palladium (statue), transport to Rome, 21

Pandey, Nandini, x; on rescue from antiquity, 21, 55
Panzer divisions, "snail offensives" of, 128n79
*paruus*, connotations of value, 9. See also smallness; small things
Passienus Crispus. *See* Crispus, Passienus
the past: brokenness of, 3; transhistorical contact with, 18, 20–21
Paulus, Lucius Aemilius: divorce of, 76, 77
Peiraicos, food paintings of, 12
Peirano, Irene, 4
Penates, 24, 125n101; Aeneas's sacrifice to, 21, *fig.* 5; collective past in, 21; little, 21. See also deities, Roman
Pence, Mike, 119
Perec, Georges: on the infraordinary, 4, 17, 124n83
Persius, condensation of Horace, 124n64
pests, irritating people as, 83, 86, 87. See also flies; irritants, small
Philaeni brothers, 126n25; martyrdom of, 36
Philemon: on snails, 47
Philip of Macedon, anecdotes of, 54
Phillips, Adam, 20
philosophy, Greek: Cicero's diminutives describing, 116; the infinitesimal in, 15; Pre-Socratic, 9
Piso, C. Calpurnius, 55; Juvenalian scholion on, 130n25
Plass, Paul: *Wit and the Writing of History*, 59, 60
Platner, Samuel B.: on diminutives, 101, 110, 140n45
Plato: on *pleonexia*, 39; small-large dialectic of, 9, 10. Works: *Alcibiades 1*, 113; *Phaedo*, 10; *Republic*, 37; *Sophist*, 20
—*Symposium*: Aristophanes' hiccups in, 19–20, 28, 30; the casual in, 19–20; erotic desire in, 125n97; generation of nostalgia, 125n97; nonlinearity of, 20; order of speeches, 19, 125n90; Socrates in, 19, 20
Platt, Verity, 3
Plautus: on annoyances, 77; diminutives of, 100, 107, 140n30; diminutive titles, 105–6; language of contempt, 87; reflections in, 114; snail imagery of, 42. Works: *Amphitryo*, 114, 140n30; *Bacchides*, 87; *Cistellaria*, 106; *Persa*, 87; *Pseudolus*, 53, 100, 130n12; *Stichus*, 107
*pleonexia* (desire for more), 39
Pliny the Elder, *Natural History*: on African snails, 13; on Catullus, 13; on insects, 13–14; on the macroscopic/microscopic, 13–14; on matter, 19; on miniature structures, 22; on minimalist art, 12; paired experiences in, 18;

on Passienus Crispus, 63–64; on sudden death, 17, 75, 91; use of *pupilla*, 114
Pliny the Younger: *Panegyricus*, 60; on triviality, 14
Plutarch: anecdotes in, 54, 55, 58; on Antony, 27; on details, 54, 55; on plant intelligence, 41–42. Works: *Life of Alexander*, 54; *Life of Lucius Aemilius Paulus*, 76, 77, 93
Poe, Edgar Allen: *The Gold Bug*, 106
poetry, ancient: backward extrapolation in, 11
poetry, Latin: small irritants in, 83–86; small things in, 9
poetry, modernist: the ordinary in, 4; the small in, 9
Pompeii, magic squares of, 132n58
Pompey, defeat of, 130n106
Pomponia (wife of Quintus Cicero), 93
Porter, Jim, 10
Posidippus, pebble epigram of, 10
Power, Tristan, 60, 61, 132nn52,53
Praxilla, *Hymn to Adonis*, xii
precision: diminutives' expression of, 97, 104, 114–15; in Sallust, 34
Pre-Socratics, large/small polarity of, 9
*Priapea* (poetry collection), *cinaedi* in, 98
Probus, life of Vibius Crispus, 132n63
Ptolemy Philadelphus, x
*punctum* (point, pinprick), 14–15, 96, 118; aesthetics of, 16; Barthes on, 18–19; human life as, 15–16; photographic, 19; Seneca on, 14–15, 18–19. *See also* small things
*pupillae* (girls): *pupulae* and, 113–14
*pupulae* (pupils): puns on, 115; *pupillae* and, 113–14
Purves, Alex, 4

queerness: in Catullus, 103, 113; orientation and, 127n54; trees and, 40–41
Quintilian: on Domitia, 68; on Homer, 10; on Junius Bassus, 61; on Passienus Crispus, 130n25; on the quotidian in Cicero's rhetoric, 128n76; on Vibius Crispus, 133n81

racism, psychological effects of, 78
randomness, of death, 17–18
Rankine, Claudia: *Citizen*, 122n20
Raus, Erhard, 128n79
Razzall, Lucy: *Boxes and Books in Early Modern England*, 106
reality effects, literary, 16, 35; metonymy and, 36; of Seneca the Elder, 17. *See also* Barthes, Roland
Regulus, blinding of, 89
Rehm, Albert, 128n61
Reinhardt, Tobias, 116

reversal of attraction (the "ick"), 75
rhetoricians, on unimportant things, 123n57
Richlin, Amy, x, 55; on *Pseudolus*, 130n12
Riggsby, Andrew, 43; on *cubicula*, 106
Rigney, Ann, 131n44
Rimell, Victoria, 3, 106
Roman Empire, human scale of, 26
Ronsard, Pierre de: diminutives of, 100
Roy, Arundhati: *The God of Small Things*, 5–6, 122n22
rubbing, at irritants, 91, 94, 137nn75,78
Rumwold, Saint, 130n18
Rutilius Gallicus, reconstructed biography of, 53

*sacculi* (purses), Catullus's: full of emptiness, 109–10
*sacraria* (shrines), Roman emperors', 23
salience, 17, 30, 34, 44, 50
Sallust: as *brevitatis artifex*, 126n18; on Carthage, 126n19; claim to industry, 50; as collector, 49; governorship of Africa Nova, 32; historiographical principles, 30, 42; intellectual life of, 33; invasion of Cercina, 38–39; moral messages of, 32; postmodern historiographers on, 33; relationship to Passienus Crispus, 57; on Roman imperialism, 33, 36, 39; universalizing by, 37; use of dramatization, 34
—*Catiline*, 32, 49; Catiline's mind in, 128n74; grafting imagery of, 127n57; Plato's *Republic* and, 37; Roman imperialism in, 33
—*Jugurtha*, 28; African landscape of, 37–38, 42, 43–44, 47, 49, 127n37; allegorical reading of, 36; causality in, 73; challenge to elites in, 32; climbing in, 41; credibility of, 35; data gathering in, 46; dualities of, 37; good fortune in, 36; greed in, 36, 40, 41; horizontal/vertical axes of, 40; horn players, 48–49, *fig.* 17; human/landscape relationship in, 37; human types in, 46; humility tropes, 35; ilex tree, 33–35, 36, 37, 40–41; Ligurian in, 33–42, 45–47, 49, 96, 126n29; Marius in, 32–36, 46, 49; Marius's simplicity in, 38; Metellus in, 32, 33; metonymy in, 36; moralizing in, 50; moral oppositions in, 40; nomadism in, 37, 38; Numidians of, 38, 46–47, 48, 127n35; ordinary men of, 33, 39; parallels with Herodotus, 35, 36, 48; patterns of growth in, 40–41; predictability of nature in, 36; reality effect of, 35; scale in, 32, 36; small things in, 36; snail, 33–34, 37, 39, 41, 73; snail's pace in, 42, 47, 49, 50; snail/tree hierarchy of, 41; Sulla in, 33, 36

Sallustius Passienus Crispus, C. *See* Crispus, Passienus
Sather lectures (University of California, Berkeley), ix
Saunderson, William, 54
scale, paradoxes of, 15, 123n57
scarab, engraved (Greek, fifth century), *fig.* 4
scholia, Juvenalian: on Passienus Crispus, 55, 60; on Piso, 130n25
Scipio Aemilianus, 14, 27, 58, 118
Scipio Africanus, ruined bathhouse of, 26
*scortilla* (sluts), Catullus on, 102, 103
Scots, Northern: diminutives of, 139n3
*scrupuli* (snags, sharp stones), 91–95; in Apuleius, 91–92; in Cicero, 92–95; moral sense of, 91, 92; Servius Sulpicius's, 91; in Terence, 91
seal-ring, replication of self, 122n11
Sedgwick, Eve Kosofsky: *Epistemology of the Closet*, 106
Ségalas, Robin, 128n74
Sejanus, melted statue of, 123n31
Seltzer, Mark, 122n20; on "one-downsmanship," 5
Sempronius Musca, Aulus and Marcus: joke on name, 81, 86
Seneca the Elder, 125n117; reality effects of, 17; on sordid details, 17
Seneca the Younger: on bees, 124n59; on courtiers' servitude, 133n72; diminutives used by, 73, 104, 141n45; on emotional restraint, 74; on enduring emperors, 69; on *fastidium*, 87; on involuntary responses, 74; Nero's dissembling with, 65, 70; on Scipio, 26; on small pains, 73, 77; on small things, 14–16, 26; on suicide, 15; superfluities in, 14; on syllogisms, 141n68. Works: *De beneficiis*, 70; *De brevitate vitae*, 14; *De clementia*, 87; *De ira*, 63, 74; *Letters*, 15, 112; *Natural Questions*, 14–15, 66, 77, 118; *Thyestes*, 39–40
senses: in antiquity, 77; engagement with small things, 1, 16. *See also* emotions, minor; irritants, small
*Senses in Antiquity* series (Routledge), 134n14
Servilia (wife of M. Lucullus), Memmius's seduction of, 93–94, 138n100
Shackleton Bailey, David R., 89, 93; on *scrupulus*, 94
Shakespeare, William: anecdotes of, 54; snail imagery of, 129nn81,82
Shield of Achilles: small/large opposition in, 10
shoes: Augustus's superstition concerning, 91; badly fitting, 76, 86, 93, 134nn11,12; Milo's, 45; stones in, 91, 92–93

shrines, Roman: miniature, 22–23, 26
Sidonius, on small irritants, 75
similes, Homeric: small things in, 9
Simons, Patricia: "The Salience of the Snail," 30
size: disorientation caused by, 1; relationship to power, 6. *See also* smallness
slaves, Roman: as infections, 87; records of misfortune, 53–54
smallness, x; largeness compressed into, 11–12; modern aesthetic of, 4, 122n14; physical/psychological need for, 3; politics of, 5; in popular culture, 6; postpandemic, 118; repetitive, 4; of snails, 42; tactile engagement with, 6; in twentieth-century thought, 4; vanishing point of, 104
small things: causality and, 73–74; collections of, 6; communicative power of, 1; disproportionate power of, 73; eighteenth-century, 52, 122n11; haptic challenges of, 122n25; histories of, 53; importance of, xi–xii; inspiration from, 119; literary, 16–21; malevolent, 73; meaning of, xi; nostalgia fostered through, 21; prompting of loss, 21; scholarship on, 3–4; sensory engagement with, 1, 16; societal engagement with, 2; survival of, 2, *fig.* 2; symptomatic of the large, 4. *See also* details; diminutives; enclosures, small; irritants, small
snails: on acanthus frieze (Pompeii), *fig.* 14; African, 38; Burgundian, 35; in del Cossa's Annunciation, 30, 35, *fig.* 9–10; Hesiod on, 47; Horace on, 47; individuality of, 41; literary, 30; Martial on, 35; mechanical, 42; as miniature nomads, 47; mosaic (Aquileia, fourth century CE), 35, *fig.* 11; navigation of obstacles, 50; on Roman column (Volubilis, Morocco), 129n97, *fig.* 18; served without shells, 47; Shakespeare's imagery of, 129nn81,82; slow locomotion, 42, 46, 47, 49, 50m 128n79; smallness of, 42; sweetness of, 39; symbolism of, 30; *testudines* of, 47–48; in time experiments, 42–43, *fig.* 13; in World War II imagery, 128n79. *See also* Sallust, *Jugurtha*
Socrates: on abstract forms, 125n96; Aristophanes on, 20; on tall/short contradictions, 10
Sophocles, death of, 17
sound, link with touch, 78
spatialization, induced by repetition, 43
Spiegelman, Art, 87
spirals, natural, 42; on snails' shells, 128n64

Squire, Michael, 3, 122n11
Statius: on miniature structures, 22; Saturnalian gifts of, 34; small things of, 9. Works: *Achilleid*, 11; *Silvae*, 41
Stephen, Leslie, 52
Stewart, Kathleen, 55; *Ordinary Affects*, 5, 6
Stewart, Susan, 3, 21; on childhood, 7; on diminutives, 118; on miniatures, 42; on nostalgia, 126n118
Stoicism: Cicero's diminutives for, 116; small irritants and, 77
Strabo, C. Julius Caesar: in *De oratore*, 78–79, 80–81
stumbling blocks, 91
Suetonius: on Augustus's nursery, 26; on children's rooms, 26; life of Passienus Crispus, 56, 60, 70, 131n33. Works: *Life of Domitian*, 71; *Viri illustres*, 55
suicide, as escape from servitude, 133n72
Sulpicius, Servius, 142n73; "snag" of, 89, 91, 93
Syme, Ronald, 34

*Tabulae Iliacae*, 122n11
Tacita Muta, ritual of, 142n76
Tacitus: dialectic of terror, 60; on dissimulation, 131n33; on imperialism, 131n50; on Nero, 65; on Passienus Crispus the elder, 57, 58; on Passienus Crispus the younger, 69; use of negatives, 59–60; on Vibius Crispus, 133n81
tactlessness, Greek, 82
Telò, Mario, 106
temples, Roman: miniature, 23, 24; relative sizes of, 26
Terence, use of *scrupulus*, 91. Works: *Adelphoe*, 97–98; *Andria*, 17, 124n81
Terentia (wife of Cicero), 136n62; Cicero's letters to, 88, 137n76, 138nn101,102; marital strife of, 94, 138n101
Tertullian: on little jewelry boxes, 12–13, 104
*testudines* (tortoises), and snails, 47–48
*testudo* (battle formation), 47–48; on Trajan's column, *fig. 15*
Theocritus, on painful thorns, 73
Theophrastus, *Characters*: irritants in, 82
"Think Small" conference (Toulouse, 2015), 7
Tiberius, Emperor, 136n55; as dissimulator, 69; Passienus Crispus and, 56, 60, 131n49; relationship with Caligula, 69
time: historians' expressions of, 42–43; impression on sensory organs, 128n66; perception in memory, 42; small units of, 42, 45; snail experiments, 42–43, *fig. 13*
time/space relationships, in *Jugurtha*, 43–44, 50, 128n70
Tobin, Beth Fowkes, 122n25
topography, subdivisions of, 108
touch, human: circular mechanism of, 2. *See also* senses
toys: horse on wheel, *fig. 1*; reality of, 122n29. *See also* dolls
Trajan's Column, 123n43
trees: anthropomorphized, 64–65; eccentric fondness for, 63–65; as mistresses, 65, 66; nemus Caesarum, 65; as queer, 40–41; as symbols of colonialism, 39, 127n46; worship of, 64; Xerxes's homage to, 64
trees, ilex: giant, 64, 65; in *Jugurtha*, 33–35, 36, 37, 40–41
trivia: of ancient urban life, 14; inspiring of study, 27
Trollope, Anthony: small irritants in, 76, 134n11
The Troubles (Northern Ireland), 79
*tubae* (trumpets), 49, *fig. 16*
Tullia (daughter of Cicero): marriage to Dolabella, 94; monument to, 88, 90; Cicero's grief for, 90, 116
Turchin, Gary: "A Thousand Little Irritants," xii–xiii
Turton, William, 126n18

Updike, John: "Museums and Women," 1–2; object relations in, 2, 121n2
urban life, triviality of, 14

Valla, Giorgio, 56
value, ancient: hierarchies of, 13; relationship to size, 7, 9, 12–13
Varro: on compartments, 107, 110; organization scheme of, 107–8. Works: *De lingua latina*, 76–77, 105; *De re rustica*, 107–8
Vermeer, Johannes: anomalous details in, 16
Vibius Crispus, of Vercellae. *See* Crispus, Vibius
villas: Cicero's, 90; Curius's, 26; eye metaphors for, 90
Virgil: farm pests in, 117–18; on great burdens, 79; large/small juxtaposition, 11, 122n24. Works: *Georgics*, 27, 117–18
—*Aeneid*: diminutives of, 99, 139n12; Ligurians in, 127n47; Penates in, 21
Virgil, pseudo-: *Culex*, 11, 99, 135n33; *Moretum*, 11, 99
Vitellius, Emperor: Vibius Crispus on, 133n79
Von Baer, Karl Ernst, 128n66; on "the moment," 42
votives, size of, 26

Warhol, Andy: Michals's photograph of, 19
Washington, John David, 63
Wigston Smith, Chloe, 122n25
Williams, William Carlos, 4, 9
women: Cicero's diminutives for, 116; irritating, 76, 77, 86; stereotypes of smallness for, 97; worries of, 97–98
Woods, David, 132n52
Woolf, Virginia, 5. Works: *Flush*, 130n3; *To the Lighthouse*, 16; *The Waves*, 1

World War II, snail's pace imagery in, 128n79
Wren, Christopher: anecdotes of, 54

Xerxes, homage to plane tree, 64

Yarrow, Liv, 39, 127n46
Young, Elizabeth, 98

*Zeitschichten* (layers of time), 45
Zeno, syllogisms of, 116
Zetzel, J. E. G., 115–16

Founded in 1893,
UNIVERSITY OF CALIFORNIA PRESS
publishes bold, progressive books and journals
on topics in the arts, humanities, social sciences,
and natural sciences—with a focus on social
justice issues—that inspire thought and action
among readers worldwide.

The UC PRESS FOUNDATION
raises funds to uphold the press's vital role
as an independent, nonprofit publisher, and
receives philanthropic support from a wide
range of individuals and institutions—and from
committed readers like you. To learn more, visit
ucpress.edu/supportus.